A PEOPLE'S HISTORY OF CHRISTIANITY

ONE VOLUME STUDENT EDITION

A PEOPLE'S HISTORY OF CHRISTIANITY

ONE VOLUME STUDENT EDITION

DENIS R. JANZ

Editor

FORTRESS PRESS

Minneapolis

A PEOPLE'S HISTORY OF CHRISTIANITY—ONE VOLUME STUDENT EDITION

Cover design: Laurie Ingram

Cover image © Album / Art Resource, NY

Library of Congress Cataloging-in-Publication Data

Print ISBN: 978-1-4514-7053-6

eBook ISBN: 978-1-4514-7967-6

The paper used in this publication meets the minimum requirements of American National Standard for Information Sciences — Permanence of Paper for Printed Library Materials, ANSI Z329.48-1984.

Manufactured in the U.S.A.

CONTENTS

CONTRIBUTORS

Richard A. Horsley is Distinguished Professor of Liberal Arts and the Study of Religion at the University of Massachusetts, Boston. His work has ranged widely, from ancient Galilee to contemporary religious and cultural themes. He is the author of numerous influential books, including *Jesus and Empire* (2003); *The Message and the Kingdom* (with Neil Asher Silberman, 2002); *Galilee: History, Politics, People* (1995); *Jesus and the Spiral of Violence* (1992); and *Bandits, Prophets, and Messiahs* (1985).

Andrew McGowan is Warden and President of Trinity College, The University of Melbourne, and Joan Munro Professor of Historical Theology, The University of Divinity. He is the author of *Ascetic Eucharists: Food and Drink in Early Christian Ritual Meals* (1999) and *Ancient Christian Worship* (2014).

Derek Krueger is Joe Rosenthal Excellence Professor of Religious Studies and Women's and Gender Studies at the University of North Carolina at Greensboro. A student of Byzantine monasticism, saints' lives, devotional art, and hymns, he is the author of *Symeon the Holy Fool* (1996); *Writing and Holiness: The Practice of Authorship in the Early Christian East* (2004); and *Liturgical Subjects: Christian Ritual, Biblical Narrative, and the Formation of the Self in Byzantium* (2014).

Gary Dickson is an Honorary Fellow in the School of History, Classics, and Archaeology, University of Edinburgh, where he was Reader in History until his retirement. His latest book, *The Children's*

Crusade: Medieval History, Modern Mythistory, clarifies the history of the Children's Crusade in 1212 and explores the way that dramatic event has been reimagined by writers from the thirteenth century to the late twentieth. In 2007 a Festschrift was published: *Images of Sanctity: Essays in Honour of Gary Dickson*, edited by Debra Strickland.

Peter Matheson has taught at Edinburgh University and Otago University and is now Principal Emeritus at the Uniting Church of Australia's Melbourne College. His publications include writings on New Zealand and the Third Reich, but focus mainly on the German Reformation, including *The Imaginative World of the Reformation* (2001); *The Rhetoric of the Reformation* (1997); *The Collected Works of Thomas Müntzer* (1988); and *Argula von Grumbach (1492–1554/57): A Woman Before Her Time* (2013), the first woman writer to be published during her lifetime.

James M. Stayer most recently taught at Queen's University in Ontario before retiring in 2000. He has been associated with the post-confessional trend in the study of the German Reformation, particularly with a secular approach to Reformation radicalism, and more recently with a critical reappraisal of German Luther historiography in the Weimar era. Recent published works include *A Companion to Anabaptism and Spiritualism, 1521–1700* (edited with John D. Roth, 2007), and *Bernard Rothmann and the Reformation in Münster, 1530–35* (with Willem de Bakker and Michael Driedger, 2008).

Amanda Porterfield is the Robert A. Spivey Professor of Religion and History at Florida State University.

Carlos Eire is T. Lawrason Riggs Professor of History and Religious Studies, Yale University.

Mary Farrell Bednarowski is professor emerita of religious studies at United Theological Seminary of the Twin Cities, Minnesota. Her books include *American Religion: A Cultural Perspective* (1984); *New*

Religions and the Theological Imagination in America (1989); and *The Religious Imagination of American Women* (1999).

Margaret Bendroth is director of the Congregational Library in Boston and a historian of American religion. She is the author of several books, including *Fundamentalism and Gender, 1875 to the Present* (1993), and *Fundamentalism and the City: Conflict and Division in Boston's Churches, 1885–1950* (2005), and has edited several other volumes, including *Women and Twentieth Century Protestantism* (2002). Her most recent books include *A School of the Church: Andover Newton Across Two Centuries* (2008), written to mark the school's bicentennial year, and *The Spiritual Practice of Remembering* (2013).

Luis N. Rivera-Pagan is emeritus professor of ecumenics at Princeton Theological Seminary. His many publications include an edition of the report of the assembly of the World Council of Churches *God, in Your Grace . . .* (2007).

ILLUSTRATIONS

Figures

INTRODUCTION: INVITATION TO A PEOPLE'S HISTORY OF CHRISTIANITY

DENIS R. JANZ

The academic discipline known as church history takes upon itself the study of an impossibly large subject.[1] At one end stands, let's say, the rugged, illiterate agricultural day laborer in first-century Galilee who in some way identified himself with the earliest Jesus movement. At the other end, perhaps on a recent Sunday morning, is the well-heeled, educated American businesswoman stepping out of her SUV in front of a suburban church, two children and a husband in tow. These are the bookends, from proto-Christianity to post-Christianity. What happened in the interval? Change—the contrast is obvious, stark, almost grotesque. And continuity—these two people, plus roughly ten billion human beings in between, have thought it important to orient their lives in one way or another on the person of Jesus of Nazareth. This "in between" is what church historians care about.

Why? Obviously because they see this as being of major importance, not only for current "church people," but for all of us. Calling themselves "Christians," these ten billion individuals have, for better or worse, shaped the course of Western history more profoundly than any other group, religious or secular. In large measure, it is precisely this cultural inheritance that has made us who we are. And thus, we will never make sense of who we are, or of our current world-historical situation, or of humanity's prospects for the future, without knowing something about it. Church history, to paraphrase Paul Tillich, is in this sense the depth dimension of the present. Without it we are condemned to superficiality.

Focused on this massive set of data from ten billion people, church history as a discipline has existed now for at least two centuries. Until very recently, its agenda has been dominated by certain facets of Christianity's past, such as theology, dogma, institutions, and ecclesio-political relations. Each of these has in fact long since evolved into its own subdiscipline. Thus the history of theology has concentrated on the self-understandings of Christian intellectuals. Historians of dogma have examined the way in which church leaders came to formulate teachings that they then pronounced normative for all Christians. Experts on institutional history have researched the formation, growth, and functioning of leadership offices, bureaucratic structures, official decision-making processes, and so forth. And specialists in the history of church-state relations have worked to fathom the complexities of the institution's interface with its sociopolitical context, above all by studying leaders on both sides.

NEW DIRECTIONS

As comprehensive as this may sound, the fact is that this discipline has told the history of Christianity as the story of one small segment of those who have claimed the name "Christian." What has been studied almost exclusively until now is the religion of various elites, whether spiritual, intellectual, or power elites. Without a doubt, many of the saints, mystics and theologians, pastors, priests, bishops, and popes of the past are worth studying. But at most they altogether constitute perhaps 5 percent of all Christians over two millennia. What about the rest? Does not a balanced history of Christianity demand that attention be paid to them?

Besides the issue of imbalance, there is also the issue of historical injustice. Ever since the study of history was born as a professional academic discipline two centuries ago, it has been fixated on the "great" deeds of "great" men, and little else. What was almost always left out of the story, of course, was the vast majority of human beings: almost all women, obviously, but also those who were socially inferior, the economically distressed, the politically marginalized, the educationally deprived, or the culturally unrefined. For various elites to despise these people was nothing new. Cicero, in first-century-BCE Rome, referred to them as the "urban filth and shit." Thirteenth-century Dominicans, commissioned to preach to them, referred to them as the "stulta," the stupid. In the sixteenth century, the Paris theological faculty agreed that when Jesus spoke of casting pearls before swine and dogs in Matthew 7:6, he was referring to the laity. In eighteenth-century London, Edmund Burke called them the "swinish multitude." Throughout Western history, this loathing of "the meaner sort" was almost universal among the privileged. Since the nineteenth century, historians perpetuated this attitude, if not by outright vilification then at least by keeping these people invisible. Thus, to pay attention to them now is not only to correct an imbalance, but in some sense to redress an injustice, to rehumanize these masses, to reverse this legacy of contempt.

The new approach to church history tries to do this. It insists that "church" is not to be defined first and foremost as the hierarchical-institutional-bureaucratic corporation; rather, above all, it is the laity, the ordinary faithful, the people. Their religious lives, their pious practices, their self-understandings as Christians, and the way all of this grew and changed over the last two millennia— this is the subject matter. In other words, the new church history is a "people's history."

NEW METHODS

It is one thing to ask new questions about the past and quite another to develop ways to answer them. Difficult as this may be, it is unavoidable: a disciplinary reorientation necessarily entails developing new ways of approaching the subject matter. Disciplines are not generally born with full-blown, highly sophisticated, neatly laid out methodologies. Rather these develop slowly, sporadically, incrementally, by trial and critique, by a willingness to set aside well-worn research procedures and to take chances on new ones. The path to disciplinary maturity is by its very nature a messy and painful one. Those who chart the growth of the natural sciences can attest to this. The novel field of study before us is now experiencing precisely this. Methodologically speaking, it is beyond its infancy, but certainly not yet out of its adolescence.

The detritus of the past that has washed down to us and that we can study can be classified into two basic types: material and literary. Conventional historians have most often sought to understand the past through its literary remains. The problem here, of course, is that the extant written sources for at least the first 1,700 years of Christian history are almost always the products of elite culture. As such they give us access to the religious lives of nothing more than a tiny minority. The illiterate masses simply did not leave to posterity a clear account of their beliefs, values, and devotional practices, let alone their unspoken longings, fears, joys, and sorrows.

For this reason the new people's history increasingly turns its attention to material survivals of the past, to the interrogation of artifacts rather than literary texts. Not that these are transparent: like literary texts, they must be "read" with great caution, with the so-called "hermeneutic of suspicion." Thus, for instance, the discovery of toys that children of Christian families played with in the late ancient world gives us tantalizing hints about parental values and maybe even about how this neglected segment of the Christian people was socialized into the community. So, too, the archaeological uncovering of modest homes with tiny chapels and altars from this same period is suggestive. Women's jewelry from Christianity's Byzantine branch may well indicate distinctively feminine devotional practices. What is the significance of the communion rail, introduced into church architecture in fifth-century North Africa? Can one infer from this, as some now do, that parishioners madly rushed to the altar to receive communion when the time came? The exhumation of medieval bodies in peasant cemeteries has led to the discovery of ubiquitous "grave goods." Surely such data indicates something about the religious consciousness of the laity. But what is notable in each of these examples is that we are not operating here in the realm of proof or fact or certainty. Rather, until methods are refined and research is broadened, we remain in the realm of hints, indications, suggestions, and probabilities.

Important as material culture is for studying people's history, this venture can by no means abandon the literary remains of the past. For one thing, while it is true that the vast majority of lay Christians over the last two millennia have been illiterate, there are exceptions, and their writing must be attended to carefully. We also have graffiti from semiliterate laypersons. And illiterate believers at times, for example, dictated letters and wills and epitaphs, or gave transcribed testimony in courts of law. Few and fragmentary though they may be, such sources allow us at least a glimpse into the popular Christianity of the past.

The writings of various elites within the church also retain some considerable importance for a people's history. Rather than turning a blind eye to these documents, what is needed is the development of new ways of reading them. Practitioners of the new church history refer to such approaches as the "tangential," "oblique," "regressive," or "mirror" reading of texts. The most promising writings to be considered are those that are in some way addressed to the laity. And the researcher's primary question in every case is not, "What is the author trying to say?" but rather, "What can we infer from the text about popular piety?"

NEW ISSUES: POWER, SEX, AND POLITICS

The new history of Christianity is built on the assumption that a meaningful and helpful distinction can be made between "elite" and "popular" (or whatever other labels one chooses to apply). Already in their formative stages, religious groups, like all social groups, differentiate themselves into leaders and followers. The process is similar, whether it took place yesterday as the neighborhood ten-year-old boys organized a baseball game, or in the first century in Galilee as the earliest Jesus movements took shape. And it seems to happen no matter how egalitarian the initial impetus to group formation was. Religious groups in their earliest stages often have an informal, spontaneous, charismatic leadership. If these groups survive, this is inevitably institutionalized, formalized, and professionalized at some point. When it is, it makes sense to distinguish between elite and popular within the group.

Reversing the bias of conventional church history, we now intentionally sideline the various leaderships and elites. And yet, paradoxically perhaps, as we do this we also focus on them again, albeit in a new way. For while popular piety is given center stage, it cannot be understood in a vacuum. From the basic distinction between popular religion on the one hand, and elite, clerical, official religion on the other, there immediately arises the crucial question of how these two interact with one another. And thus, inevitably and unavoidably, the issue of power relations confronts us.

To state the obvious, leaders at every point try to lead. Working on the assumption that they know what is best for the rest, they try to influence, sometimes to dominate, even to control. In Christianity, they instruct on what should be believed; they try to form consciences, inculcating values and moral standards; they work to shape attitudes; they advocate for a particular lifestyle; they admonish, exhort, enjoin, warn, dissuade, implore, cajole, reprove, and harangue. All this is done in countless ways, but most directly perhaps in sermons, catechesis, confession, counseling, and so forth.

And to what effect?

Here, no simple answer is possible. It may be that at certain points in the history of Christianity, ordinary Christians accepted official church teaching, moral instruction, and the like, almost in its entirety. No significant gulf separated clergy and laity when it came to these matters. In this case, official religion and popular religion nearly coincided. This was in fact the tacit assumption of earlier generations of church historians. Today, as the study of popular religion progresses, there appear to be fewer and fewer persuasive examples of this scenario.

Far more often in the history of Christianity, we find evidence that everyday Christians said no and resisted: in these cases, popular and official religion obviously diverged, though to varying extents in different contexts. This "no" spoken by popular religion to elite religion could take the relatively mild form of indifference. Thus, in fourteenth-century Western Europe, for instance—as the church hierarchy emphasized that missing Sunday mass was a mortal sin and threatened punishment temporal and eternal, physical, and spiritual—attendance hovered around 50 percent (if we are to believe reports of village priests).

But the laity's "no" could also take the form of stubborn resistance. For instance, village priests in thirteenth-century France complained that no amount of haranguing could convince their illiterate peasant parishioners that fornication was a mortal sin. At its most extreme, saying no could even take the form of physical violence. Take, for example, the Peasants' Revolt in England in 1381. Hoards of peasants rampaged through the countryside. When they arrived in towns, they sought out the local bishops and beheaded them—a rather vehement repudiation of official religion. Whatever the level of resistance, popular religion does not always buy what elite religion is trying to sell.

Perhaps most commonly in Christian history, the people have said a simultaneous yes and no to their leaders. Absolute refusal to follow is rare: its result is schism, and new group formation in which virulent anti-clericalism inevitably gives way sooner or later to a new clericalism. Blind following is even more uncommon: the image of mindless masses eagerly embracing pronouncements and proscriptions from on high bears virtually no semblance to reality.

We can illustrate aspects of this question of power relations by focusing for a moment on the history of Christian attitudes toward human sexuality. Today, on this score, we have more questions than answers. For instance, why did the church hierarchy struggle so mightily for so many centuries to control this aspect of the lives of the laity? In the case of marital sexuality, why did the clergy go to such great lengths to regulate when, how, how often, and so forth? Did Christianity, as some now suggest, really develop into a sex-hating religion by the end of the Middle Ages, or was this only the clergy? Did the progressive demonizing of sexuality in the Middle Ages have anything to do with the growing enforcement of the celibacy rule for priests? To what extent did average Christians adhere to the magisterium's rules, such as the absolute prohibition of sex during Lent? Was the insistence on detailed confession of sexual "sins" to celibate priests really about sex, or was it about power? Many of these questions may be largely unanswerable today with the present state of scholarship. These questions are notable for two reasons. First, they are the kinds of questions that drive current research and discussion. Second, in every case they focus our attention on the nexus between the popular and the elite. In a people's history, the problem of power relations is inescapable.

It should immediately be added that these elementary reflections on power barely scratch the surface. Experts would immediately ask, for instance, whether such a binary schema is really adequate to the complexity of the issue, or whether the assumption of a one-way influence can account for the data. Practitioners of the new discipline who have begun to focus on this know that we are entering here into an issue of massive complexity. How power within religious groups is negotiated, conferred, wielded, and so forth, or how the location of power migrates within a group—these are the fascinating questions that people's historians of Christianity have barely begun to formulate, let alone answer.

Wherever there is a power differential between members of a group, there is also, of course, politics. In this sense, church politics becomes the subject matter of the new kind of Christian history. We care about official statements emanating from the World Council of Churches, for instance, but only insofar as they make a difference in the lives of ordinary believers. We pay attention to who was made pope in 2006, but only if we suspect this has impacted the religiosity of the Catholic laity. When church leaders made decisions in the past, we ask in every case whose interests were served by those decisions. Thus the new church history is political in the sense that the church politics of the past is thematized.

But it is also political in another sense, one that should be openly acknowledged. Church history in the old style was never objective, value-free, or apolitical. Sides were always chosen. Standing with the "official" Christianity of leadership elites, traditional historiography portrayed popular piety for the most part as emotional, irrational, and superficial—a hopeless bog of sub-Christian superstition, indifference, and stubbornness. Surely "the church" was justified in its massive efforts throughout history to inform, influence, mold, shape, dominate, domesticate, and control this. And surely we church historians are justified in ignoring it.

The new historiography also chooses sides. It starts with the assumption that the elites may have been wrong, that popular piety in fact may have a validity of its own, that it may be an authentic manifestation of this religion centered on Jesus of Nazareth, that it may be worthy of our attention after all. In this sense, people's history is slanted, biased, disrespectful—even subversive perhaps.

NEW RESULTS?

What, finally, is to be gained by this new venture? What outcome can we anticipate? Practitioners of the discipline must, in all humility, admit that at this early stage, it is far too early to say. Perhaps in a generation or in a century, lines of development that we can now barely glimpse will appear obvious to our successors.

One thing that can already be said, however, is that the new portrait of Christianity's past will be vastly more expansive and detailed than the current one. The chapter on the fifth century, for instance, will not be able to ignore Augustine's reflections on the mediation of grace, but neither will it dare to omit those Christians who tied fox-claw amulets onto their bodies for healing. Take accounts of the thirteenth century, for example. Perhaps the intellectual achievement of Thomas Aquinas will still be featured prominently. But what about the vast majority of Christians in his day who had never heard of him? What about the Italian peasants who, we are told, admired Thomas greatly, not for his intellect or his sanctity, but for his remarkable girth and stature? And should not at least some space be given to the thirteenth-century peasant village in the Auvergne, where the cult of St. Guinefort, the holy Greyhound, flourished? So too, balanced treatments of the sixteenth century, while they couldn't ignore Luther and Calvin, would have to inquire into religious life in peasant villages, where the Gospel of John was still read to the wheat fields to ensure a good harvest. And perhaps space should be allotted to the English farmer who had faithfully attended his parish church for thirty years, but who, when asked by his vicar, still could not say the Lord's Prayer, nor, for that matter, how many persons comprise the Trinity? (And what about the disillusionment of the vicar, to whose sermons he had listened for thirty years?) All this and much more will be part of the new picture. If today we have mainly close-ups, what we can anticipate is that the camera will pan out to show us a panorama, and it will do this somehow without losing the fascinating micro-historical detail.

But far more is involved here than merely the accumulation of additional data. Historians are not simply collectors of facts about the past, or chronologists, or antiquarians. The mass of data must be interpreted. The search for meaning and direction in human history, for the contours of a narrative—surely this is what makes it significant. Put differently, the historian's goal is understanding. Mountains of fresh data about the past are worthless unless they lead to a new, more integrated, more adequate, more "true" comprehension of the past, one that then informs and deepens our self-understanding in the present.

The shape of that new plot, if you will, is not yet apparent. But there are already signs that the old one is loosening its grip on the discipline. Take, for example, the growing discontentment among church historians with the traditional periodization. The conventional division of Christian history into New Testament, Patristic, Medieval, Reformation, Modern may have been appropriate for the history of theology, and it may still provide us with handy divisions for the sake of course requirements, but is it helpful for understanding the history of Christianity, especially now when we can no longer ignore "the people"? If, for instance, lay piety is made the central theme of the narrative, does it really make sense to posit some borderline between medieval and Reformation? The frequency of such questions today indicates that we are in transition. The old configuration is crumbling, and the new has not yet appeared.

What you have before you in these volumes is a varied assortment of some of the best current work, all of it at the cutting edge of the new orientation I have described. Chronologically, this collection moves from the earliest Jesus movements to post-modern Christianity. And geographically, it ranges from first-century Palestine to twenty-first-century Latin America and beyond. And yet it is only a sampling. It showcases a discipline in its early development, and invites all who are interested and who glimpse its promise to come aboard.

JESUS MOVEMENTS AND THE RENEWAL OF ISRAEL

RICHARD A. HORSLEY

The Middle Eastern peasants who formed the first movement that focused on Yeshua bar Yosef (whom we know as Jesus) eked out a living farming and fishing in a remote region of the Roman Empire. At the outset their movement was similar in form and circumstances to many others that arose among people of Israelite heritage. Their families and village communities were steadily disintegrating under the increasing pressures of offerings to the Jerusalem Temple, taxes to Herodian kings, and tribute to their Roman conquerors. Large numbers of Galilean, Samaritan, and Judean peasants eagerly responded to the pronouncements of peasant prophets that God was again about to liberate them from their oppressive rulers and restore cooperative community life under the traditional divine principles of justice. The other movements ended abruptly when the Roman governors sent out the military and slaughtered them. The movements that formed around Yeshua bar Yosef, however, survived the Roman crucifixion of their leader as a rebel "king." In fact, his martyrdom became a powerful impetus for the expansion and diversification of his movements.

To understand the earliest Jesus movements in genuinely historical terms requires some serious rethinking of standard assumptions and approaches in conventional New Testament studies, which developed as a foundation for Christian theology. Standard interpretation of the Gospels in particular focuses on Jesus as an individual figure or on the Christology of one of the Gospels. It is simply assumed that the Gospels and other scriptural books are religious and that Jesus and the Gospels were pivotal in the origin of the new, universal, and truly

Fig. 1.1. Map of Palestine in the first century CE.

spiritual religion, "Christianity," from the old, parochial, and overly political religion, "Judaism." In the ancient world in which the Gospels originated, however, religion was not separated from political-economic life. In fact, at the time of Jesus there was no such thing yet as a religion called Judaism, judging from our sources such as the Gospels, the Dead Sea Scrolls, or the contemporary Judean historian Josephus. Similarly, something that could intelligibly be called Christianity had not developed until late antiquity, well after the time when the books that were later included in the New Testament and related literature were composed by leaders associated with the movements focused on Jesus.

It makes sense to begin from the broader historical conditions of life under the Roman Empire that constituted the historical context of Jesus' mission and to focus first on the many other Judean, Samaritan, and Galilean movements that illuminate the form of the earliest Jesus movements.

POPULAR RESISTANCE AND RENEWAL UNDER ROMAN IMPERIAL RULE

The ancient world was divided fundamentally between rulers and ruled, in culture as well as in political-economic structure. A tiny percentage of wealthy and powerful families lived comfortably in the cities from the tithes, taxes, tribute, and interest that they extracted from the vast majority of people, who lived in villages and worked the land. We must thus first examine the historical dynamics of that fundamental societal division in order to understand the circumstances in which the early Jesus movements formed and expanded.

At the time of Jesus, the people of Israelite heritage who lived in the southeast corner of the Mediterranean world, Judea in the south, Galilee in the north, and Samaria in between, lived under the rule of Rome. A Roman army had conquered the area about sixty years before Jesus' birth. The Romans installed the military strongman Herod as their client king to control the area. He in turn kept in place the Temple and high priesthood. The temple-state and its high priestly aristocracy had been set up by the Persian imperial regime centuries earlier as an instrument of their rule in Judea, the district around the

Fig. 1.2. Judean silver shekel, from the time of the first Jewish revolt against the Romans (66–70 CE). Obverse shows a chalice and the Hebrew inscription "year 2," "shekel of Israel"; reverse shows pomegranates and the inscription "Jerusalem the Holy." The minting of coins was itself an act of rebellion against Rome. Israel Museum, Jerusalem; photo: Erich Lessing / Art Resource, NY.

city of Jerusalem. Subsequent imperial regimes retained this political-economic-religious arrangement for the control of the area and collection of revenues. With the decline of Hellenistic imperial power, the Hasmonean high priests extended Jerusalem's rule over Idumea to the south and Samaria and Galilee to the north, little more than a century before the birth of Jesus. After the Roman conquest, however, the high priestly aristocracy at the head of the temple-state in Jerusalem was again dependent on the favor of the imperial regime. Dependent, in turn, on the favor of the high priesthood were the professional scribal groups (such as the Pharisees) that worked for the priestly aristocracy as administrators of the temple-state and custodians of the cultural traditions, traditional laws, and religious rituals in which its legitimacy was articulated.

The old construct of a monolithic Judaism glosses over the fundamental division and multiple conflicts that persisted for centuries in Judean and Galilean history. Conflicts between rival factions in the priestly aristocracy, who competed for imperial favor, and the corresponding factions among scribal circles came to a head in the Maccabean Revolt of the 160s BCE. Further conflict developed as the Maccabean military strongmen consolidated their power as the new high priestly regime. The groups known as the Pharisees, Sadducees, and Essenes, whom we now understand to have been closely related to the Qumran community that left the Dead Sea Scrolls, cannot be understood in early modern terms as sects of Judaism. They were rather rival scribal factions or parties who competed for influence on the high priestly regimes or, in the case of the Essenes, withdrew into the wilderness when they lost out.

The history of Judea and Galilee in the two centuries preceding and the century immediately after Jesus' mission, however, was driven by the persistent conflict between the peasantry and their local and imperial rulers. In fact, according to our principal sources for these centuries—such as the books of the Maccabees, the *Jewish War* and the *Antiquities of the Jews* by the Judean historian Josephus, and later rabbinic literature—it was actions by Judean and Galilean peasants that drove most of the major historical events. The period of history around the time of Jesus was framed by four major peasant revolts: the Maccabean revolt in the 160s BCE, the revolt at the death of Herod in 4 BCE, the great revolt against Roman rule from 66 to 70 CE, and the Bar Kokhba revolt in 132–35 CE. In the immediate period of Jesus' mission and the first generation of Jesus movements, furthermore, peasants and ordinary people in Jerusalem mounted numerous protests and formed a number of renewal and resistance movements, most of which the Romans suppressed with brutal military action. Almost all of these revolts, protests, and movements were directed both against the foreign imperial rule of the Romans and against the Herodian and high priestly rulers in Jerusalem.[1]

Such popular revolts are rare in most areas of the world and periods of history. In response to their perpetual subjection to exploitative practices of the elite, peasants regularly engage in hidden forms of resistance, such as sequestering portions of their crops before the tax collectors arrive. Peasants generally do not mount serious revolts, unless their backs are against the wall or they are utterly outraged at their treatment by their rulers. They do, however, organize vocal protests against their conditions and treatment.

We can see the remarkable level of organization and discipline that popular protests were capable of generating in the strike against the emperor Caligula mounted by Galilean peasants a few years after Jesus' mission there (Josephus, *Ant.* 18.269–84). Gaius Caligula, incensed that diaspora Jews refused to render him divine honors, ordered his statue installed in the Jerusalem Temple by military force. As the military expedition prepared to march through Galilee, large numbers of peasants organized a strike, refusing to plant the crops. The Roman Legate of Syria as well as the Herodian officers in control of Galilee knew well that they faced the prospect of a "harvest of banditry" instead of the crops on which their expropriation of tribute depended. Gaius's timely death prevented an escalation of the conflict. Clearly, Galilean and Judean people were capable of mounting serious widespread protests and other movements of resistance.

As the Galilean peasant strike illustrates, most of the widespread peasant revolts, urban protests, and popular renewal-resistance movements were rooted in and inspired by Israelite tradition. The central social memories of the origin and formation of Israel as an independent people focused on their liberation from foreign rule of the pharaoh in Egypt and on their Covenant on Sinai with their true, divine king (God), to the exclusion of oppressive human rulers ("no gods other than me"; "no images"). Judeans' and Galileans' loyalty to these formative traditions shaped their very identity as a people and led them to oppose foreign and Jerusalem rulers who conquered them and interfered with their community life directly under the covenantal rule of God.

Perhaps the most vivid example is the Passover celebration of the exodus from foreign oppression in Egypt. Jerusalem rulers had long since centralized this celebration in Jerusalem so that it would associate the formative memory and identity of Israel as a people with the Temple and its priesthood. Celebration of the exodus by pilgrims to Jerusalem, however, became a time of heightened awareness of their own subjection by the Romans and intense yearning to be independent again, in accordance with God's will and previous deliverance. In response to regular outbreaks of protest at festival time, the Roman governors made a habit of posting Roman soldiers on the porticoes of the Temple courtyard to intimidate the Passover crowds. But that merely exacerbated the intensity of popular feeling. Under the governor Cumanus at mid-first century, the crowds burst into a massive riot, provoked by a lewd gesture by a Roman soldier—and were slaughtered by the troops (*War* 2.223–26; *Ant.* 20.105–12).[2]

Most distinctive and widespread resistance and renewal efforts among the Galilean, Samaritan, and Judean people were the popular messianic movements and the popular prophetic movements. The many movements that took one or the other of these two distinctively Israelite forms are surely most important in understanding why the Galilean and Judean peoples, more than all others subjected by the Romans, persisted in mounting repeated resistance against Roman rule. These movements are most important for understanding the social forms taken by the Jesus movements. Both the popular prophetic movements and the popular messianic movements were following distinctively Israelite "scripts" based on memories of God's original acts of deliverance led by the great prophets Moses and Joshua or by the young David as the people's "messiah." Memories of these founding events were still alive in villager communities, ready to inform the people's collective action in circumstances of social crisis.[3]

When Herod finally died in 4 BCE, after a long and intensely oppressive rule over the people he had conquered with the aid of Roman troops, widespread revolts erupted in nearly every district of his realm (*War* 2.56–75; *Ant.* 17.271–85). In Galilee, Perea across the Jordan River, and Judea itself, these revolts were led by figures whose followers acclaimed them king, according to Josephus. They attacked the royal fortresses and storehouses, "taking back" the goods that had been seized and stored there, and they raided Roman baggage trains. In Galilee the movement led by Judas, son of the famous brigand-chief Hezekias, was suppressed within a few months, with great slaughter and destruction in the general area around Nazareth—shortly before Jesus came to live and grow up there. In Judea the movement led by the strapping shepherd Athronges and his brothers managed to maintain the people's independence in the Judean hill country for three years. Roman troops were finally able to ferret it out, again with much slaughter and the crucifixion of thousands as a means of terrorizing the people into submission.

Again in the middle of the great revolt of 66–70 CE, Judean peasants acclaimed Simon bar Giora as king (*War* 2.652–53; 4.503–34, 574–78; 7.29–36, 153–55). The Romans having been temporarily driven out, he moved around the countryside in the area of Hebron, where the young David had gotten his start. He liberated (debt-) slaves, restored people's property, and in general effected justice for the people. Having amassed a peasant army of thousands, he entered Jerusalem, joining other forces from other areas of the countryside that had taken refuge in the fortresslike city to resist the inevitable Roman reconquest. After being captured in the Roman reconquest of the city, Simon was taken in chains to Rome. There he was formally executed as the vanquished enemy general (the "king of the Judeans") by the emperor Vespasian and his son Titus in the lavish celebration of their glorious triumph.

All of these movements appear to have been patterned after the messianic movement led centuries earlier by the young David. As the Philistines continued their attacks against the Israelite peasantry, the people acclaimed David as their messiah-king (2 Sam. 2:1-4; 5:1-4) to lead them against the oppressive foreign rulers and to reestablish justice among the people. In his accounts of the movements in 4 BCE and 66–70 CE, Josephus does not use the term "messiah" ("anointed"), probably because he was writing for a Greek-speaking audience. But if we translate his accounts back into the Hebrew-Aramaic culture of Judea and Galilee, these movements must be understood as messianic movements patterned after the liberating revolts led by David and other popularly acclaimed messiah-kings in formative Israelite tradition.

That several such messianic movements emerged a generation before and a generation after the time of Jesus' mission is significant when we recognize that literature produced by the Judean scribal elite rarely mentions a messiah. This is in sharp contrast to previous Christian understanding, according to which the Jews were eagerly expecting *the* Messiah to lead them against foreign rule. But as scholars finally began to recognize about forty years ago, there was no such job description just waiting for Jesus to fulfill (in his own way). The Judean elite, of course, would not have been interested, since their positions of power and privilege depended on the Romans, who appointed oppressive kings such as Herod. Perhaps it was against just such an illegitimate king set in power by the Romans that the memory of the popularly acclaimed messiah-king David and other popular kings was revived among the Judean and Galilean peasantry and came to life in numerous movements for the independence and renewal of Israel right around the time of Jesus.

After the revolt led by Judas, son of Hezekias (4 BCE), this Israelite cultural "script" of a popular messianic movement would certainly have been alive in the area around Nazareth, the very area in which Jesus supposedly grew up. And its brutal suppression by the Romans would have left a collective social trauma of villages pillaged and burned and family members slaughtered and enslaved by the Romans. Such historical events and cultural memories cannot have been without their effect on popular life in Nazareth and other Galilean and Judean villages.

In another distinctively Israelite form, a number of popular movements led by prophets in anticipation of new acts of deliverance by God appeared in mid-first century. According to the ever hostile Josephus, "Impostors and demagogues, under the guise of divine inspiration, provoked revolutionary actions and impelled the masses to act like madmen. They led them out into the wilderness so that there God would show them signs of imminent liberation" (*War* 2.259), and

"For they said that they would display unmistakable signs and wonders done according to God's plan" (*Ant.* 20.168).

The first of these movements led by prophets was among the Samaritans (circa 36 CE). A prophet led a crowd up to Mount Gerizim, the most sacred mountain, promising that they would recover the holy vessels from the tabernacle of the formative exodus-wilderness experience of Israel, buried at the spot where Moses had put them. But the Roman governor, Pontius Pilate, dispatched cavalry as well as infantry, killed some, took many prisoner, and executed the leaders (*Ant.* 18.85–87).

Perhaps the most famous prophetic movement was led about a decade later (circa 45 CE) by Theudas, who "persuaded most of the common people to take their possessions and follow him to the Jordan River. He said he was a prophet, and that at his command the river would be divided and allow them an easy crossing. . . . A cavalry unit killed many in a surprise attack [and] having captured Theudas, cut off his head and carried it up to Jerusalem" (*Ant.* 20.97–98; also mentioned in the Book of Acts 5:36). About another decade later (56 CE), just prior to Paul's visit to Jerusalem after his mission in Corinth, Ephesus, and Macedonia, a Jewish prophet from Egypt rallied many thousands in the countryside. He led them up to the Mount of Olives, opposite Jerusalem, declaring that the walls of the city would fall down and the Roman garrison would be overpowered, giving them entry into the city. The Roman governor Felix, with heavily armed cavalry and infantry, killed hundreds of them, before the prophet himself and the others escaped (*Ant.* 20.169–71; *War* 2.261–63).

Fig. 1.3. The hill of Gamla, in Israel. Fortified by Josephus during the First Jewish revolt, the town finally fell to Vespasian's troops in 67 CE. Photo: Erich Lessing / Art Resource, NY.

As with the messianic movements, so these prophetic movements were peasant movements clearly patterned after formative events in

Israelite tradition. In the general characterization by Josephus (who called those who performed signs of liberation in the wilderness "prophets") and in the case of Theudas, who told his followers to take their goods along and expected the waters to be divided, these figures stepped into the role of a new Moses (or Joshua), leading a new exodus (or entry into the land, which had been more or less collapsed with the exodus in popular memory). The Judean prophet from Egypt patterned his role and the anticipated divine act of deliverance after Joshua's leadership of Israel in taking over their land from oppressive kings in their fortified cities, particularly the battle of Jericho. Judging from the terms used in Josephus's hostile accounts, these prophets and their followers were acting under inspiration.

The most noteworthy aspect of these movements to the ruling elite, of course, was the threat they posed to the imperial order. Josephus says that they were out to make "revolutionary changes." The Israelite traditions they were imitating, the exodus led by Moses and the entry into their own land led by Joshua, moreover, suggest that these movements anticipated a restoration of the people as well as a liberation from alien rule. Given our limited sources, of course, we have no indication of how they imagined the future of an Israel again living in independence of foreign domination. Although Josephus claims that the Samaritans were armed, his accounts of the others suggest that, unarmed, they were acting in anticipation of God's action to deliver them. The Roman governors, however, saw them as serious threats to the imperial order and sent out the troops to crush them and kill their prophetic leaders.

In all of these protests and movements the ordinary people of Galilee, Samaria, and Judea were taking bold action, often involving considerable organization and discipline, in making history. The people, facing acute economic distress and a disintegrating political order, took control of their own lives, under the leadership of popular kings (messiahs) like Judas ben Hezekias or popular prophets such as Theudas. These movements of social renewal and political resistance put the Roman and Jerusalem rulers on the defensive. The peasants were challenging the Roman imperial order! In response, the Roman governors, along with the Jerusalem high priesthood in some cases, took brutal, sometimes massive military action, often symbolically decapitating or ceremonially executing the prophetic or messianic leader.

Most striking is how, with the exception of epidemic banditry, these protests and movements took distinctively Israelite social forms. The protests were driven by outrage at the violation of traditional Mosaic covenantal principles. Both the messianic movements and the prophetic movements were decisively informed by (or patterned after) social memories deeply embedded in Israelite tradition. That there were so many of these movements that took one or another of two basic social forms strongly suggests that these distinctive cultural memories, these "scripts" for movements of renewal and resistance, were very much alive in the village communities of the peoples of Israelite heritage in Palestine around the time of Yeshua bar Yosef.

THE EARLIEST JESUS MOVEMENTS

It is in precisely this context of persistent conflict between the Judean and Galilean peasantry and their Jerusalem and Roman rulers that we must understand the origins and development of the earliest Jesus movements. Given how prominent the popular prophetic and messianic movements were in the immediate historical context, moreover, we might expect that the earliest movements that formed in response to Jesus' mission would exhibit some similar features and patterns.

Several closely interrelated factors in the traditional Christian theological scheme of Christian origins, however, have worked to isolate Jesus from his historical context, even to keep Jesus from having any direct relation to Jesus movements. First, since he was supposedly a unique person and revealer, Jesus is treated as separate from the social roles and political-economic relationships in which historical figures are usually engaged. Second, rather than being read as complete stories, the Gospels have been taken merely as containers in which to find individual sayings. Jesus' sayings are then understood as artifacts that have meaning in themselves, rather than as genuine communication with other people in historical social contexts. Third, Jesus is viewed as a revealer, separated from the formation of a movement in the context of the village communities in which people lived.

Not Jesus himself but the disciples were supposedly the ones who established a community—in Jerusalem after the outpouring of the Holy Spirit at Pentecost, from which they then founded "churches" in Judea and beyond.

The net effect of these interrelated factors of theologically determined New Testament interpretation is a combination of assumptions and procedures that would be unacceptable in the regular investigation of history. When historians investigate popular movements and their leaders (for example, the civil rights movement and its leaders such as Martin Luther King Jr.), they consider multiple contextual and relational factors.[4] Since there are no leaders without followers and no movements without leadership, *leader-follower interaction* is central. Leader and movement would not emerge in the first place, moreover, unless there were a *problematic historical situation*. Yet we do not understand why the leader and followers who form a movement find their situation intolerable unless we know something of the previous *historical developments* that led to the problems. And we cannot understand why they found the situation intolerable unless we have a sense of their cultural values. Indeed, we cannot understand how and why the leader's message and program resonate with followers such that they form a movement without a sense of the *cultural traditions and values* that provide the media in which they communicate.

To investigate the earliest Jesus movements, including possible similarities with contemporary Galilean and Judean movements, we will follow just such a relational and contextual approach—simply bypassing the problematic assumptions, approaches, and concepts of previous New Testament interpretation. We will focus mainly on what are by consensus the earliest Gospel sources, the Gospel of Mark and the sequence of Jesus speeches that appear in closely parallel versions in Matthew and Luke but not in Mark, and known as Q (for *Quelle*, the German word for "source").[5]

The Agenda

Both of the earliest Gospel texts, Mark and Q, represent Jesus and followers as a prophet-led movement engaged in the renewal of Israel that condemns and is condemned by the Jerusalem (and Roman) rulers.[6]

The people who produced and used the sequence of Jesus speeches that is called Q understand Jesus as—and themselves as the beneficiaries of—the figure whose activities fulfilled their yearnings for a prophet who would heal and bind up the people and preach good news to the poor (Q/Luke 7:18-35). They even see his exorcisms as manifestation of a new exodus, done "by the finger of God," a clear allusion to Moses' divinely empowered performances in the exodus (Q 11:14-20). In the longest speech of Q (6:20-49), moreover, Jesus speaks as the new Moses, enacting a renewal of the covenant as the guiding principles for cooperation and solidarity in community relations. Jesus' speech sending envoys out into villages indicates that the movement of renewal of Israel is expanding by sending delegates to more and more village communities. In speeches that take the distinctively Israelite form of prophetic woes and oracles, Jesus pronounces divine condemnation of the Jerusalem rulers and their representatives. He pronounces a series of woes against the scribes and Pharisees and prophetic oracles of lament over the aristocracy who presume on their lineage, the Jerusalem ruling house (Q 11:39-52; 13:28-29, 34-35). The speeches heard by the Q people thus represent Jesus as the latest in the long line of Israelite prophets to be killed by the oppressive rulers.

The people who produced and used Mark's Gospel had an even more vivid sense of Jesus, his disciples, and themselves as engaged in a renewal of Israel against, and under attack by, the Jerusalem and Roman rulers. Jesus called and commissioned the Twelve as the representative heads of the twelve tribes of Israel as well as disciples who extend his mission of renewing Israel in village communities. The hearers of Mark's story resonated to the clear allusions to the origins of Israel under Moses and the renewal of Israel led by Elijah in the sequences of sea-crossings, exorcisms, healings, and wilderness feedings in the middle of the Gospel (3:35—8:29). That a renewal of Israel is under way is confirmed by the disciples' vision of Jesus with Moses and Elijah on the mountain. And in a series of dialogues (Mark 10:2-45) Jesus presents Torah-like instruction to the communities of his followers, teaching that constitutes a renewed Mosaic covenant, indicated by the recitation of the covenantal commandments. After he marched up into Jerusalem with his entourage, he had condemned the Temple itself in a forcible demonstration reminiscent of Jeremiah's famous pronouncement that God would destroy the Temple because of the rulers' oppressive practices (Mark 11; Jeremiah 7 and 26). Finally, just before he was arrested, tried, and executed by the Romans, Jesus celebrated the Passover at the "last supper," a meal that renewed the Mosaic covenant with the Twelve representatives of Israel, and announced that the cup was "my blood of the covenant" (an allusion to the original covenant meal (Exodus 24).

Mark and Q are different in overall literary form, the one a complex story in a sequence of episodes, the other a series of speeches on different issues. They appear, moreover, to have been produced and used by different communities or movements. Yet they both represent Jesus as a Moses- and Elijah-like prophet engaged in the renewal of Israel in its village communities and pronouncing prophetic condemnations of the Jerusalem Temple, its high priestly rulers, and its Pharisaic representatives. That the two earliest Gospel sources, so different from one another in form, share this portrayal of Jesus as leader of a movement suggests the same role and relationship with followers at the origin of the respective communities or movements. Within the overall agenda shared by both texts, we will focus our investigation on a few key aspects of both movements: the sending of workers on the mission of building and expanding the movement, covenant renewal, and persecution by hostile authorities.

Before moving to those key aspects, however, we may note some distinctive features of Mark and Q that seem to distinguish their communities from other movements of Jesus followers. Mark appears to be setting its movement's identity off against the Jerusalem community headed by Peter and others of the Twelve. The story portrays the disciples as increasingly misunderstanding Jesus' mission and, in the crisis in Jerusalem, betraying, denying, and abandoning him. Mark represents Jesus' role as in a sense patterned after a messianic role in addition to his dominant prophetic role. Yet the narrative qualifies and criticizes the messianic role in decisive ways. Mark also downplays Jesus' resurrection so seriously that it is merely instrumental to calling the hearers of the story back up to Galilee to continue the movement that Jesus had started. The Q speeches indicate no knowledge of a resurrection at all. Jesus' death is understood as the climax of the long line of prophets killed by the rulers. And Q's

Jesus demonstrates virtually no messianic traits in his dominantly prophetic agenda.

In these ways and more Mark's story and the Q speeches appear to address movements that originated in Galilee and spread into the bilingual villages of nearby areas (Aramaic and Greek). They are both different from other communities or movements of Jesus loyalists, such as the Jerusalem community known from Acts and the assemblies that Paul addresses in his letters. Before we explore these earliest sources and Jesus movements, however, it makes sense to have a more precise sense of the historical conditions in which the Jesus movements developed.

Conditions in Galilee[7]

Galileans were people of Israelite heritage. They shared with their more southerly cousins in Judea and Samaria the formative traditions of Israel. Most basic were stories of the exodus led by the prophet Moses, celebrated annually in the Passover, and of Israel's covenant with its divine king mediated through Moses on Sinai. Memories of northern Israelite prophets such as Elijah and Elisha would also presumably have been particularly prominent in Galilee.

Galilee, however, had recently come under Jerusalem rule, about a hundred years before Jesus' birth, after being under separate imperial jurisdiction for hundreds of years. During the lifetime of Jesus, Galilee was again placed under separate imperial jurisdiction, no longer under rule by the Jerusalem temple-state. Galileans thus may well have been ambivalent about Jerusalem rule. On the one hand, they were again reunited with others of Israelite heritage, which could well have generated a revival of Israelite traditions. On the other hand, they may not have been overly eager to pay tithes and offerings to the Temple in addition to the taxes demanded by King Herod and the tribute taken by Rome.

Moreover, in Galilee more than in Judea there would have been a discrepancy between the Judean-Israelite "great tradition" cultivated by scribal circles in Jerusalem, partly embodied in the scrolls of the Pentateuch, and the "little" or popular Israelite tradition cultivated in village communities.[8] When the Jerusalem high priesthood took over

Galilee, they imposed "the laws of the Judeans" (presumably including the Pentateuch) on the inhabitants. It is difficult to imagine that a century of Jerusalem rule provided sufficient time for Galilean peasants, who lived largely in semi-independent village communities, to assimilate much from the official "laws of the Judeans"—even if they were being pushed on the people by scribal and Pharisaic representatives of the temple-state. The only close contemporary evidence we have, Josephus's accounts of the great revolt in 66–67, indicates that collective actions by Galileans were motivated by their adherence to the basic principles of the Mosaic covenant, and these accounts give no evidence for Galilean acquaintance with laws in the Pentateuch.[9]

The Galilean people eagerly asserted their independence of both Jerusalem and Roman rule at every opportunity. After the Romans imposed Herod as "king of the Judeans" in 40 BCE, Galileans repeatedly resisted his attempts to control their territory (*War* 1.304–16, 326; *Ant.* 14.415–33, 450). When Herod died in 4 BCE, peasants in the area around Nazareth, having acclaimed Judas ben Hezekiah their king, attacked the royal fortress in Sepphoris (*War* 2.56; *Ant.* 17.271). Seventy years later, at the beginning of the great revolt, the peasants quickly asserted their independence of their rulers. In western Galilee they periodically attacked the city of Sepphoris, which remained loyal to the Romans. In eastern Galilee they repeatedly resisted attempts to bring them under control, whether by the Herodian officers in Tiberias or by Josephus, who had been delegated by the provisional high priestly regime in Jerusalem (Josephus recounts these events in his *Life*).

The Roman imposition of Herod Antipas following the revolt in 4 BCE meant that for the first time the ruler of Galilee was located in Galilee itself and not at a considerable distance. The location of the administration within view of nearly every village meant greater efficiency in tax collection. That efficiency and Antipas's need for extraordinary revenues to underwrite the huge expense of building two capital cities, Tiberias as well as Sepphoris, must have exacerbated the economic burden on the peasant producers. Both cities, built in Roman style by a ruler who had been educated in Rome, must have seemed like alien urban society set down into the previously Israelite rural landscape remote from the dominant high culture.

With peasant families forced into escalating debt in order to pay taxes and still support themselves, village communities were threatened with disintegration. There is simply no solid evidence to support the romantic notion of the last generation that Jesus attracted primarily the marginalized members of society, such as "sinners" and prostitutes or rootless individuals who had abandoned their lands and families. Evidence for economic conditions and land tenure in Palestine at the time of Jesus suggests that peasants in the hill country of western Judea had indeed been losing their lands to wealthy Herodian landlords. By contrast, that Herodian officers in Galilee had their estates on the east side of the Jordan River suggests that villagers in Galilee were still on their ancestral lands.[10] Mark and Q themselves, moreover, represent Jesus as engaging the poor peasantry in general. The frequent attention to debts and their cancellation point to an audience still on the land but unable to make ends meet, given the demands for taxes and tribute. The people available for hire as day laborers in some of Jesus' parables were previously assumed to be landless laborers. But those looking for work in a society such as Galilee were more likely villagers who needed to supplement the dwindling subsistence living they were still eking out on their land or peasants working off debts. And as studies of peasant revolts have found, it is villagers in just such circumstances who tend to become involved in popular movements and revolts. On the other hand, those who have already lost their land become heavily dependent on wealthy elite families or their agents and hence are less free to join movements.

Mission

Our earliest Gospel sources offer a number of indications that a movement developed and expanded in Galilee and areas beyond, catalyzed by and focused on Jesus. These indicators come into focus once we cut through previous assumptions regarding Judaism and Christianity that turn out to be historically unfounded.

In contrast to the portrayal of Paul in Acts as founding a new *ekklesia* ("assembly") as a counterpart to the Jewish *synagoge* ("assembly"), in Galilean, Judean, or Syrian villages it was not necessary to form new communities. As in most agrarian societies, the fundamental form of societal life in Galilee and Syria was the village community, comprised of a larger or smaller number of households. The latter were the basic productive and reproductive unit, while village communities had mechanisms for mutual cooperation and aid to help maintain each household as a viable multigenerational unit in the community.

The speeches in both Q and Mark's story portray Jesus and his disciples as developing a movement based in village communities. In Q, the covenant renewal discourse (6:20-49), which addresses local social-economic relations, makes sense only in the context of local communities. The Lord's prayer, with its mutual cancellation of debts, and the discourse on anxiety (11:2-4, 9-13; 12:22-31) also presuppose village communities. Mark's story, moreover, has Jesus repeatedly teaching and healing in villages or "towns" and "places." Most significant, surely, is how Mark's story, almost in passing (as if it would be obvious), has Jesus and his envoys carrying out their teaching and healing in the village *assemblies*. The Greek term *synagoge*, like the Hebrew and Aramaic *knesset* in rabbinic texts, meant "assembly." In the Gospels and in most references in contemporary Judean texts it refers to the local village assembly. According to later rabbinic texts, these village assemblies met twice a week (compare the community fasts mentioned in the *Didache* 8:1). As the religious-political form of local cooperation and self-governance of the semi-independent village communities, the assemblies dealt with common concerns such as the water supply and held community prayers and discussions.[11]

Independently, Mark (6:6-13) and Q (10:2-16) both have Jesus deliver a speech that commissions workers to assist in the program of extending the movement (of renewing Israel) to other village communities.[12] That these "discourses" exhibit the same basic structure, with different wording, suggests that such sending of Jesus envoys was a standard practice in the earliest phases of the Jesus movements. In both versions of the commissioning, the workers are sent out in pairs to other villages where they were to stay with, and accept subsistence support from, a household in the community. Given the small houses and crowded conditions known from archaeological excavations (several houses of two rooms roughly six feet by nine feet off central courtyards), we can assume they were not working with individual families, but wider village communities. Charged to expand Jesus' own mission of preaching and healing, these workers were apparently also, in effect, carrying out what might be called community organizing. The expectation, surely based on experience, was that a whole village might be receptive or hostile. In the former case it apparently became associated with the wider movement. In the latter, curses might be called down upon it for its rejection of the opportunity offered: "Woe to you Chorazin! Woe to you Bethsaida!"[13]

Fig. 1.4. "Peter's House," ruins of a modest first- or early-second-century house in Capernaum, Israel. Capernaum was one of several densely populated towns surrounding Lake Genessaret (the Sea of Galilee) and figures prominently in the accounts of Jesus and his disciples in the Gospels. Photo: Erich Lessing / Art Resource, NY.

In this connection we should follow up the few clues Mark gives about how the most prominent leaders of the movement—Peter, James, and John—may have come from a somewhat different personal and familial situation from the villagers among whom they built the movement. Their fishing enterprise involved the collaborative effort of several men.[14] Herod Antipas, needing to expand his revenues in order to fund his ambitious city-building, developed fishing into an industry. Working through brokers as intermediaries, the king supplied the equipment, especially the costly large (twenty-six-foot) boats that required a crew of five or six (compare the size of boat required in Jesus' seacrossings in Mark). Collaborative crews evidently contracted to deliver a certain percentage or amount of their catch to the processing depots in return for keeping the rest (somewhat like sharecroppers). The principal processing center for the fish was the burgeoning boomtown of Magdala, "tower of fish" in Aramaic, where people cut loose from their ancestral lands and village communities found work. We might speculate also that the Mary known as "from Magdala," evidently an independent woman (not identified by her attachment to either father or husband), may have been such a destitute person cut loose from her family of origin.

Cross-cultural studies suggest that it is precisely such people with experience beyond a village and contact with outsiders who tend to become leaders in movements of renewal or resistance. Some of the principal leaders of the Jesus movements were apparently "downwardly mobile" people with direct experience of indebtedness to

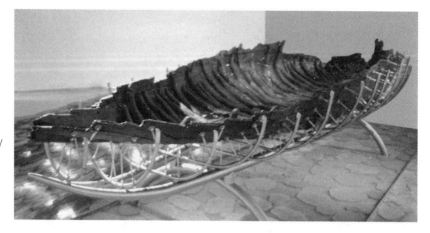

Fig. 1.5. This Roman-era boat was recovered from the Sea of Galilee in 1986. The remains are 8.2 meters long and 2.3 meters wide. Numerous repairs, made with different types of lumber, show the boat had a long working life. Yigal Allon Center, Ginosaur, Israel. Photo: Erich Lessing / Art Resource, NY.

the very power holders who were oppressing the people with heavy taxation and interest on loans prohibited by Israelite covenantal law. These leaders would have had an unusually poignant sense of how the Israelite ideal of a life of cooperation and justice in semi-independent, self-sustaining communities was disintegrating. Such people would have responded eagerly to a message of God's imminent restoration of Israel. Having already been cut loose from the land, moreover, they would have been free to move about from village to village on speaking-healing-organizing missions, in contrast to villagers who needed to remain in place in order to work the fields.

Fig. 1.6. Modern reconstruction of a Roman fishing boat based on the archaeological remains of a boat from first-century Galilee. The size of the craft indicates the scale of the Roman fishing industry, requiring a hired crew much larger than a family operation. Photo: Richard A. Horsley.

The earliest Gospel sources portray the Jesus movements as having developed initially in Galilee. Mark represents Jesus as having his base of operations in Capernaum, a village on the northern shore of the Sea of Galilee—an account that is generally accepted as historically credible. That also fits the idea of Peter and Andrew and James and John's having been fishermen. In the mission speech in Q, Jesus utters curses on Capernaum, the nearby village of Chorazin, along with Bethsaida, a town across the border in Herod Philip's territory. Such curses presuppose that the mission was active in those communities but that they later backed away or rejected the mission.

Mark then also has Jesus and his disciples extend their mission beyond Galilee into the villages of Tyre to the northwest, those of

Fig. 1.7. Ruins of the synagogue of Chorazim, situated above Lake Genessaret (the Sea of Galilee). Hellenistic architectural style. Photo: Erich Lessing / Art Resource, NY.

Caesarea Philippi to the north, and those of the Decapolis to the east and south of the Sea of Galilee. This may well reflect the movement's extension by the time Mark's story was composed and being performed in the constituent communities a few decades after Jesus' own mission. It should not be surprising that movements of local renewal and resistance to rulers among one people would become appealing to others and extend over the frontiers. The Syro-Phoenician-woman episode in Mark's story indicates that the inclusion of a women specifically known as from the dominant Hellenic culture was a serious issue for the Jesus movements. Yet the rapid expansion of the Jesus movements beyond the primarily Aramaic-speaking Galilee into Syrian villages, including some Greek-speaking communities, suggests that villagers of previously non-Israelite culture fairly easily identified with Israelite tradition. This is indicated by the very existence of Mark and Q in Greek as texts performed in communities of a movement.

Covenant Renewal

Closely coupled with the exodus, in the formative traditions of Israel, was the covenant with God made on Mount Sinai. The Mosaic covenant and its fundamental principles of political-economic relations (the Ten Commandments) played a crucial role in the people's repeated resistance to oppressive rulers and struggles to restore just social relations. According to Josephus's accounts of the social turmoil of the great revolt, roughly a generation after Jesus' mission in Galilee, violations of covenantal principles by the elite were what mobilized Galilean peasants to collective action. Clearly, the covenantal principles still provided the operative foundation for social-economic relations in village communities and for their political-economic relations with their rulers.[15]

Ostensibly, of course, covenantal principles and mechanisms were still observed by the temple-state as well as the peasantry. There was society-wide observance, for example, of the seventh-year rest for fields and the seventh-year cancellation of debts, traditional covenantal mechanisms designed to keep subsistence peasant households viable on their land. Hillel, the distinguished elder of the Pharisees, had promulgated the famous *prosbul* as a bypass of the sabbatical cancellation of debts, ostensibly to "ease credit" for already indebted peasants. The covenant was thus clearly still well-known among scribal groups such as the Pharisees, who strove to adapt or vitiate covenantal principles in order to allow the consolidation of power in the Jerusalem temple-state. As we know now from the Dead Sea Scrolls, the dissident scribal and priestly community that withdrew to the wilderness at Qumran used the Mosaic covenant as the basic model for their utopian attempt at the renewal of Israel.

It should not be surprising therefore that in both Mark's story and the Q speeches, in which the main theme is the renewal of Israel over against its rulers, covenant renewal should figure prominently. In Mark the covenant theme runs throughout the narrative, with a covenant discourse and a covenant meal at crucial points in the story. In Q the longest and most substantive speech is a renewal of the covenant. The prominence of covenant renewal in the earliest Gospel sources suggests that it was prominent in the Jesus movements that produced and used them.

The basic components of the Mosaic covenant even provide the structure of the longest speech in Q (6:20-49).[16] In the original pattern, a declaration of God's deliverance (focused on the exodus) as a basis of obligation prefaced the principles of social relations that constituted the core demands of the covenant, which were then sanctioned by blessings and curses. These components can be observed at many conspicuous points in the books of the Hebrew Bible: in covenant making, covenantal laws, and covenantal teachings. They are also prominent in key texts of the Qumran community found among the Dead Sea Scrolls.

Most significant for the covenant speech in Q is how the pattern of components is creatively transformed in the initiation ceremony for those entering the renewed covenantal community in the Qumran Community Rule (1QS). The covenant speech in Q exhibits a similar adaptation of the basic components. In both the blessings and curses components, a previously sanctioning motivation has been transformed into a new declaration of God's deliverance, only now in the present and future ("Blessed are the poor, for yours is the kingdom of God"). Other materials now provide the sanction (double parable of building houses on the rock or sand). Still central, of course, are the covenantal principles (laws, teachings, focal instances) that allude to and adapt traditional covenant principles, as guidance for community social and economic interaction.

The covenantal discourse in Q, moreover, is couched in performative speech, that is, speech that makes something happen (for example, "I now pronounce you husband and wife"). The speech enacts a renewal of the Mosaic covenant in the assembled community. The blessings pronounced on the poor, hungry, and mourning announce God's new deliverance happening in the mission of Jesus and the formation and life of the movement, with the corresponding pronouncement of woes on the wealthy. The declaration of covenantal principles (the "love your enemies" set of sayings) gives focal instances of ways in which community members are to quit their local quarrels, insults, and conflicts and return to the covenant ideals of cooperation and mutual support. They are to "love your enemies, do good, and lend." The thrust is to restore the mutuality and solidarity of village community life. That presumably would strengthen the village community with regard to the pressures that are contributing to its disintegration, most obviously the heavy taxation resulting in indebtedness to the cursed wealthy, which exacerbates their poverty and hunger.

Closely associated with the covenant commandments in Israelite tradition were the time-honored mechanisms of prohibition of interest on debts and sabbatical cancellation of debts and release of debt-slaves. Debts were the bane of peasant life and could become a downward spiral from which a family could never recover. That is why Israelites and most other peasantries developed mechanisms of what has been called a "moral economy," mechanisms that could keep each constituent multigenerational family economically viable.[17] The "Lord's Prayer" in Q, also performative speech, is thus also a covenantal economic as well as religious prayer. The "third petition" is a combination of a plea to God for cancellation of debts and the corresponding commitment to cancel whatever debts were owed by fellow villagers. As expressed in the parallel petitions of the prayer, cancellation of debts along with the provision of subsistence food ("daily bread') is what the kingdom of God means.

Parallel to the covenantal speech in Q, Mark presents a covenantal discourse in a series of dialogues (Mark 10) that deal successively with marriage, status in the community, economic relations, and leadership. These dialogues feature a number of covenantal law–like pronouncements ("What God has joined together, let no one separate!" 10:9) as well as recitation of the covenant commandments (10:19). Like the original covenant principles, the principles enunciated in this series of dialogues (like the focal instances in Q 6:27-39) govern particular facets of local social-economic relations, that is, prohibition of divorce protecting marriage at the core of the family unit (no adultery), sanction against the desire for surplus goods (wealth; no coveting, no stealing of others' goods), and a declaration that leaders must be servants, not aspire to power (one of the purposes of the covenant as a whole).

Besides this covenantal renewal discourse directed to social-economic-political relations within the community of the movement, Mark includes other dialogues with covenantal themes. The most pointed is his charge against the scribes and Pharisees from Jerusalem who urge peasants to "devote" (korban) their property to the Temple. He declares that such demands violate the basic covenant commandments. He gives the example of "honoring father and mother" to illustrate that the goods and produce of peasant families are needed for local subsistence, as in supporting the elders who can no longer labor productively (Mark 7:1-13). This appeal to the original covenantal "commandment of God" in order to condemn the predatory devices of the representatives of the Temple reinforces peasant families' and village communities' attempts to resist the oppressive demands of their rulers. Similarly, Jesus declares that the scribes based in the Temple "devour widows' houses" (household or possessions). He then illustrates how this happens in the widow's donation of the last copper coin of her "living" to the Temple, again reinforcing the popular resistance to Temple demands. Mark's story thus has Jesus use covenantal references both as principles of community welfare and cooperation and as principles of resistance to the ruling institutions and their representatives.

The covenant renewal discourses and other covenantal teaching in the two earliest Gospel sources offer further indications that the Jesus movements that used these texts were based in local communities that they were attempting to restore to the ideals of mutuality and cooperation of Israelite tradition. Other peasant peoples usually had traditional principles and mechanisms that corresponded to Israelite covenantal commandments and sabbatical cancellation of debts. Thus the (renewed) Israelite covenant that forms a central aspect of Jesus movements would have been easily adapted by village communities across the frontier in Syria.

Persecution and Repression

Ancient and medieval rulers seldom kept their peasants under surveillance. The Judean historian Josephus makes it sound highly out of the ordinary even when Herod arranged for informers on the residents of Jerusalem. About the only time that rulers paid any heed to the semiautonomous village communities over which they "ruled" was at harvesttime, when they sent officers to the threshing floors to appropriate taxes. The Roman approach to "pacification" was to terrorize the populace by brutal slaughter and enslavement of villagers and gruesome public crucifixion of insurgents. As noted above, the Roman governors and their clients in Jerusalem and Galilee seem to have been regularly taken by surprise by protests, prophetic movements, and rebellions. Only after disruptions arose did they send out massive military force to destroy them.

It may be all the more telling, therefore, that Q and Mark contain so many references to persecution of movement members: the likelihood of being arrested, brought to trial, even crucified (Mark 13:8-9; Q 12:2-3; 14:26). In fact, one of the standard speeches shared, in different versions, by Mark and Q is an exhortation about remaining steadfast when brought to trial and faced with the threat of execution (Mark 8:34-38; Q 12:2-12). The people who heard Q apparently understood themselves to be in the long line of prophets who had been persecuted and killed (11:47-51; 13:34-35; compare 6:22-23). All of these references and passages suggest that the movements had come to the attention of the rulers of Galilee and other territories, who periodically took repressive action to check the growth of the movement. This parallels the experience of other movements of Jesus-followers: periodic attacks by the high priestly or Herodian rulers on the leaders of the Jerusalem community as portrayed in Acts and Paul's arrest and imprisonment as mentioned in his letters. The gist of the warnings and exhortations about repression in both Mark and Q is that it is only to be expected. The people are not to worry about it, however, but to be ready to face martyrdom, as had Jesus, in the trust that they would receive divine inspiration in the hour of testing and would be vindicated in the divine judgment.

WHAT HAPPENED TO THESE JESUS MOVEMENTS?

There is no obvious reason to imagine much continuity between any of the early Jesus movements or Christ-believers and what later became established Christianity, since the latter was shaped by later generations of "bishops and councils." It was later church councils, for example, that canonized the four Gospels. By the time of those fourth- or fifth-century councils, however, Mark was being read differently from the way it was understood in the early communities for which it was produced. The principal way in which Mark and the Q speeches found minimal continuity with later developments was through their absorption and transformation into the Gospels of Matthew and Luke. As the first Gospel in the canon, Matthew became the most widely influential in the next several centuries. The initial absorption of Mark and Q into the composition of Matthew's Gospel, however, did not dramatically alter the identity and agenda of the movements addressed in Mark and Q. Like its sources, Matthew's Gospel and its community still understood themselves as a renewal of Israel, not a new religion.

We simply do not know what the outcome of the Jesus movements in Galilee and southern Syria may have been, how long their influence lasted in the village communities in which they took root. It must be due to the rapid spread and dramatic impact of Jesus' mission in the first generation that we have records of such popular movements in the first place. Peasant movements generally leave no records. Galilean villages in which the movement took root may have been among those decimated in the Roman reconquest in the summer of 67. Villages further north and east in Syria were probably much less affected.

It would be unwarranted to conclude that these movements represented by Mark and Q simply died out and left no trace after a generation or two and that the diverse branches of later Christianity developed only on the basis of the urban communities established by Paul and others. The letters of Pliny provide evidence that the movements of Jesus-followers or Christ-believers continued to spread into village communities as well as cities as far away as northern Asia Minor into the second century. It is tempting to imagine that the teachings included in the movement manual or handbook known as "The Teaching of the Twelve Apostles" *(Didache)* may have been directed to Greek-speaking village communities of a movement in Syria similar to the one addressed in the Q speeches. The issues addressed and the teachings given appear as a likely later stage in the development of a movement parallel to the one addressed in the Q speeches. For example, the covenant discourse that opens "The Teaching" is expanded with traditional Israelite covenantal teachings, but lacks the performative power involved in the Q speech's transformation of the covenantal components. And the workers ("prophets") sent out in the mission discourses in Q and Mark have now become a problematic drain on the economic resources of subsistence communities when they want to prolong their prophetic "mission." The communities to which the Didache is addressed do not appear to be the same as those addressed in Q or Mark. The instructions for the eucharist assume that Jesus stands in continuity with "the Holy Vine of David," that is, the popular messianic tradition, not the popular prophetic tradition of Moses and Elijah, and baptism is done with a full-blown trinitarian formula. The communities addressed in the *Didache,* however, are a network of village and small-town assemblies that parallel those addressed in Q and Mark.

THE RENEWAL OF ISRAEL

The earliest Jesus movements, known from the earliest Gospel sources Mark and Q, did not comprise a new religion. Rather, they were movements whose agenda was the renewal of Israel in resistance to the imperial rulers of the people. These movements did not form new communities but set about renewing the social-economic relations of already-existing Galilean village communities according to the basic principles of the Mosaic covenant. They quickly spread to villages across the frontier under the jurisdiction of other Roman client rulers. But they continued to cultivate the Israelite tradition and covenantal principles, as adapted and transformed in Jesus' teaching and practice. And they continued their distinctively Israelite identity even after they took root in Greek-speaking communities and performed the story and speeches of Jesus in Greek.

In their origins the earliest Jesus movements are part of the history of the Galileans, Judeans, and Samaritans under the rule or continuing authority of the high priestly rulers in Jerusalem. Jesus and the movements that formed in response to his mission are closely parallel in basic ways to other popular movements at the time among the Judeans and Samaritans as well as the Galileans. All of these popular movements formed in resistance to the Jerusalem as well as the Roman rulers, consistent with the general division in ancient societies between rulers and ruled. In social form these Jesus movements parallel the popular prophetic movements insofar as both Mark and Q, with numerous allusions to Israelite tradition, represent Jesus as a Moses- and Elijah-like prophet leading a renewal of Israel. Mark complicates this somewhat with some messianic motifs, yet cautiously and critically so.

Whereas the other popular prophets called their followers away from their village communities into the wilderness, however, the Jesus movements focused on renewal of village communities themselves. And that may explain why the rulers of Galilee and nearby areas did not destroy the Jesus movements in the same way that the Roman governors simply eliminated the Samaritan and Judean prophetic movements. The imperial authorities, however, after executing Jesus as a rebel leader, did carry out periodic repression of his movements. In so doing they perhaps sensed that these movements aimed to strengthen village independence, mutual support, and solidarity in resistance to the imperial order and its disintegrative effects on the subject peoples.

FOR FURTHER READING

Fiensy, David. *The Social History of Palestine in the Herodian Period.* Lewiston, N.Y.: Mellen, 1991.

Horsley, Richard A. *Hearing the Whole Story: The Politics of Plot in Mark's Gospel.* Louisville: Westminster John Knox, 2001.

———. *Jesus and Empire: The Kingdom of God and the New World Disorder.* Minneapolis: Fortress, 2003.

———. *Jesus and the Spiral of Violence: Popular Jewish Resistance in Roman Palestine.* Minneapolis: Fortress, 1993 [1987].

———, with John S. Hanson. *Bandits, Prophets, and Messiahs: Popular Movements in the Time of Jesus.* Harrisburg, Pa.: Trinity Press International, 1999 [1985].

———, and Neil Asher Silberman. *The Message and the Kingdom: How Jesus and Paul Ignited a Revolution and Transformed the Ancient World.* Minneapolis: Fortress, 2002 [1997].

Scott, James C. *The Moral Economy of the Peasant: Rebellion and Subsistence in Southeast Asia.* New Haven: Yale University Press, 1976.

FOOD, RITUAL, AND POWER

ANDREW MCGOWAN

> A woman...went up to the priest after Mass and said..."Father, I went to communion without going to confession first." "How come, my daughter?" asked the priest. "Father," she replied, "I arrived rather late, after you had begun the offertory. For three days I have had only water and nothing to eat.... When I saw you handing out the hosts, those little pieces of white bread, I went to communion just out of hunger for that little bit of bread."[1]

It takes some effort to perceive the eucharist of later Christian tradition as food, let alone as a meal. Contemporary Westerners may certainly find it hard to imagine that rudimentary meals centered on bread could ever have been of any interest or importance beyond some supposed spiritual or sacramental benefit. Yet Christian liturgical tradition has eating and drinking at its origin, not merely as incidental actions in religious ritual, but as actual food. The power of the story from contemporary Latin America told above lies in the fact that, in most societies, the pursuit of staple food such as bread has been a central part of daily living, with hunger a constant threat. Establishing the meaning of any meal for most of its participants involves considering food and its value in the most prosaic of terms.

The physical necessity of food does not, however, exhaust the significance of meals. Food itself is not merely fodder, and meals are complex rituals that involve many elements beyond food—participants, places, times, words, and rituals—as means of expressing, forming, and transforming religious, social, and other commitments, as well as of meeting physical necessity. All these seemingly prosaic elements have the capacity to convey and construct meaning.[2]

Meals were at the heart of ancient Greco-Roman household life. They not only served as occasions for physical sustenance, but were the venue for basic values to be expressed, confirmed, or critiqued, and the power and status of different diners (or nondiners) displayed or developed. Meals were also central to groups or associations formed for purposes we might describe as religious, political, vocational, and social. Such dining clubs, often referred to as *collegia*,[3] might be the most recognizable social formation through which we may understand the life of the first Christian communities and the centrality of meals within them.[4]

Meals of particular festivity and formality—banquets, we might say—had a prominence in the culture somewhat disproportionate to their literal place in the feeding process. Relatively few people dined often with the niceties depicted on painted vases and in philosophical dialogues, or with the types and quantities of food portrayed in such artistic or literary works. Yet the models of procedure and behavior that center on these prominent banquets—"meal ideology," as it has been called—had an influence that extended even to those who could participate in them only rarely.[5] If few banqueted often, many dined in some semblance of formality and festivity at least sometimes.

Ancient images and debates about issues like types of food, portions, and placement of diners are thus potentially relevant to the variety of ways in which Christians participated in the ancient meal tradition, even in less exalted settings. These elements will all be given at least some attention in this chapter, since diversity must be taken into account if we are to reenvision ancient eucharistic meals from the eaters' perspectives. As in wider banqueting practice, the specifics of food and ritual and other aspects of the Christian meal tradition varied across time and space. And the potential value of belonging to Christian communities will have included the enhanced dietary and social opportunities involved in access to an important practice. Even the same meal could be experienced quite differently. The meals of the first Christians did often bring together women and men of different social class and ethnicity, transcending expected boundaries and offering experiences to benefit and empower participants beyond their normal expectations.[6] Yet many aspects of eating, from the food available to the company kept and roles taken, reflected or created distinctions among eaters, as well as between those present and those absent or excluded. The eucharistic gatherings of the early Christians could thus reinforce or reconfigure power relations, existing or new.

So, too, the theologies that informed and arose from the meal were varied. Christian banquets were not just a universal imitation of one particular model such as the Last Supper. Various groups seem to have had different explicit understandings and purposes in mind and to have used eating and drinking together in a variety of ritual forms. Meals were a way of addressing bodily needs and of expressing and constructing community, but also of remembering Jesus in various ways, experiencing the Holy Spirit, sharing traditional and inspired forms of wisdom, and more besides.

Although there were different Christian meals, supposed essential distinctions based on later nomenclature—opposing eucharist to *agape* ("love feast"), for instance—do little to help interpret these varied gatherings. Different terms were certainly used, and various meanings were attached to the events themselves and to the food elements, but a supposed duality between a more sacred token meal (eucharist) and a more everyday substantial community meal *(agape)* does not really help make sense of the evidence for Christian eating in the first two hundred years.[7]

Of course, the diverse meals of the first few centuries of Christian history were eventually to give rise to the event—less obviously a meal in the usual sense—that is known as eucharist in subsequent tradition. That process of attenuation or abbreviation of the meal into a food ritual—still retaining certain trappings of ancient banqueting practice—was related to the emergence of the church as an imperial religion. Yet processes of change were well under way before Emperor Constantine's conversion and the consequent appearance of the eucharistic meal in a form fully suited for civic ritual. The development was not one of transition from real meal to mere ritual or from open community to structured liturgy; from the earliest point, the Christian meal gatherings were about both ritual and feeding, and they involved the subtleties of symbol as well as the clear trappings of power. Even in its eventual state as a token food ritual, characteristics of a meal were and are still sometimes visible at the eucharist.

FOOD AND FOODS

Bread and Wine

Bread and wine were the staple foods of the ancient world, and the most obvious thing about finding and eating them in a communal context would have been how ordinary they were.[8] Stories of Jesus sharing food and drink of this kind, whether in the wilderness or in an upper room, certainly influenced the sacralization and consumption of bread and wine in early Christian settings, but would not have been necessary to explain their use.

The best-known rationale for a Christian meal of bread and wine is the story of Jesus' Last Supper, presented in three of the canonical Gospels and the writings of the apostle Paul. Jesus, taking bread and cup, presents them to his companions as his own body and blood (1 Cor. 11:23-25). These startling word-images, with sacrificial connotations as well as new overtones of cannibalism that still puzzle scholars, seemed to mean that the simplest food elements could bear within themselves a power otherwise associated with the more expensive and exclusive food offerings of animal sacrifice.[9] Thus the actual food content of the best-known Christian meal tradition may not have been especially appealing, except to those who were literally hungry; yet the capacity of the simplest meal to become a vehicle for power and forms of divine presence otherwise associated with civic ritual and elite dining is significant.

Not by Bread Alone

Bread and wine were not, however, the only foods that might have appeared at all Christian banquets. Typical meals in Greco-Roman households might have centered on bread and been accompanied by wine, but included smaller amounts of other valued and flavorful foods such as cheese, olives, meat, or fish. So too some eucharistic meals seem to have involved a more expansive menu.

In Christian communities where bread and wine were the core of the meal, the complexity or variety of the foods may well have depended on the importance of the occasion, as in many other cultures. In the second and third centuries, milk and honey might be added when baptisms were held in conjunction with the meal. These foods carried with them various symbolic associations of plenty and peace, but they were prized and somewhat luxurious items regardless.[10] Even in the fourth century, when the eucharistic meal had become largely token or symbolic in scale, one liturgical document not only prescribes milk and honey in addition to bread, wine, and water for a baptismal eucharist but also gives blessings for cheese and olives at the ordination of a bishop, another dietary expression of festivity (*Ap. Trad.* 6, 21.27–28).[11]

Ironic as it may seem, much of the early evidence for Christian meals involving foods other than bread and wine actually comes from strict ascetic traditions and communities, who might otherwise have been assumed to eat fewer foods, and less of them. Novelistic literature from the ancient Christian milieu makes these concerns and choices especially prominent. The Pseudo-Clementine *Homilies,* from the second or early third century, reject meat eating and wine drinking but depict a sacred meal of bread and salt for the newly initiated recipient of sacred books (*Letter of Peter to James* 4:3; *Letter of Clement to James* 9:1-2). The apocryphal *Acts of Paul and Thecla* present simple meals of, for example, bread, vegetables, and water (not wine) as the substance of the communal meal known as an *agape* (25). Another early Christian novel, the *Acts of Thomas,* depicts its apostolic hero presiding at a sacred meal with surprising ingredients: he took "bread, oil, vegetables and salt, blessed them and gave them to them" (29). Both these sets of *Acts* also oppose the use of meat and wine altogether. Although these cases are idealized within fictional narratives, they probably reflect real practices. Their extra elements actually reflect a common concern to avoid certain other foods, that is, meat and wine, both connected with pagan meal and sacrificial custom and entirely avoided in these documents and communities.

There are more direct witnesses to this type of avoidance and its tendency to produce meals with other elements: for instance, a group of Christians in Asia Minor connected with the charismatic New Prophecy movement (also known as Montanism) were nicknamed the *Artotyritai* ("bread-and-cheesers") because of the form their eucharistic meal took (Epiphanius, *Panarion* 49.1); again wine was absent, but cheese or perhaps coagulated milk was used, as in the more festive cases already noted. Here the ascetic impulse that rejected impure or idolatrous foods seems to have led to a different pattern of relating eucharistic to everyday meals. In this understanding, all food had to be pure or even sacred, and the distinction between specific community meals with ritual elements and other forms of eating was relativized.

Meat and Fish

Fish and meat raise quite different questions. In the Greco-Roman world meat was generally expensive and desirable, and a prominent feature at banquets in wealthier circles as well as on festive civic or domestic occasions. Central in the sacrificial rituals of Judaism and in the many other temples surrounding the newly emergent Christian movement, eating meat was often a form of sociability with the god to whom it had been offered. As Paul's First Letter to the Corinthians indicates, the production and distribution of meat could thus be fraught with the connotations of pagan religion, since even meat in the market had often been sacrificed in the temples. Paul's own approach was a "don't ask, don't tell" policy, where only meat explicitly known to have been offered to a deity was to be refused.

Eat whatever is sold in the meat market without raising any question on the ground of conscience, for "the earth and its fullness are the Lord's." If an unbeliever invites you to a meal and you are disposed to go, eat whatever is set before you without raising any question on the ground of conscience. But if someone says to you, "This has been offered in sacrifice," then do not eat it, out of consideration for the one who informed you, and for the sake of conscience—I mean the other's conscience, not your own.

—1 Cor. 10:25-29

There is no particular evidence for meat eating at specifically Christian meals, although an argument from silence cannot be definitive. The increasing sense in some communities of Jesus' body and blood in or as other foods at eucharistic meals may have made the actual use of meat, a different sacrificial element, awkward.

At least two specific attitudes to meat eating in addition to Paul's prag-matism emerged early and were also influential among Christians. As we have already seen, some took a more radical stance and refused all meat eating as well as wine drinking in whatever setting, both elements seen as tainted with idolatry because of their prominence in sacrifice. At the other extreme, some diners relied on a superior understanding whereby faith or knowledge (gnosis) allowed them to partake of any food, regardless of origin (1 Cor. 8:1-7). If the pagan gods were not real, what harm was there in eating their offerings? This sort of attempt to reinterpret or ignore qualms about idolatry on the basis of theological sophistication may have opened the social as well as dietary benefits of relatively prestigious banquets to high-status converts for whom they were an important part of life.[12]

The significance of these alternative approaches was sharpened as persecution of Christians grew, and sacrifice—including the eating of meat offerings—became a key element in testing faith and apostasy. Those Christians for whom gnosis allowed greater freedom found that their position allowed not just social advantage but literal sur-vival, since they could eat sacrificial meat with impunity, not merely when it was desired, but when demanded. A century or more after Paul's encounter with this suggestion, it was still powerful enough to influence many. A Jewish critic could then be imagined as pointing out that there were many "Christians [who] eat meats offered to idols, and declare that they are by no means injured in consequence" (Justin Martyr, *Dialogue with Trypho* 35.1). A bishop in late second-century Gaul, Irenaeus of Lyons, attributes meat eating and a range of other socially accommodating behaviors specifically to such so-called gnos-tic Christians (*Her.* 1.6.3, 1.24.5, 1.26.3).

On the other hand, the more ascetic alternative of refusing meat altogether likewise became rather more than a lifestyle matter or expression of dietary dissent when sacrifice became a matter of com-pulsion rather than of choice. Vegetarian Christians, who included groups labeled Montanists, Marcionites, and Encratites, were often prominent among martyrs, expecting a heavenly banquet as reward for their earthly abstemiousness.[13]

Despite intriguing literary references in the Gospels (for example, John 21:13) and early Christian artistic depictions (fig. 6.1), there is

Fig. 2.1. This third-century fresco depicts a fish and a basket of bread that bears the image of a glass of wine, thereby linking meal traditions involving bread and wine with the story of the miracle of the loaves and fishes. Catacomb of S. Callisto, Rome, Italy. Photo credit: Scala / Art Resource, NY.

no clear evidence for Christian use of fish as a specifically sacral food. Fish probably was a more acceptable luxury food for Christians than meat. This may again be related to sacrifice and idolatry; although there are various symbolic as well as aesthetic reasons fish might have been prized, the fact that it was not regularly sacrificed was probably crucial to its use, real or artistic. Intriguingly, what may be the oldest surviving depiction of the Last Supper, from the sixth-century decoration of S. Apollinare Nuovo in Ravenna, depicts Jesus reclining with the twelve at the proper *sigma*-shaped table, but with two fish rather than the expected paschal lamb before the diners (fig. 6.2). Conflation of the scene with another Gospel story, a miraculous feeding (Mark 6:30-44), avoids the potential difficulty of depicting both the animal and the human victims in one setting.

My Flesh Is Real Food

Bread was the element most often emphasized in Christian meal traditions. Although it was of course used in Jewish temple offerings (for example, Exod. 25:30) and in the ritual meals of Passover, the symbolic usefulness of bread for the early Christians may have been precisely its ordinariness. The ubiquity of bread gave it a capacity to carry a whole variety of associations, rather than just one.

If bread was as common and as necessary in the ancient Mediterranean as such staples are in subsistence-level societies, then the economic value of participating in meals based on bread may have

Fig. 2.2. Jesus and his disciples dine on fish at the Last Supper. S. Apollinare Nuovo, Ravenna, Italy. Photo credit: Erich Lessing / Art Resource, NY.

been greater than often assumed, at least for the poorest. Yet one of the most distinctive elements of many Christian meals was the tendency for bread to be treated as central, honored, and sacralized. Those who ate this sacred bread received implied benefits like those otherwise accessible only to meat eaters; thus a characteristic of some eucharistic gatherings was a sort of dietary expression of social reversal.

The most distinctive and powerful understandings of the sacralization of bread invoke the body or flesh of Jesus, which was often understood to be literally present in or as the food (see Ignatius, *Smyrneans* 7.1). This imagery drew upon the words of Jesus in the Last Supper stories and John's Gospel interpretation of the miraculous feeding of five thousand, where Jesus insists on his followers eating his flesh and drinking his blood (John 6:53-56).[14] Paul's Corinthian correspondence also made a number of comparisons between the meal of the Christians and the carnivorous banquets of their neighbors and associates. Although it is hard to know exactly what Paul himself understood the bread of the meal to be or become, eating the bread and drinking the cup amounted to a participation in the body and blood of Christ (1 Cor. 10:16), and he understood these to be objectively powerful and potentially beneficial or dangerous (1 Cor. 11:30). Ignatius, a Christian leader in Antioch just after the end of the first century, reflects a similar seriousness about the significance of the eucharistic food. He calls on his correspondents in Ephesus to go on "breaking one bread, which is the medicine of immortality, the antidote preventing us from dying, so that we might live for ever in Jesus Christ" (Ignatius, *Ephesians* 20).

These letters also imply that alternative views and practices existed. Paul complains that some eat and drink "not discerning the body," which seems to be a concern both about behavior at the meal and about the understanding of the meal elements (1 Cor. 11:26-30). Ignatius also bemoans the fact that some do not participate in the preferred form of meal precisely because of difficulty with the belief that the elements are the body and blood of Jesus, the objection apparently tied to an understanding of him as a spiritual rather than a material being (*Smyrneans* 7).

Yet these Christians who were less comfortable with a literal consumption of eucharistic foods as the remnants of Jesus' sacrificial immolation do seem to have had their own versions of a common meal. The slightly later apocryphal *Acts of John* give some idea of the understanding and practice of communities who approached the meal, and Jesus himself, differently (see sidebar). That narrative of deeds attributed to the apostle John reflects the ascetic sort of meal practice already discussed, now with an accompanying eucharistic theology replete with symbolism, but not with the specific and difficult imagery of Jesus' body and blood. This different way of sacralizing food is based as much on a different sense of community as on a particular Christology; rather than singling out bread and wine alone among the elements of a sacred meal, these practices attribute a generally sacred character to all acceptable food and to its eaters. The theological emphasis comes not on the distinction between the bread and wine of the eucharistic meal and normal food, but on that between the pure food of the community and the tainted food of idolaters outside.

Where the more focused understanding on the eucharistic foods as Jesus' body and blood held sway, the fearful and fascinating properties of bread-become-flesh could overshadow the importance of the meal setting itself. Although Ignatius had urged common meals with the presence of the local leader or bishop in Asia Minor, not long afterward Roman Christians were carrying fragments of the eucharistic bread away from the community meal to the sick and others unable to attend the banquet (Justin Martyr, 1 *Apol.* 67). By 200 CE, fragments of the blessed bread were being distributed quite independently of the banquet in North Africa, and carried home for later consumption, especially for breaking fasts (Tertullian, *On Prayer* 19.1–4). Around 250 the Carthaginian bishop Cyprian depicts devotees wearing lockets with the eucharistic bread around their necks as talismans, and these receptacles bursting into flames or their contents turning to ashes in the hands of the unworthy (*Laps.* 25–26). These practices were signs of a shift that would fundamentally change the nature and place of the banquet.

> And when he had said this John prayed, and taking bread brought it into the sepulcher to break and said:
>
> We glorify your name that converts us from error and pitiless deceit;
> We glorify you who have shown before our eyes what we have seen;
> We testify to your goodness, in various ways appearing;
> We praise your gracious name, O Lord, [which] has convicted those that are convicted by you;
> We thank you, Lord Jesus Christ, that we confide in [...], which is unchanging;
> We thank you who have separated the nature that is being saved from that which is perishing;
> We thank you that you have given us this unwavering [faith] that you alone are [God] both now and for ever;
> We your servants, that are assembled and gathered with [good] cause, give thanks to you, O holy one.
>
> And when he had made this prayer and glorified [God] he gave to all the brethren the Lord's Eucharist, and went out of the sepulcher.
>
> —*Acts of John* 85–86[15]

FROM FOOD TO MEAL

Ancient sensibilities could distinguish between mere eating—meeting the needs of hunger—and the more powerful and socially enriching process that makes a meal. Then, as more recently, factors including the identity of the diners, their places at table, the order of proceedings, and the forms of discourse or entertainment would all have to be taken into consideration, along with the food itself, to construct a meal.

Order at the Meal

The typical banquet consisted first of a meal where diners reclined at a U-shaped *(sigma)* table, thus facing one another to some extent (fig. 6.3). After various food courses, tables were removed, and the second part, the *symposium* or drinking party, ensued. During this time conversation and entertainment were expected, as a number of bowls of wine were mixed, with prayers and libations, for the company. The story of Jesus' Last Supper as given in most of the New Testament accounts fits this expected order of meal followed by drinking party. A description of a Christian meal gathering or *agape* from North Africa around 200 CE reflects an adaptation of this structure and process to reflect the specific interests and concerns of one community (see sidebar).

> Our feast explains itself by its name. The Greeks call it *agape,* i.e., affection. Whatever it costs, our outlay in the name of piety is gain, since with the good things of the feast we benefit the needy. . . . If the object of our feast is good, consider its further regulations in the light of that. As it is an act of religious service, it permits no vileness or immodesty. The participants, before reclining, taste first of prayer to God. As much is eaten as satisfies the cravings of hunger; as much is drunk as befits the chaste. They say it is enough, as those who remember that even during the night they have to worship God; they talk as those who know that the Lord is one of their auditors. After washing of hands, and the bringing in of lights, each is asked to stand forth and sing, as he can, a hymn to God, either one from the holy Scriptures or one of his own composing—a proof of the measure of our drinking. As the feast commenced with prayer, so with prayer it is closed.
> —Tertullian, *Apol.* 39

Other versions of the Christian meal tradition were less immediately comparable to the typical Greco-Roman banquet of a meal followed by drinking. Sometimes ritual cups were blessed and drunk at the outset of the eucharistic meal, and not just at the end. This pattern appears in the earliest known outline of prayers for a Christian meal ritual (called "*Eucharistia*" or "thanksgiving"), presented in the *Didache* or *Teaching of the Twelve Apostles*, perhaps from Syria in the late first century. The same order of cup and bread is also found in the *Mishnah* as well as in meals prescribed in the Dead Sea Scrolls, suggesting this pattern may have been a distinctly Jewish tradition.[16] These cases should still be understood as part of the wider banqueting culture of the Greco-Roman

Fig. 2.3. A Christian funeral banquet is boisterously under way, as represented on this third-century Christian sarcophagus. Museo Nazionale Romano (Terme di Diocleziano), Rome, Italy. Photo credit: Scala / Art Resource, NY.

world, since it is clear that Jewish meal traditions, including the Passover seder itself, were influenced by the rest of the banqueting genre, even if there were distinctive formal elements (in addition to well-known Jewish dietary rules). In context, this reversed order of proceedings may have reflected the same concern for moderation and proper behavior evident in Tertullian's North African *agape* account; taking the cup at the beginning seems to have avoided the dubious *symposium* and the connotations of raucous behavior connected with it.

The *Didache* also has no knowledge of, or no interest in, either the Last Supper itself or Jesus' death as the basis for its procedure of thanksgiving. This has led some to suggest that the *Didache* meal has a different character than what Paul refers to as the Lord's Supper. Up to a point this may be true, but it is misleading to suggest that there were two specific forms of meal (least of all eucharist and *agape*) with essentially different meanings, foods, and procedures and that the diversity of early Christian evidence should be allocated to one category or the other. Rather, these different terms, models, and understandings constituted a variety of ways in which the Jesus tradition and other elements of early Christian theology and belief interacted with ancient meal customs, giving rise to a variety of forms and understandings of the banquet.

And concerning the Eucharist, hold Eucharist thus: First concerning the Cup, "We give thanks to you, our Father, for the Holy Vine of David your child, which you made known to us through Jesus your child; to you be glory for ever." And concerning the broken Bread: "We give you thanks, our Father, for the life and knowledge which you made known to us through Jesus your child. To you be glory for ever. As this broken bread was scattered upon the mountains, but was brought together and became one, so let your Church be gathered together from the ends of the earth into your Kingdom, for yours is the glory and the power through Jesus Christ for ever." But let none eat or drink of your Eucharist except those who have been baptized in the Lord's Name. For concerning this also did the Lord say, "Give not that which is holy to the dogs."

—*Didache* 9[17]

By the later third or early fourth century, this local diversity would yield to processes of influence and standardization. The outcome was not single or simple, but rather a normative tokenized eucharist with a variety of continuing meal and food practices in its orbit. The preeminent offering remained in some relation not only to a somewhat secularized banquet known as *agape* but to a variety of other rituals connected with consumption of the eucharistic food, meals celebrated in tombs and in honor of saints, and more. At earlier points, however, both eucharist and *agape* had been terms by which particular communities referred to their whole meal tradition, rather than to specific and clearly defined alternative procedures.

Prayers and Discourse

Appropriate talk could be one of the most important elements of a meal, as the literary tradition about banquets reveals. This is not to say that the philosophical dialogues of Plato represent real expectations for discourse at most ancient banquets. Yet for Christians as for others, meal gatherings may often have been the settings at which teaching, argument, or other forms of formal and serious conversation and debate took place. Many of the written works that have survived from the early centuries of the Christian movement may actually have been formed or used in such traditional *symposia*, whether or not they make any reference to it. For instance, Paul in writing to the Corinthians refers to various forms of utterance at the meal gathering (1 Cor. 12:8-10), and Tertullian's *Apology* depicts individual diners as singing when called upon at their pleasant Carthaginian evening, but their own works may also have been read in these settings.

The prayers and blessings used in the actual meal ritual have been the major focus of much study of the eucharistic tradition and can receive less treatment here accordingly.[18] At the outset it can probably be assumed that they were relatively brief utterances—the meal prayers of the *Didache* are the earliest example and are somewhat comparable to contemporary Jewish blessings (for example, *Mishnah* Berakoth). The *Acts of John* provide quite different forms of prayer, connected only by the sense of thanksgiving with those of the *Didache,* but whose list of epithets for Christ still only amounts to a short discourse.

Neither of these makes any reference to the actual story of Jesus' Last Supper, later regarded as the core of prayer appropriate to the eucharistic meal, but at this point somewhat marginal to the actual performance of its ritual. In some cases, that story may have functioned as a rationale for the meal—told and retold, perhaps, in the course of the Christianized *symposium,* but not originally used as a blessing for food. In others, that story was probably simply unknown or irrelevant, with other stories or images of Jesus serving to inform and ground the proceedings.

The development already traced, from substantial meal gathering to an assembly focused on the distribution of token amounts of bread and wine, had its impact on the words spoken also. The link with Jesus' death so central in later, and particularly Western, understandings of the eucharist was to be accentuated in the same developments that brought the eucharistic elements to their eventual place on altars in basilicas rather than at domestic tables.[19] And as the reception of the sacral food was separated from banquets and became a more self-contained process undertaken not at meals but at morning liturgical assemblies, the expectation of extended discourse shifted somewhat. While there were still elements of instruction, the communal *symposium* was no longer part of the process. Sermons and catecheses, on the other hand, continued or expanded, as did the actual prayers and blessings, almost in inverse proportion to the size and scope of the meal itself. As less was eaten, more and more seems to have been said over the sacral foods.

Equality, Inclusion, Diversity

The Greco-Roman meal tradition was a vehicle for competing understandings of its own character and purpose. That is to say, banquets were the place where proper meal conduct was debated—at least in the literary tradition. This was no less the case in Christian circles than otherwise. Luke's Gospel, for instance, depicts teaching by Jesus concerning meal behavior taking place at actual meals (Luke 11, 14). The communities in which this and other Gospels were formed had to confront these same basic questions such as appropriate washing, foods, and seating order when they ate together.

The question of who might even properly be present at Christian meals is an important and difficult one. Although New Testament stories about Jesus at table reflect an early tradition of open commensality, Christians retold these in a somewhat different context, where community formation and boundary maintenance had typically become important. Diners did sometimes move between different groups and their meals, and people who were not identifiably or clearly members of the Christian community may perhaps have taken part in eucharistic meals at times. Generally, however, the Christian meal seems to have drawn and created a distinctive group of participants, usually defined further in terms of baptismal initiation (*Did.* 9.5). As elsewhere, inclusion in the group that celebrated regular meals meant participation in a specific network of support and friendship, at times the creation of a sort of constructed familial structure. The Christian meal was certainly perceived as an exclusive event and often viewed by outsiders with corresponding suspicion and concern.

These meals may nonetheless be described as inclusive, in the sense that those who did dine together were somewhat diverse in terms of class or status, gender, and ethnic or religious background. Although the range of such participants may have signaled transcendence of such distinctions, the proceedings may have reinforced or reflected some new and some existing differences. Diners sometimes found their status outside the meal reflected in their treatment at it, and, in addition, the new social formation of the church created its own specific structures related to the conduct of the meal.

The question of equality and hierarchy at table was a vexed one in antiquity. Gender was not always marked or treated in the same way, with local and cultural variations determining the participation of women as diners as well as in the expected roles of food preparation and service.[20] This was, of course, a highly stratified society otherwise, and serious critics of that reality were relatively few. Meals were often an expression of that class structure in a variety of ways: at a given banquet, the seating and even the foods given to different guests might be an unapologetic depiction of wider social realities.[21] Yet there was also a different and prominent tradition that diners were equals and that sharing meals created forms of sociability in some degree of tension with the wider structures and understandings of hierarchy.

Again, Paul's correspondence with the Corinthian Christians reflects these debates. For some of those more elite diners, separate meals in a common venue was already condescension enough toward their lower-status colleagues, and those of lower status need not have expected anything different. Paul, however, argues strongly that the sharing of self shown by Jesus at his Last Supper demanded a more equitable approach. The Letter of James also reflects a concern that the order of seating at the meal not reflect class distinctions (James 2:1-7), but the necessity of making the point shows that this was not always clearly accepted.

Scrutiny of Paul's own letters also suggests caution about assuming just what sort of equality was really intended. Just as his own rhetoric of "weakness" serves to establish his authority, Paul seems to have intended the poor at Corinth to experience acceptance and inclusion within the church, but not necessarily any transformation of their relationships with wealthier Christians outside the meal gathering (1 Cor. 7:24). This approach fits with other ancient constructions of equality, where friendship could actually serve to bind diners into the networks of patronage that dominated social relations.

> Now in the following instructions I do not commend you, because when you come together it is not for the better but for the worse. For, to begin with, when you come together as a church, I hear that there are divisions among you; and to some extent I believe it. Indeed, there have to be factions among you, for only so will it become clear who among you are genuine. When you come together, it is not really to eat the Lord's supper. For when the time comes to eat, each of you goes ahead with your own supper, and one goes hungry and another becomes drunk. What! Do you not have homes to eat and drink in? Or do you show contempt for the church of God and humiliate those who have nothing? What should I say to you? Should I commend you? In this matter I do not commend you!
>
> —1 Cor. 11:17-22

Presiding and Patronage

The physical setting and the roles exercised by individuals at the meal played an important part in the creation of patronage, the fundamental structure of obligation and dependence in ancient Roman society. The most natural patron at a domestic meal was the householder who invited others to dine, but associations also had their own office-bearers who might exercise authority in matters such as seating, recite prayers and blessings, and by implication benefit from the honor attributed to the host's role. The ministerial offices of the early Christian communities were inevitably linked with such ideas of leadership and patronage at banquets. These roles included the ceremonial; Gospel accounts attribute such actions and words to Jesus in certain cases (see, for example, Mark 6:41), and apostles likewise preside in the accounts of canonical and apocryphal *Acts*. The *Didache* specifies that prophets are to use whatever form of words they are inspired to utter when they pray over cup and bread, implying that set prayers are for the bishop (10.7); in other words, either of these persons might have led the meal.

A tension between the roles of actual householders and church office-bearers could emerge. Ignatius of Antioch, writing early in the second century, insisted that the presence of the bishop was necessary for the *agape* to take place (*Smyrneans* 8). Others clearly thought differently and either persisted in a different form of household leadership or even had a flexibility of leadership roles akin to rotation (see Tertullian, *Prescrip.* 41).

Women may have taken leadership roles at eucharistic meals; as householders they could serve as patrons or hosts and also sometimes as appointed clerics, although these cases were often resisted in emergent catholic structures. In second-century Asia Minor the new Prophecy movement later known as Montanism certainly included women who were leaders and eucharistic hosts. Irenaeus, in Gaul at the same time, gives a rather pejorative description of the eucharistic blessings associated with one community (perhaps comparable with that behind the *Acts of John*). The leadership of this group seems to have included not only a prominent male leader, Marcus, but a number of women (see above, p. 51).

Irenaeus undercuts his own picture of that "Marcosian" church as just a group of gullible women bewitched by a mountebank when he also indicates that they practiced a sort of liturgical lottery to allocate roles in the expected discourse following the meal. Tertullian, writing just a little later, speaks of another Valentinian group who also had a sort of rotational system for the meal presiders, with the full participation of women (*Prescrip.* 41). Yet the assumption that women's leadership and Gnosticism or other heresies were always and everywhere connected is undermined by evidence that ancient Christian women in the catholic part of the church did sometimes hold offices relevant to the meal celebration, such as deacon, presbyter, and perhaps also bishop.[22]

Third- and fourth-century evidence also reflects a shift away from evening banquets as the primary focus of ritual eating and drinking toward gatherings focused more narrowly on the distribution of sacramental food elements by the bishops. By this time Christian groups were often meeting in adapted or purpose-built spaces rather than private homes, and the changes of space and of meal procedure reflect not just the growth of the church but also the consolidation of the role of clerics as the exclusive hosts and patrons in terms of the sacred food of the eucharist.[23]

By the fourth century, substantial meals in households and in other small gathered settings were also distinguished clearly from the eucharistic gatherings of whole Christian communities. Various subgroups of what was now a much larger church might still be invited for specific suppers by private hosts, and these might include some specific rituals and prayers, indicating a religious purpose (fig. 6.4). These domestic gatherings of selected Christian invitees often carried with them the term *agape* that had previously been applied to eucharistic banquets of the wider Christian community. The meal gatherings of the emergent monastic movement were another

---

Pretending to eucharistize cups prepared with mixed wine, and extending greatly the word of invocation, he contrives to give them a purple and red color, so that Grace, who is one of those that are superior to all things, should be thought to drop her own blood into his cup through means of his invocation, so that those who are present should be led to rejoice to taste of that cup, in order that by doing so, Grace, who is set forth by this magician, may also flow into them. Again, handing mixed cups to women, he tells them to eucharistize these in his presence. When this has been done, he himself produces another cup of much larger size than that which the deluded woman has eucharistized, and pouring from the smaller one eucharistized by the woman into the one brought forward by himself, he at the same time pronounces these words: "May she who is before all things, Grace who transcends all knowledge and speech, fill your inner human, and multiply in you her own knowledge, sowing the grain of mustard seed in good soil." Having uttered such words, and thus goading on the wretched woman, he then appears a wonder-worker when the large cup is seen to have been filled out of the small one, so as even to overflow from out of it. By accomplishing several other similar things, he has completely deceived many, and drawn them away after him.

—Irenaeus, *Against the Heresies* 1.13.2 (adapted from *ANF*)

Fig. 2.4. What kind of meal is depicted on this third-century Christian fresco? Given the variety of existing practices as well as the diversity of possible meanings attributed to eating and drinking, it is not always easy to categorize Christian meals. Catacomb of S. Callisto, Rome, Italy. Photo credit: Scala / Art Resource, NY.

selective—and often very ascetic—form of banquet that continued alongside the identifiable eucharistic celebration. Interestingly, the dietary concerns of these ascetic specialists continued the exclusion of meat and wine that had earlier distinguished a highly sectarian strand among the diversity of Christian groups.

In other and especially later forms of Christian meal, the fictive equality of the ancient banquet seems to have given way to more explicitly hierarchical expressions of the community's self-understanding. In the fourth-century Syrian *Apostolic Constitutions,* the bishop is encouraged to arrange the church according to a nautical metaphor: "When you call an assembly of the Church as though you are the commander of a great ship, ensure the assemblies are made with all possible skill, charging the deacons as sailors to prepare places for the brothers and sisters as for passengers, with all due care and decency." The possibility of rocking the ecclesiastical boat now invokes a sensibility almost opposite to that of the Letter of James: "if any one be found sitting out of place, let them be rebuked by the deacon, as a manager of the foredeck, and be removed into the place proper for them; for the Church is not only like a ship, but also like a sheepfold" (*Ap. Const.* 2.57).

The detailed instructions for this eucharistic voyage (see sidebar) give a particularly strong emphasis to gender. This is not an entirely new concern, given Paul's awkward instructions about women's participation (1 Cor. 14:13), but the elaborated concern may also reflect that the cultic element of the meal—never entirely absent from formal dining, in any case, it must be admitted—has all but overwhelmed the conventions of banqueting. The arrangement of persons in space now seems to owe more to sacrificial ritual and its characteristic impact on the use of space as hierarchical, and especially gendered.[24] The character of the Christian assembly as the meal of a specific association within society, marked by its own limited equality among diners, has given way to the notion of the church as a kind of polis with internal distinctions of many kinds.

Other forms of power and patronage had also emerged during the age of the martyrs, with their own dietary expressions. Food gifts were already a means of extending the significance of common eating beyond the group physically able to be present. Justin Martyr's eucharistic meal in second-century Rome had already invoked this sort of practice in the custom of sending eucharistic bread home to the sick (1 *Apol.* 67). When Christians were imprisoned during times of persecution, food gifts of a more general kind were a very practical means of connection with those martyrs who might otherwise have starved in inhospitable surroundings before their own scheduled and spectacular immolation (see Tertullian, *Mart.*).

Let the young persons sit by themselves, if there be a place for them; if not, let them stand upright. But let those that are already stricken in years sit in order. For the children which stand, let their fathers and mothers take them to them. Let the younger women also sit by themselves, if there be a place for them; but if there be not, let them stand behind the women. Let those women which are married, and have children, be placed by themselves; but let the virgins, and the widows, and the elder women, stand or sit before all the rest; and let the deacon be the disposer of the places, that every one of those that comes in may go to his proper place, and may not sit at the entrance.
—*Ap. Const.* 2.57

After the conversion of Constantine and the end of institutionalized violence against catholic Christians within the empire, the care of the martyrs tended to become a form of devotion to the dead, evoking existing pagan practices of communing with ancestors as well as continuing the specific expression of interest in Christian heroism through food and meals. Christians had already been dining with the dead, as the decorations of catacombs even in the third century attest; these idealized scenes provide oblique evidence for the physical arrangements and roles at meals in other settings as well.

From the fourth century, martyrs and ancestors merged to form a collection of unseen diners with whom one might eat in one form or another. Sometimes older practices of food offerings at ancestral graves were transferred to the martyrs; North African tombs, Christian and other, even exhibit holes through which liquid offerings could be poured, so the faithful dead could partake in what were sometimes rowdy cemeterial picnics. Attempts to guide these practices toward the more orderly celebration of the eucharist proper had mixed success.[25] Perhaps more startling still is evidence that animal sacrifice was assimilated to the cult of the saints, baptized rather than banned in at least one Italian setting around 400.[26] Thus old patterns of using food and meals for earthly and divine patronage were taken up and transformed in these meal rituals, both at and beyond the primary focus of the eucharistic altar.

CONCLUSIONS

Christian eucharistic gatherings in the early centuries are best understood as meal forms exhibiting features comparable to those of other ancient Greco-Roman banquets. The diversity of forms and meanings makes it difficult to generalize any further about the ways in which various diners—wealthy and poor, female and male, African and Syrian—experienced these events. At times both inclusive and exclusive, egalitarian and hierarchical, festive and ascetic, they nonetheless constituted a near-universal element of early Christian experience.

The growth of the Christian churches through the second and third centuries raised concrete issues or problems such as the size of the community and more symbolic ones such as the appropriate function of a meal ritual. Both contributed to the change in the nature of the eucharist itself from associational meal to quasi-civic ritual, even before the Christianization of the civic rituals of the empire. Other meals and food rituals were still to play various important parts in the life of the Christian community, beyond the time of the apparent submersion of the shape of the ancient Christian banquet beneath the surface of the medieval mass. Versions of the actual evening banquet or *agape* continued for some time after the disappearance of the sacralized eucharistic foods into their separate liturgical context. Such "church suppers" continued to have social and economic significance, although within the empire the realignment of the boundaries of church and Roman society meant that such gatherings no longer constituted and reflected the church as such, but defined smaller networks and subcommunities.

Yet the transformed eucharist itself also retained features indicative of its origin. The sequence of bread and cup still echoes the order of the ancient *symposium*; the mixed chalice, the regular manners of the moderate ancient drinker; and the broken bread, the basic needs and pursuits of thousands.

FOR FURTHER READING

Teresa Berger. *Women's Ways of Worship: Gender Analysis and Liturgical History.* Collegeville, Minn.: Liturgical, 1999.

Paul Bradshaw. *The Search for the Origins of Christian Worship.* Rev ed. New York: Oxford University Press, 2002.

Kathleen E. Corley. *Private Women, Public Meals: Social Conflict in the Synoptic Tradition.* Peabody, Mass.: Hendrickson Publishers, 1993.

Gillian Feeley-Harnik. *The Lord's Table: Eucharist and Passover in Early Christianity.* Philadelphia: University of Pennsylvania Press, 1981.

Peter Garnsey. *Food and Society in Classical Antiquity.* Cambridge: Cambridge University Press, 1999.

Nancy Jay. *Throughout Your Generations Forever: Sacrifice, Religion and Paternity.* Chicago: University of Chicago Press, 1992.

Enrico Mazza. *The Origins of the Eucharistic Prayer.* Collegeville, Minn.: Liturgical Press, 1995.

Andrew McGowan. *Ascetic Eucharists: Food and Drink in Early Christian Ritual Meals.* Oxford Early Christian Studies. Oxford: Clarendon, 1999.

Dennis E. Smith. *From Symposium to Eucharist: The Banquet in the Early Christian World.* Minneapolis: Fortress, 2003.

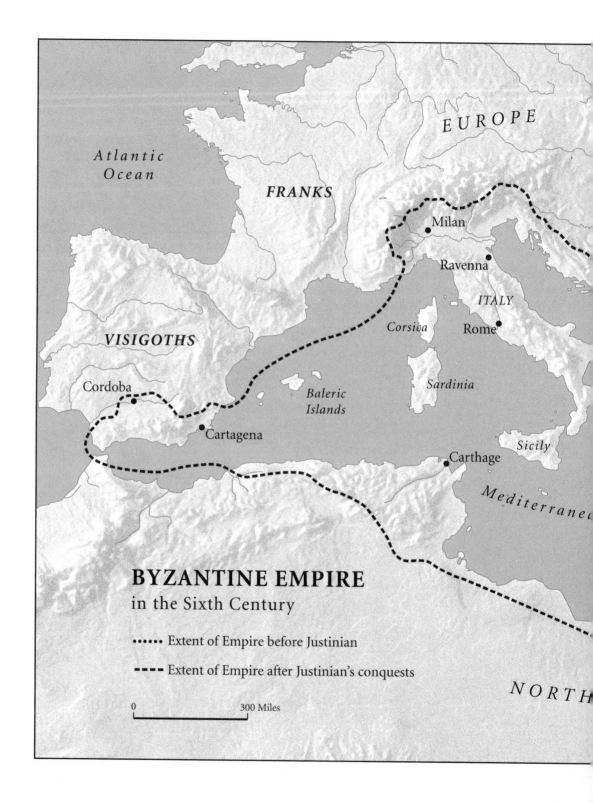

Atlantic
Ocean

EUROPE

FRANKS

Milan

Ravenna

ITALY

VISIGOTHS

Corsica

Rome

Cordoba

Baleric
Islands

Sardinia

Cartagena

Sicily

Carthage

Mediterranea

BYZANTINE EMPIRE
in the Sixth Century

•••••• Extent of Empire before Justinian

- - - - Extent of Empire after Justinian's conquests

0   300 Miles

NORTH

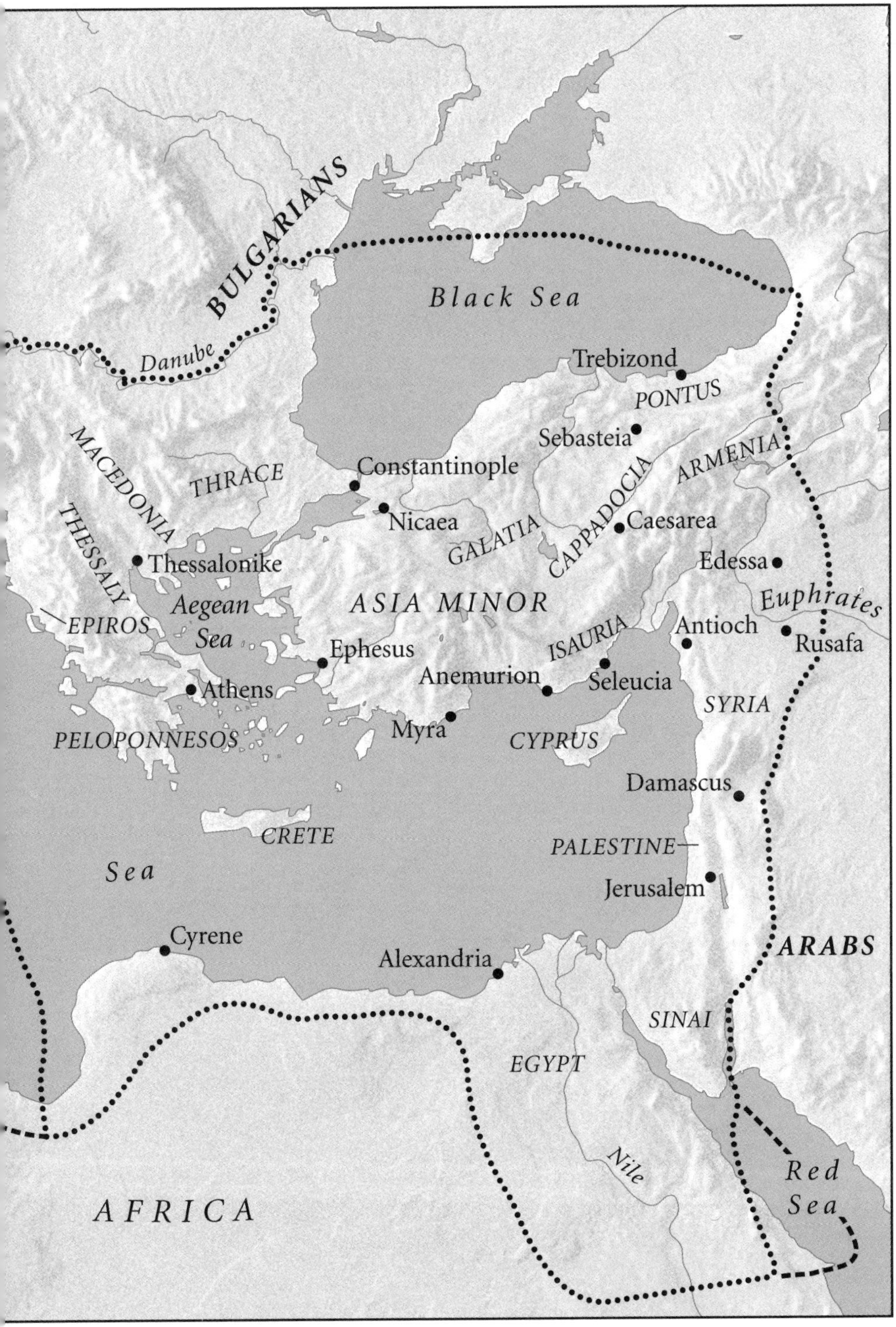

Fig. 3.1. Map by Lucidity Information Design.

Map labels: BULGARIANS, Black Sea, Danube, Trebizond, PONTUS, Sebasteia, MACEDONIA, THRACE, Constantinople, ARMENIA, CAPPADOCIA, GALATIA, Caesarea, THESSALY, Nicaea, Edessa, Thessalonike, Euphrates, ASIA MINOR, Aegean Sea, Antioch, Rusafa, EPIROS, Ephesus, ISAURIA, Anemurion, Seleucia, SYRIA, Athens, Myra, CYPRUS, PELOPONNESOS, Damascus, CRETE, PALESTINE, Sea, Jerusalem, ARABS, Cyrene, Alexandria, SINAI, EGYPT, Nile, Red Sea, AFRICA

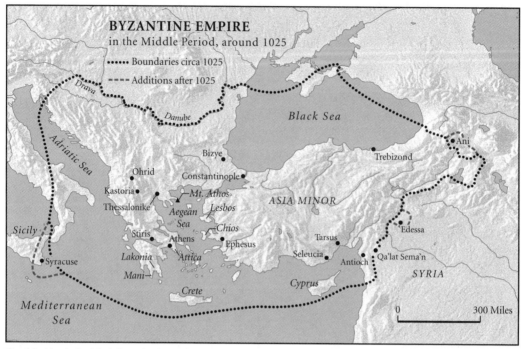

Fig. 3.2. Map by Lucidity Information Design.

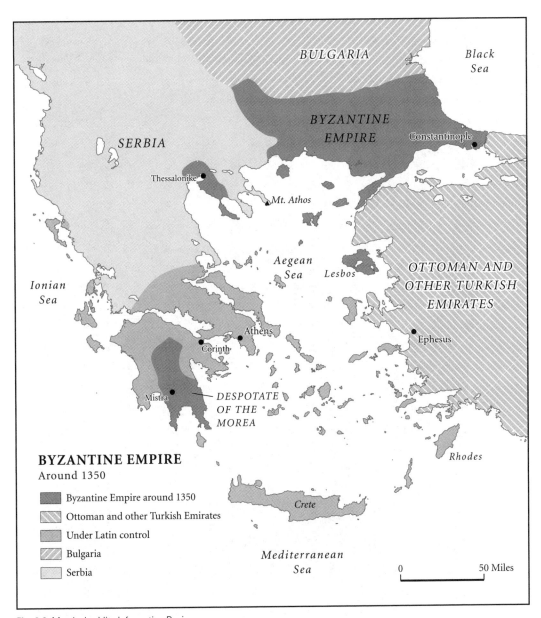

Black
Sea

BULGARIA

SERBIA

BYZANTINE
EMPIRE

Thessalonike

Constantinople

Mt. Athos

Aegean
Sea

Lesbos

OTTOMAN AND
OTHER TURKISH
EMIRATES

Ionian
Sea

Athens

Corinth

Ephesus

Mistra

DESPOTATE
OF THE
MOREA

Rhodes

BYZANTINE EMPIRE
Around 1350

Byzantine Empire around 1350
Ottoman and other Turkish Emirates
Under Latin control
Bulgaria
Serbia

Crete

Mediterranean
Sea

0   50 Miles

Fig. 3.3. Map by Lucidity Information Design.

Fig. 3.4. Wooden panel icon of the Virgin Mary and child, two saints, and two angels painted in the sixth or seventh century, now at St. Catherine's Monastery at Mount Sinai, Egypt. During the early Byzantine period, Mary came to be venerated as *Theotokos* or "God-bearer." Photo: Erich Lessing/Art Resource, NY.

THE PRACTICE OF CHRISTIANITY IN BYZANTIUM

DEREK KRUEGER

CHAPTER THREE

In sixth-century Palestine a circle of women gathered to weave curtains for two monasteries in the Judean desert. In the seventh century a merchant from the island of Chios spent three months living and sleeping at the shrine of St. Artemios in Constantinople waiting for the saint to heal his hernia. In eighth-century Constantinople young mothers routinely adorned their babies with amulets to protect them from demons.[1] In the twelfth century, in a small church in the Peloponnesos, villagers attended liturgical services surrounded by life-size images of the saints; in another church, in the mountains of Cyprus, colorful scenes of major events in the lives of Christ and the Virgin, painted throughout the church, enveloped congregants in the world of the Bible. In fifteenth-century Thessalonike mourners marked the third, ninth, and fortieth day after a family member's death by bringing offerings of boiled wheat with nuts and raisins to the parish church.[2] Such acts shaped lay Christianity in Byzantium.

This essay, dedicated to Byzantine Christianity, explores the practices of lay Christians during the eleven centuries between the foundation of the city of Constantinople in 324 and its fall to the Ottoman Turks in 1453. Lasting from Late Antiquity to the threshold of the early modern period, the Byzantine Empire began as the eastern half of the Roman Empire and ended as a small medieval state. In the intervening centuries, Byzantine Christianity developed as a distinct system of religious practice and devotion, different from the medieval Roman Catholicism emerging simultaneously farther west. While some doctrinal issues divided the Orthodox East and the Catholic West, most differences stemmed from cultural practices. Different ways of performing Christianity produced separate identities for these two groups of medieval Christians. Even as their empire shrank, Byzantine emperors and churchmen exported their Eastern Orthodoxy to neighboring peoples. The direct heirs of Byzantine Christianity remain numerous among Greeks, Slavs, Arabs, and others to this day. Today there are more than 200 million Orthodox Christians worldwide.

This essay introduces the religion of the Byzantine Christian laity by asking the question "What did Byzantine Christians do?" To answer, we must consider how people prayed and how often they attended services; how they celebrated, married, and mourned; how they interacted with priests, monks, nuns, and holy people; where they went on pilgrimage and why they visited shrines; how they transmitted religious values to their children; and how they performed acts of charity. Indeed, questions about what ordinary Christians did in church or in their homes or workshops, about their veneration of saints or their use of icons, about their visual and material culture, and about the place of religion in the course of their lives illuminate a people's Christianity.

Fig. 3.5. The Church of the Holy Apostles, Athens, Greece. Built in the eleventh century, the building's modest scale, central plan, elaborate brickwork, and domed cupola are typical of Byzantine church architecture after the ninth century. Photo: Vanni/ Art Resource, NY.

Many Western readers tend, not surprisingly, to know less about Orthodoxy than about Catholic and Protestant forms of Christianity. And while Byzantine sources offer fairly detailed and accessible documentation for the religious lives of Byzantine aristocrats, clergy, and monastics, the piety of ordinary Christians and the patterns of their religious lives remain less familiar even to scholars. Researching the lives of ordinary Byzantines can be difficult. Most written sources derive from powerful church leaders who used their texts to shape proper practice rather than leave behind an unbiased and unfiltered description of what people did. Yet careful interpretation of sermons, saints' lives, hymns, canon law, and histories, together with architecture, icons, church decoration, and devotional objects, enables a rich description of lay religion among nonelites. Drawing on the techniques of social and cultural history, this essay contributes to a historical anthropology of Byzantine Christianity.

The focus on religious practice complements and sometimes challenges other ways of telling the history of Christianity in Byzantium. Neither the history of Christian doctrine nor the institutional history of the Byzantine church is sufficient in itself to tell the story of Byzantine religious life. Townsfolk and tradesmen, women and children, village peasants, the poor and the powerless rarely feature as agents in these narratives. The history of popular religious practice affords perspectives on religion in their everyday lives. Moreover, the interest in practice rather than doctrine draws on recent insights within the modern academic study of religion. Scholars increasingly understand religions not simply as the assent to a series of intellectual propositions but rather as richly embodied cultural systems. To understand people's religious lives, we must explore their customs and habits. Only in this way can we begin to understand the logic that grounded Byzantine piety, the basic assumptions that made such widespread practices as visiting the saints or worshipping before icons a matter of common sense.

While Orthodox theology investigated ways to understand God and creation, humanity's participation in Christ's work of redemption, and how the divine might be present in images, much Byzantine religious activity sought solutions to practical problems. Christianity offered therapies for physical ailments, protection from illness and demons, and the salvation of the soul after death. Observing pious activity uncovers patterns of Christian devotion both public and private. Festivals and vigils provided opportunities for collective expressions of devotion to Christ and the saints, often standardized through hymns and liturgies. Christians performed their piety, engaging in behavior to be witnessed by other worshippers, by the saints, or perhaps only by God and the self. Modern scholars have little access to the interior religious life of individual persons, but we can begin to reconstruct collective practice. Depending on the era, forms of private devotion—such as wearing small cross-shaped reliquaries, collecting and saving holy oil, or kissing icons—were often consistent across the broader population. Even intimate acts displayed common modes of self-presentation and comportment before the holy. To provide a people's history of Byzantine Christianity, this essay investigates a wide variety of religious expressions as they developed and changed over time.

CHRISTIANITY IN BYZANTINE HISTORY

Modern scholars divide Byzantine history into four periods, marking distinct phases in the territorial expansion and contraction of the empire, together with distinct forms of political and military organization, social and economic structure, and cultural and religious life.

The period from 324 to 641, early Byzantium, overlapped with the later Roman Empire and maintained many continuities with antiquity. At its height, under Emperor Justinian, who reigned from 527 to 565, the empire stretched from the eastern Mediterranean to include North Africa, the Italian Peninsula, and southern Spain. This multicultural, multiethnic, and multireligious empire boasted the great cities of Constantinople and Alexandria, with as many as half a million inhabitants each; other large cities such as Antioch and Ephesus, with roughly 120,000 inhabitants; and numerous smaller cities, especially in Asia Minor and Syria, with 10,000 to 25,000 inhabitants. Despite the vitality of urban life, the vast majority of Byzantines lived on farms and in villages in rural districts. This period also saw the formation of an imperial Christianity, distinctive of Byzantium, in which the emperor had effective control over the church, convening councils and appointing patriarchs and prominent bishops. Church leaders articulated Christian teachings on the incarnation and the Trinity under imperial guidance, although the supposedly definitive articulations of the faith at Nicaea (325), Chalcedon (451), and Constantinople (553) tended to perpetuate division as well as unity. Moreover, not all the empire's inhabitants were Christians. Jews remained an integral part of Byzantine society throughout its history, and traditional polytheists (or "pagans") survived in locally significant populations into the sixth century, despite imperial edicts expropriating temples and restricting public practice.

Byzantine society and economy suffered decline in the century after the 540s, as recurrent plague, disastrous earthquakes, wars with Persia, and the rise of Islam took their toll. The loss of the Levant and the southern Mediterranean to the Arabs in the 630s and 640s marked the beginning of the Byzantine "Dark Ages," 641 to 843. The population in the remaining lands in Asia Minor, Greece, and the Balkans was primarily Greek-speaking and Orthodox, although there were significant numbers of Slavs, Armenians, and Jews. With coastal cities in decline and a collapse in trade and coinage, Byzantine high culture nearly disappeared. Many people retreated to walled fortresses, or *kastra*, built on hills and promontories for safety. While earlier Byzantine Christians had decorated churches and religious paraphernalia with images of Christ and the saints, the characteristic Orthodox veneration of icons appears to have emerged for the first time in this period, together with a violent reaction to icon piety known as iconoclasm. From 717 to 787 and again from 815 to 843, imperial policy condemned worship before images even as the practice spread among monastics and laity alike.[3]

The middle Byzantine period, lasting from 843 to 1204, saw the revival of the Byzantine state and successive centuries of flourishing culture. Although cities never regained the central status that they had achieved in late antiquity, they regularly expanded beyond their walled fortifications. New forms of church architecture and decoration spread quickly throughout the empire together with new forms of liturgy. The cultural embrace of icons meant that the interiors of even the simplest churches were covered with images of the saints and scenes from the life of Christ. During the reign of Basil II (976–1025), church authorities in Constantinople standardized the calendar of the saints and rewrote their *vitae*, or biographies, into versions short enough to read during morning prayer. The liturgy of the Great Church of Hagia Sophia disseminated from Constantinople

Fig. 3.6. A late Byzantine icon depicting Christ crucified with the Virgin Mary and John the Evangelist grieving at the foot of the cross. Thirteenth century. Icon Gallery, Ohrid, Macedonia. Photo: Photo: Erich Lessing/Art Resource, NY.

to provincial churches. In the 860s began the first of many missions to convert the Slavs to Byzantine Orthodoxy, a development with momentous consequences for the peoples of Eastern Europe, especially the Bulgarians, Serbs, and Russians. By the end of the period, the empire's population included some Muslims.

Beginning already in the ninth century, the Byzantine church found itself in conflict with Rome over such issues as the text of the Nicene Creed and papal supremacy. The Orthodox objected to the Latin addition of the *filioque* to the creed, the assertion that the Holy Spirit proceeded not only from the Father but from both the Father "and the Son." And while the Patriarch of Constantinople recognized his counterpart in Rome as a "first among equals," Byzantines rejected the claim that the pope was the sovereign of the entire church. Perhaps more important for the self-understanding of ordinary Christians, Byzantines began to distinguish their practices from what they regarded as Latin aberrations, which included priestly celibacy, crossing oneself backwards, and using unleavened bread at the Eucharist. Despite the mutual anathemas that Western and Eastern church leaders pronounced against each other in 1054, the schism between Byzantine Orthodox and Roman Catholic Christians did not have a feel of finality until the thirteenth century; even so, Byzantines and Latins were still attempting to heal the rift in the 1430s. The middle Byzantine period also saw the rise of Western Christian crusades to wrest the eastern Mediterranean and the Holy Land from Islamic control; but during the Fourth Crusade, in 1204, Latins sacked the city of Constantinople, bringing a glorious period in Byzantine history to a decisive end.

The final phase of Byzantine history, from the restoration of Byzantine rule in 1261 to the fall of Constantinople in 1453, witnessed a dramatic revival under the dynasty of the Palaiologos family. This development is perhaps odd, since the empire was little more than a rump state encompassing the regions of Constantinople, Thessalonike, and parts of the Peloponnesos. Palaiologan elites commissioned beautiful churches, rich in mosaic and fresco, while on the peninsula of Mount Athos and elsewhere, Byzantine monasticism experienced a golden age. At the same time, lay practice coalesced in forms that would survive the centuries of Turkish rule to come.

DEFINING BYZANTINE CHRISTIANITY

"Byzantine Christianity" is not quite the same thing as "Christianity in Byzantium." First, there is the problem of self-designation. The Byzantines understood themselves to be Romans (*Rhomaioi*); they did not refer to themselves as Greeks (*Hellenes*) before the thirteenth century. Their empire was the Roman Empire, and Constantinople was the New Rome, founded on the site of the earlier town of Byzantion. Only after Constantinople's fall did sixteenth-century Western humanists begin to refer to the Eastern Roman state as "the Byzantine Empire." In some sense Byzantine Christianity here could be understood as the medieval phases of Roman Orthodoxy, and indeed Arabic speakers still refer to those in communion with the Patriarch of Constantinople as "Rum Orthodox."

Then there are the problems of geographical and temporal scope. Byzantine Christianity is not a phenomenon coterminous with the shifting boundaries and temporal limits of a medieval state. This volume focuses on piety and devotional practice among Christians in the eastern Mediterranean, and particularly the north-eastern Mediterranean, in the regions that are now Turkey, Greece, the Balkans, and Syria, Israel, and Palestine. Not all of the Christians in this region, however, were (or are) in communion with Constantinople. The communities that would emerge as the Syrian Orthodox, Coptic (or Egyptian) Orthodox, and Armenian churches were distinct in doctrine and organization. These groups, which split decisively with Byzantine Orthodoxy and the Patriarch of Constantinople in the course of the sixth century, in part because of the controversies following the Council of Chalcedon (451), lie beyond the scope of this volume.[4] Even so, and despite different conceptions of the relationship between the human and the divine in the person of Christ and allegiances to separate—and often competing—hierarchies, these Christians often shared the everyday practices typical in Byzantium, even when these communities found themselves beyond the bounds of Byzantine political control.

After the rise of Islam in the eastern Mediterranean, many Greek Orthodox Christians in Syria and Palestine, under the patriarchates of Antioch and Jerusalem, respectively, continued their allegiance to the Byzantine church, even as they began increasingly to speak Arabic. Moreover, through diplomacy and missionary work, the Byzantines exported their imperial orthodoxy northward, beyond the bounds of their empire, among various Slavic peoples, including Bulgarians, Serbs, Ukrainians, and Russians. For the most part, and regrettably, these Arabic- and Slavic-speaking Christians fall beyond the scope of these essays.

Byzantine Christianity also outlasted Byzantium. As parts of eastern Anatolia fell to Seljuk Turks beginning in the eleventh century and the rest of Anatolia and the Balkans to the Ottoman Turks in the fourteenth and fifteenth centuries, more and more Byzantine Christians found themselves practicing Christianity beyond the bounds of the imperial territories. Even after the fall of Constantinople in 1453, Christians in former Byzantine lands continued to practice Christianity in many of the same ways, engaging in similar practices at home, in church, and throughout the course of their lives. Greek Orthodoxy today is both an heir of Byzantine Christianity and the product of a long encounter with modernity that began in the seventeenth century and endures into the present. This essay's focus on Christianity in Byzantium tells only part of Byzantine Christianity's story.

THE PEOPLE'S RELIGION

The quest for the people's Christianity in Byzantium implies, at least in part, that the religion of the common people differed from that of political and ecclesiastical authorities and religious specialists. And yet the religious lives of the elites and of the masses were not truly distinct. Rather, all Byzantine Christians participated in a shared system of religious practice, even as they experienced and took on different roles.

Many forms of piety spread throughout the social ranks. For example, one important locus of Byzantine piety was the healing shrine. The tombs of saints and repositories of their relics dotted major cities such as Constantinople and Thessalonike and were scattered throughout the eastern Mediterranean basin. Supplicants came to these shrines in search of relief from a wide variety of ailments, applying salves of holy oil and wax to their afflicted parts or ingesting infusions of water and holy dust. Some of the sick would sleep at the shrine, hoping that the saints would appear to them in a vision. The same saints would also appear to supplicants sleeping in their own beds. While modern scholars have often regarded such behavior as "popular religion," and earlier scholars might have thought of this as "folk religion," such labels are misleading. Byzantines at all social levels engaged in such practices, from peasants to members of the imperial family. According to the sixth-century historian Procopius of Caesarea, Sts. Cosmas and Damian appeared to the emperor Justinian in a vision when he was gravely ill (*On the Buildings* 1.6.5–8). The difference between the emperor and the average layperson, of course, was that, after the cure, Justinian had the means to entirely remodel the Church of Cosmas and Damian just up the Golden Horn from the capital (at modern Eyüp) as a token of his gratitude. Nevertheless, humbler Christians shared the impulse to adorn the shrines of the saints with votive offerings.

Fig. 3.7. Pilgrims continue to visit the shrine containing a miracle-working icon of the Virgin Mary at the Greek Orthodox Convent of Our Lady of Seidnaya, Syria. Since before the Crusades, the faithful have made supplications, collected holy oil, and presented votive plaques to commemorate their healing. Photo: Derek Krueger.

The religious lives and outlooks of the lower ranks of the clergy, in particular, may not have differed so greatly from those of their lay parishioners. Even as they presided over the liturgy, administered sacraments, and offered spiritual guidance, ordinary priests, together with deacons and subdeacons, were usually long-standing residents of the communities they served. Unlike their Western counterparts, Byzantine priests could marry and raise families. In rural districts, the priest often farmed his plots alongside his fellow villagers. Some priests were dependent peasants on large estates.

And while the rhythms of monastic life shaped monks and nuns differently from laypeople, it would be a mistake to overemphasize the differences between monks and the laity. Byzantine monasticism tended to be less institutional and hierarchical than its Western counterparts; in the absence of a standardized Rule, such as the *Rule of St. Benedict*, or of centralized systems of interrelated monasteries, as in the Cistercian movement, monasteries remained in a dynamic relationship with the lay world from which their members were drawn. In many cases, wealthy lay patrons founded monastic communities, and often members of the family would join these monasteries and govern them. Although, beginning in the late tenth century, monks might retire to the remoter wilderness of Mount Athos in increasing numbers, many monasteries were situated within the walls of cities and towns or on their edges. Here the laity might go for counsel or healing; here they might easily join. Indeed, the twelfth-century poet and historian John Tzetzes sneered that "every disgusting and thrice-accursed wretch has only to put on a monastic habit . . . dress himself up to look self-effacing in an ostentatious and highly theatrical way . . . [and] immediately the city of Constantinople showers him with honors."[5] Such comments reveal an uneasy tension with monasticism, but also its abiding presence.

The influence of monastic life on ordinary Christians was enormous. Church authorities sought to shape lay observance in the image of monasticism. Already in the fourth century, in Easter letters to communities of Christians up and down the Nile, Athanasius of Alexandria called on lay Christians to spend Lent "imitating the behavior of the saints," cultivating self-control through prayers and vigils, the renunciation of sex, and fasting.[6] An elaborate system, completely in place by the eleventh century, prescribed fasts for forty days before Christmas and seven weeks before Easter, for a variable period after Pentecost, for the first two weeks of August, during vigils preceding communion, in advance of various minor feasts, and on Wednesdays and Fridays. Some fasts forbade only meat, others meat and cheese, and some, such as the Easter vigil, demanded total abstinence from all food and drink. The rules demanded that, while fasting, lay Christians also avoid sexual relations. Thus all Christians were called to periods of rigorous, semimonastic observance: monks and nuns provided the model for a form of lay life that was particularly ascetic in character.

Even the distinction that obtained in the early Byzantine period between the cathedral and parish liturgies on the one hand and monastic liturgies on the other disappeared after the ninth century, as monastic leaders imposed their offices on lay parishes. And yet, while the laity came to observe the monastic rites, the boundaries between parishioners and their clergy during services increased. In the early Byzantine period, the urban laity participated in stational liturgies that processed through city neighborhoods between major churches and shrines and rendered the entire city a ritual space. By the eighth century the outdoor processional liturgies had come to an end, and most religious activity moved indoors. Processions still took place within the church building, but with less active lay participation. In the Little Entrance, during the first half of the liturgy, the laity sang psalms and hymns while the deacons and priests processed with the Gospel book. In the offertory, or Great Entrance, the laity watched as deacons and priests brought eucharistic gifts from the nave to the altar. Especially in the sixth and seventh centuries, lay Christians participated in elaborate vigils on the eves of feasts, listening to readings and sermons and singing hymns. Over time, church architecture changed to mark a stronger boundary between laity and clergy. Toward the end of the middle Byzantine period and increasingly in the late Byzantine period, the low barrier, or *templon*, separating the laity in the nave from the clergy in the sanctuary around the altar, grew in height to become a wall covered with images of Christ and the saints, an "iconostasis." Services became less participatory. Lay Christians could no longer see the priest during much of the service. Churches became smaller; the number of private chapels increased. What had once been a public service was increasingly private and screened from view.

Even the later Byzantine tendency to separate clergy from laity in liturgical settings, however, does not change the fact that laypeople shared—and shared in—many practices with clergy and monks. Moreover, the laity included most members of the upper classes. Therefore, an interest in lay Christianity does not and cannot exclude insights into elite modes of worship and observance. Indeed, lay piety is a useful lens through which to understand the common religion of most Byzantines, regardless of their class or status. Supplementing and broadening other ways of doing church history, this project explores a common history from another vantage point.

FOR FURTHER READING

The Blackwell Dictionary of Eastern Christianity. Ed. Ken Parry et al. Oxford: Blackwell, 1999.

Cunningham, Mary. *Faith in the Byzantine World*. Downers Grove, Ill.: InterVarsity, 2002.

Meyendorff, John. *Byzantine Theology: Historical Trends and Doctrinal Themes*. 2nd ed. New York: Fordham University Press, 1979.

The Oxford Dictionary of Byzantium. Ed. Alexander P. Kazdan and Alice-Mary Talbot. 3 vols. New York: Oxford University Press, 1991.

The Oxford History of Byzantium. Ed. Cyril Mango. Oxford: Oxford University Press, 2002.

Safran, Linda, ed. *Heaven on Earth: Art and Church in Byzantium*. University Park: Pennsylvania State University Press, 1998.

MEDIEVAL REVIVALISM

GARY DICKSON

Whether medieval or modern, Catholic or Protestant, revivalism has not always received a good press. The portrait of the professional enthusiast has rarely been flattering. Think of Chaucer's Pardoner, Molière's Tartuffe, and Sinclair Lewis's Elmer Gantry, and one imagines a rogues' gallery of zealots, fanatics, fraudsters, manipulators, blasphemers, and conniving hypocrites. But just as the revivalist has been scorned, revivals—occasions of collective religious enthusiasm—have also been disparaged. Such a reaction has a long history. According to the author of Luke-Acts, the spectators witnessing Christianity's first instance of collective enthusiasm, Pentecost, "were amazed and perplexed, saying to one another, 'What does this mean?'" That same query has echoed down the centuries. Those who witnessed medieval revivals were similarly bewildered. Lack of understanding could find expression in mockery, just as at Pentecost: "Others sneered and said, 'They are filled with new wine'" (Acts 2:12-13).

Unsurprisingly, explanations of this kind, both from eyewitnesses and academics, have been used ostensibly to account for the uncomfortably perplexing behavior of religious enthusiasts—but in reality to dismiss it. Writing in 1905, at a time when scientific-sounding medical or psychological explanations had become fashionable, F. M. Davenport called attention to revivalism's supposedly "primitive traits" left over from humanity's "mental and social evolution." Using medical parlance, he wrote of "the social and religious epidemics of western Europe in the Middle Ages," prompting him to conclude that the "enormous amount of mental and nervous instability in evidence was due not only to special conditions, such as the massing of women in convents, but also to barbaric inheritance."[1] Allegedly hysterical nuns aside, medieval Christian revivalism, in Davenport's scheme of things, was a living link to a centuries-old pagan tribal past. Where, then, does this "evolutionary" approach to medieval revivalism lead us? It leads us nowhere.

Among American intellectuals casting a cold eye on revivalism we may count William James, psychologist and philosopher, who in his *Varieties of Religious Experience* (1902) displayed great sensitivity toward conversionary autobiography. James, however, distanced himself from revivalism, which in his day was enjoying boisterous good health; he regarded it as Wesleyan conversion "codified and stereotyped."[2] For the Harvard professor, the vulgar showmanship and noisy theatrical atmosphere of late-nineteenth-century tent meetings could not have been congenial. Moreover, James was responding to the routinization of revivalism, that is, the calculated arousal of religious excitement on the part of the preacher (and frequently his musical assistants) in order to produce the desired effect, namely, conversion on the spot. But the routinization of revivalism also has a medieval history. The church came to understand the practical uses of popular enthusiasm. Preachers became skilful at raising funds for church-building: well-managed campaigns date from at least the 1050s. Then came the crusades, which during the twelfth and thirteenth centuries demanded both recruitment and revenue.

James, however, neither demonized nor psycho-pathologized collective enthusiasm as others did and continue to do. Until recently, scholars have highlighted the "badness" (violence, social revolt, heresy, anticlericalism) or "madness" (hallucinogenic poisoning, apocalyptic fantasy, "mass hysteria") of medieval collective fervor. Norman Cohn's brilliant, if overdrawn, *Pursuit of the Millennium*, for example, is an ingeniously mixed cocktail of socioreligious "badness" and "madness." Cohn was an outstanding scholar of collective "millenarian movements," which he thought of as appealing especially to the poor and disoriented, swayed by messianic leaders and their end-of-the-world prophecies. Cohn concentrated almost exclusively upon medieval enthusiasms that ended in murderous violence—thus supporting his thesis that "millenarian movements" had as their aim the revolutionary transformation of the social order—while he takes little account of medieval revivalist peace movements and their appeal to a broad section of medieval society. Unfortunately, an unbalanced interpretation detracts from Cohn's scholarship, impressive though it is.

Today medieval revivals that manage to escape allegations of badness risk a descent into madness. A perfect illustration of this is the medieval revival known as the Children's Crusade (1212). An unofficial peasant crusade, it most likely lacked any internal controls. Exceptional for a popular crusade, however, it left no Jewish corpses behind it, butchered no priests, and gave birth to no heresies. So the usual accusations of badness are ruled out, except that the chroniclers adopted the view that the enthusiasts were the real victims of the Children's Crusade. Often ill-informed, the chroniclers relished describing how this unauthorized crusade brought suffering, dis-illusionment, enslavement, and death to the *pueri* (the youngsters) as well as to others—including elderly people—caught up in it. Because the *pueri* had disobeyed clergy and parents, their foolish enterprise came to grief. God did not will it. As a Victorian bedtime story, the sad outcome of the Children's Crusade served as a dreadful warning to girls and boys tempted to run away. In reality, the many *pueri* who did survive the long trek to the Mediterranean maritime cities remained there as immigrants. One of them, a German ex–child crusader named Otto, most likely stayed on in northern Italy, either as a student or a scholar, and pursued a clerical career.

So if badness appears implausible, then mad-ness beckons. Accordingly, one of its ablest his-torians interprets the Children's Crusade as a

The Children's Crusade (1212)

In the month of June of the same year [1212] a certain boy, by occupation a shepherd, of a village named Cloyes near the town of Vendôme, said that the Lord had appeared to him in the form of a poor pilgrim, had received bread from him, and had delivered letters to him to be taken to the king of the French. When he came, together with his fellow shepherd-boys, nearly thirty thousand people assembled around him from all parts of France. While he stayed at St. Denis, the Lord worked many miracles through him, as many have witnessed. There were also many other boys who were held in great veneration by the common multitude in many places because they were also believed to work miracles, to whom a multitude of boys gathered wishing to proceed to the holy boy Stephen under their guid-ance. All acknowledged him as master and prince over them. At length the king [Philip II], having consulted the masters of Paris about this gathering of boys, commanded them to return to their homes; and so this childish enthusiasm was as easily ended as it had begun. But it seemed to many that, by means of such innocents gathered of their own accord, the Lord would do something great and new upon the earth, which issued far otherwise.

—Anonymous Chronicler of Laon, in *Medieval Popular Religion, 1000–1500*, ed. John Shinners (Peterborough, Ont.: Broadview, 1997), 395

demented creature: "It was a release to be found, then as now, in the crowd, 'a device for indulging ourselves in a kind of temporary insanity by all going crazy together.'"[3] The study of medieval Christian revivalism surely deserves something better than this. A fresh approach, perhaps, unburdened by past prejudices? Would this allow us to cast new light upon an age-old phenomenon?

TOWARD A DEFINITION

"Medieval" is a tricky term, subject to disputed chronological frontiers. Here it will encompass the half-millennial span between the Peace and Truce of God movement (ca. 975–1038), originating in southern France, and the English Pilgrimage of Grace (1536–1537). Defining "revivalism" is trickier still. The sociologist Emile Durkheim, discussing large-scale social upheavals, observed that "there are periods in history when, under the influence of some great collective shock, social interactions . . . become much more frequent and active. Men . . . assemble together more than ever. That general effervescence results which is characteristic of revolutionary or creative epochs."[4] Durkheim's emphasis on new forms of collective behavior during certain periods of historical discontinuity is helpful, while "general effervescence" is an appropriately sparkling way of characterizing mass enthusiasm, religious or otherwise. If "general effervescence" sounds rather too celebratory, like French champagne, at least it carries no necessarily alarming message of social dysfunction.

Fig. 4.1. The Children's Crusade, 1212, J. Kirchhoff from J. Sporschil, *Geschichte der Kreuzzüge* (1843). Photo: © SuperStock.

Medieval religious enthusiasms of diverse kinds were features of extended and sometimes overlapping periods. Certain types of enthusiasm coincided with particular periods. For example, one can speak of a reformist enthusiasm roughly from circa 1000 through the mid-eleventh-century papal (or Gregorian) reform movement to the primarily monastic "Reformation of the twelfth century." This current of reformist enthusiasm certainly provoked popular responses, orthodox and heretical. And in the midst of it, interacting with it, came the long crusading epoch, which generated its own brand of religious enthusiasm, again both popular and official. Beginning with Pope Urban II's Council of Clermont in 1095, crusade enthusiasm persisted intermittently right up to Christopher Columbus's departure on his first voyage in 1492—the crusader's red cross on his caravels' white sails. Other genres of medieval enthusiasm, the cult of saints prominent among them, borrowed and absorbed characteristic features of revivalism—preachers, crowd arousal, miracles—without becoming fully fledged revivals, that is, without fully conforming to the revivalist paradigm, which was collective, conversionary, and dynamic.

Broadly speaking, medieval revivals were relatively short-lived and intense episodes of public, collective religious enthusiasm, frequently characterized by distinctive three-part structures; unusual manifestations of collective fervor; and public conversionary experiences—including conversions to monasticism, the crusades, itinerant popular movements, and personal moral regeneration. Medieval revivals were also often strongly influenced by prophetic ideas. Finally and crucially, unroutinized medieval revivals carried with them a scent of the extraordinary, an odor as identifiable as a fingerprint or DNA sample. Medieval revivals, therefore, generated an atmosphere of the miraculous at times powerful enough to overturn the routines of daily life, which, in a customary society, was liable to be disorienting but perhaps also exhilarating, rather like a Durkheimian-style general effervescence.

Crusaders and Monks

One medieval Latin word came to approximate our modern sense of "revival." That word was *devotio*, which implied a peculiarly active or ritual sense of devotion. A survey of twelfth- and thirteenth-century revivalist movements carrying the label of *devotio* should therefore illustrate some of the essential features of medieval revivalism. As André

Vauchez notes, however, *devotio* was also used by Italian chroniclers in connection with popular cults of recently deceased saints,[5] confirming what has already been said—that the characteristic traits of revivalist behavior were not limited to medieval revivals in the strict sense.

At the Council of Clermont in 1095, Pope Urban II called for a new kind of holy war. Urban's army was to be composed of people whose sole prescribed quality was pious intent—devotion alone (*sola devotione*). The product of Clermont, the crusader, came into being as a hybrid creature: a holy warrior who went by the name of pilgrim. Conventionally, the Christian pilgrim was unarmed and vulnerable, but the crusader was a new kind of pilgrim, purpose-built to seize Jerusalem as a Christian prize. The monastic chronicler Robert of Rheims writes, "When [at Clermont] Pope Urban . . . said these things . . . everyone, moved by the same feeling, shouted in unison, 'God wills it! God wills it!'"[6] Their acclamation affirmed God's providential blessing on the

Fig. 4.2. Flagellants in the Netherlands town of Tournai (Doornik), 1349. Flagellants, known as the Brothers of the Cross, scourged themselves as they walked through the streets in order to free the world from the Black Death (bubonic plague). Ann Ronan Picture Library, London. Photo: © HIP / Art Resource, NY.

new enterprise. The conciliar outcry became the crusaders' war cry. Vociferousness is audible evidence of revivalist enthusiasm. Time after time, the shouts of medieval revivalist crowds compressed complex ideas into popular slogans. At Clermont, too, taking the cross, becoming one signed with the cross (a *crucesignatus*, or crusader) meant assuming a new spiritual identity. It was a conversionary act.

Crusading experience broadened the use of *devotio*, adding motifs of penance and conversion. The spiritual meaning of the term was also enriched by the charismatic twelfth-century crusade preacher and advocate of Cistercian monasticism, Bernard of Clairvaux. Bernardine spirituality, diffused throughout Christian Europe by the rapid growth of the Cistercian order, saw *devotio* becoming a code word for religious fervor, exhibited, for example, in the gift of tears that was increasingly linked to the cult of the humanity of Christ. Nor can it be forgotten that Cistercian monasticism, along with all the other twelfth- and thirteenth-century monastic orders, was, like the crusades, dependent upon a steady stream of new recruits—in other words, converts.

Together, the crusades and a resurgent monasticism inaugurated a new medieval conversionary age, nothing less than the second conversion of Europe. Old-style missionary activity was still, of course, continuing beyond the expanding frontiers of Christian Europe, but now in Latin Christendom, instead of tribal or ethnic Christianization, the emphasis was beginning to be placed on an interiorized conversion of non-infant, already baptized Christians. For monks, as well as for crusaders, this kind of conversion resulted in a change of legal status, whether temporary (crusaders) or permanent (monks). These Christians were converted to a committed religious life, whether within the world or in flight from it. Highly relevant in this respect is that popular, collective revivalist movements also served as a setting and stimulus for individual conversionary acts. Revivalism, in short, extended the opportunities for the conversion of Christians to new forms of Christian commitment.

Popular Revivalism in the Thirteenth Century

Theorists of *devotio* in the thirteenth century, theologians such as David of Augsburg, Thomas Aquinas, and Bonaventure, were to some extent responding to the mighty waves of popular revivalism that were then sweeping over northern and southern Europe. During the same period, ideas of *devotio* were transmitted to the monastic and mendicant chroniclers who observed and commented upon popular revivalist movements. A few of these chroniclers were imbued with the teachings of the spiritual writers. A good example is the anonymous monastic chronicler of Laon. When he terms the Children's Crusade of 1212 *puerilis illa devocio* (that childish—or, better, since he is well disposed toward it, childlike—revival),[7] he reveals the spiritual imprint of Bernard of Clairvaux.

The Laon Anonymous confines his narrative to a single episode of the Children's Crusade, or *peregrinatio puerorum*, the pilgrimage-crusade of the *pueri*, which most likely began at Chartres before heading to the Paris region, then northeast into the Rhineland, finally crossing the Alps and reaching its Mediterranean terminus. The Laon Anonymous recounts that Stephen of Cloyes, together with his age-mates and fellow shepherd boys, embarked upon a pilgrimage to the king of France at St. Denis, after Stephen was entrusted to deliver letters to the king by Christ, who had appeared to him in the guise of a poor pilgrim. The contents of these letters are never divulged. The same chronicler states that Stephen attracted "nearly 30,000 people" (an exceptionally large following) to St. Denis "from all parts of France." Yet he also makes clear that Stephen's mission was part of a much wider outpouring of collective enthusiasm, for elsewhere, too, there were hordes of children—miracle-workers among them—eager to merge with Stephen's followers. Stephen, the reputed leader of the French *pueri*, was neither a cleric nor a crusader knight. Although as a lowly shepherd boy he could claim no religious authority, nevertheless Stephen emerges as the first charismatic leader of Christian Europe's earliest youth movement.

The Franciscan chronicler Salimbene designates 1233 as the *tempore illius devotionis famosi* (the date of that famous revival). Variously described as the Great Devotion or the Great Hallelujah, this powerful religious awakening swept across the cities of northern Italy, including Parma, Piacenza, and Bologna. Growing up in Parma, the twelve-year-old Salimbene eagerly responded to the thrilling processions and crowd scenes he witnessed in 1233. Vividly chronicling his childhood memories in old age, Salimbene remembers, "This *Alleluja* . . . was a time of peace and quiet, when all weapons of war were laid aside; a time of merriment and gladness, of joy and exultation, of praise and rejoicing."[8] Its initial, purely popular phase was inspired by a lay preacher. Next came the Franciscan and Dominican friars, who fashioned it into an organized peace movement and preaching campaign, for the Great Hallelujah satisfied a widespread craving for peace. Salimbene's north Italian civic milieu was a fractured, violent society, splintered by political faction and ravaged by clan vendettas. In such an environment, civic peace, temporarily achieved by inspired preachers, seemed nothing short of miraculous. But if Lombardy's Great Hallelujah of 1233 counts as one of medieval Europe's most outstanding revivalist peace movements, it was certainly not unique. The fact is that medieval Christendom gave birth to an extended family of revivalist peace movements.

Almost thirty year later, Salimbene took part in, as well as chronicled, another of the thirteenth century's most astonishing popular revivals. This too was a peace movement, although its appeal for civic amnesty and the release of prisoners was only one of its interlocking motifs. Its historical significance was much greater than that of the regional Lombard Hallelujah of 1233, for, like the Children's Crusade of 1212, this was a revival on a European scale. Salimbene calls it the *verberatorum devotio* (the revival of the flagellants).[9] Invited in 1260 to lead processions of these self-lacerating penitents, Salimbene agreed without hesitation. His responsiveness to revivalism's spiritual quickening had become part of his nature.

The penitential performance of these flagellants or *disciplinati* (from *disciplina*, whip) amounted to a new sort of Christomimetic urban theatre, a new kind of Passion play in which the scourging of Christ was not so much reenacted as imaginatively reexperienced. From Perugia in Umbria, central Italy, to Rome, then northward through Italy, Germany, and ultimately as far as Gniezno in Poland, the *disciplinati* marched through town and countryside. In the towns women also undertook the ritual, but privately, apart from men. Female participation in the movement of 1260 was repeated in nearly all the major medieval revivals. Hearing doleful chants and outcries and watching the bloodstained, half-naked penitents slowly process through the streets of the city, many spectators were overcome with awe. Some embraced the new enthusiasm, and these converts brought the *devotio* of the flagellants to new localities. Their revivalist drama was a religious movement in two crucial respects: the flagellants were both ambulatory (processional) and itinerant (peregrinatory).

But not even a thumbnail sketch of the revival of the flagellants can ignore the influence of prophecy in its origins. The year of the coming of the *disciplinati*, 1260, was, after all, the very year in which the Joachites, the adherents of the Calabrian prophet Joachim of Fiore (d. 1202), predicted that there would be an unparalleled crisis-transition in sacral history—a terrible persecution of the faithful, heralding the reign of the Antichrist. Repentance was the required response (and self-flagellation was a long-established penitential exercise, although for monks rather than laypeople). Once the transitional period had passed, however, the glorious Third Status of Christian history, the age of the Holy Spirit, would dawn. Salimbene cites two verses from Revelation, both ominously speaking of "twelve hundred sixty days" (Rev. 11:3; 12:6). Translated into the year 1260, that date became the focus for an impending universal crisis.

Fig. 4.3. *Flagellants at the Time of the Black Death.* Colored woodcut. Photo: © Image Select / Art Resource, NY.

Apocalyptic prophecy made the actual social and political crises of the year 1260 comprehensible; it also made them providential signs of what was soon to come. Evidence of a prophetic-Joachite consciousness in Perugia around the time of the flagellant movement can be detected in the iconographic program of a wall painting (ca. 1270) at the Templar church of San Bevignate, which became the home of Perugia's first confraternity of flagellants. The San Bevignate fresco appears to cast the Perugian *disciplinati* in an eschatological role, as men of history's last days. Below the dead rising from their graves in a Last Judgment, there they stand, possibly representing Joachim's *viri spirituales* or new "spiritual men."

Discovering a link between prophetic currents and revivalism in the Middle Ages, as with the *disciplinati* and Joachite thought, helps to clarify the circumstances of collective arousal. Coming forty years after the flagellants, in 1300, the first Roman Jubilee, or *anno santo* (Holy Year), is a case in point. It too arrived amid prophetic expectations, in part occasioned by the approach of the new century. This, of course, was neither the first nor the last medieval revival to appear on the hinge of the fin de siècle. Popularly initi-

Fig. 4.4. Pope Boniface VIII (r. 1294–1303) proclaims the First Jubilee (Holy Year) in 1300 from the Benediction Loggia at the Lateran Palace. Late sixteenth-century miniature, copy of a fresco by Giotto. Biblioteca Ambrosiana, Milan. Photo: © Scala / Art Resource, NY.

ated but papally legitimated, the Roman Jubilee of 1300 was the ancestor of a long line of medieval and postmedieval Holy Years. The Jubilee, the last devotio of the thirteenth century, attracted huge crowds of pilgrims to Rome from all over Christendom, Dante probably among them. Cardinal Lemoine spoke of the Christian people coming to the Roman basilicas to obtain the lavish Jubilee indulgence "with intense fervor and urgent devotion." "Not since ancient days," declaimed the cardinal, "has there been such *devotio*."[10]

The Jubilee of 1300 also highlights another of the defining manifestations of medieval revivalism: the mixed religious crowd. The medieval revivalist crowd

Pope Boniface VIII Announces the Holy Year of Jubilee (February 22, 1300)

The trustworthy tradition of our ancestors affirms that great remissions and Indulgences for sins are granted to those who visit in this city the venerable Basilica of the Prince of the Apostles. Wherefore We who, according to the dignity of our office, desire, and ought to procure, the salvation of each, holding all and each of these remissions and Indulgences to be authentic, do, by our apostolic authority, confirm and approve the same, and even grant afresh and sanction them by this our present writing. In order that the blessed Apostles Peter and Paul may be the more honored as their Basilicas in this city shall be the more devoutly frequented by the faithful, and that the faithful themselves may feel that they have been replenished by an abundance of spiritual favors in approaching their tombs, We, confiding in the mercy of Almighty God, in the merits and power of these His Apostles, in the counsel of our brethren, and in the plenitude of the apostolic authority, grant to all who, being truly penitent, and confessing their sins, shall reverently visit these Basilicas in the present year 1300, which commenced with the festival of the Nativity of our Lord Jesus Christ which has just been celebrated, and to all who being truly penitent, shall confess their sins, and shall approach these Basilicas each succeeding hundredth year, not only a full and copious, but the most full pardon of all their sins. We determine that whatever persons wish to gain these Indulgences granted by us must, if they be inhabitants of Rome, visit these same Basilicas for thirty days, whether successively or at intervals, at least once a day; if they be foreigners or strangers, they must in like manner visit the Basilicas for fifteen days. Nevertheless, each one will merit more, and will the more efficaciously gain the Indulgence as he visits the Basilicas more frequently and more devoutly. Let no man, therefore, dare to infringe or impugn this our rescript of confirmation, approval, renewal, grant, and decree. And if any one presumes to assail it, let him know that he will incur the indignation of Almighty God and of the blessed Apostles Peter and Paul.

—Herbert Thurston, *The Holy Year of Jubilee: An Account of the History and Ceremonial of the Roman Jubilee* (St. Louis: Herder, 1900), 13–14

was an all-encompassing assembly of the faithful, bringing together believers regardless of generation, gender, or social rank. Because medieval society was structured and hierarchical, mixed crowds were out of the ordinary; indeed, in some situations they could appear quasi-miraculous. More than just *popular*, the mixed crowd was *populist*. Although distinctions of social rank were never really abolished in mixed revivalist crowds, such distinctions were often momentarily stripped of religious significance.

The Roman Jubilee, a unique kind of pilgrimage whose guidelines could only be determined by the pope, preserved the populist character of pilgrimage. Thus all pilgrims, whether priests or laypeople, rich or poor, were—*as pilgrims*—of equal status. A fresco attributed to Giotto of the Jubilee pilgrim crowd at the feet of Pope Boniface VIII illustrates this very well. A mixed religious crowd appears in the lower register. The nobles (the knights or *milites*) are mounted on horseback, whereas the commoners or *pedites* appear on foot. Women as well as men are present in the throng. High above them all in the upper register is the pope surrounded by his cardinals, bishops, and priests. They are not pilgrims. Down below, a crowd of Jubilee pilgrims has positioned itself at the pope's feet, ready to catch the papal blessings.

Thus we see that medieval revivals were collective enthusiasms, behaviorally varied yet sharing common features. They were responsive to prophetic impulses; conversionary in nature; and perceived as "extraordinary"—marked, that is, by the miraculous, the charismatic, and the astonishment of observers. More generally, the medieval revivalist trajectory was brief, intense, and public. Medieval revivals could be triggered by political and social crises. Their outcomes were unpredictable, and they came in all shapes and sizes.

VARIETIES OF MEDIEVAL REVIVALISM

At the outset a distinction should be made between programmatic and nonprogrammatic revivals, despite the fact that medieval revivals were overwhelmingly programmatic—that is to say, they were "about" something. But this does not imply that a group of enthusiasts banded together to put forward a coherent set of beliefs, let alone to execute a concrete plan of action. What it does mean is that programmatic outpourings of medieval collective enthusiasm were infused with an identifiable source of spiritual energy. Quickening the pulses of potential converts, animating them, and compelling their adherence were spiritual aspirations usually combining diffuse, unsystematic religious and social ideals. We know that this is true because participants in programmatic revivals were invariably eager to disclose (and so disseminate) the fundamental spiritual ideals that energized their movements.

Programmatic Revivals: Three Modes of Expression

To communicate with the bewildered, curious onlookers who stared at them as they marched in procession through the streets or performed in town squares, medieval enthusiasts had recourse to three expressive modes. The first was behavioral iconography. In much the same way that medieval illiterates could read the language of Christian art because its conventional symbols were everywhere, so too medieval spectators of revivalist movements could easily decode the meanings of the dress, gestures, and rituals of medieval enthusiasts. Like the instantly recognizable papal keys of St. Peter in thousands of church images of that saint, the revivalists' iconographic attributes were culturally legible. And just as in the iconography of Christian art, where the saint's type (apostle, martyr, virgin, or virgin-martyr) was crucial to his or her identification, so it was with the behavioral iconography of medieval enthusiasts.

Pilgrims, for example, both individually and collectively in mass pilgrimage revivals (such as the Jerusalem-bound Great German Pilgrimage of 1064–1065), constituted a distinct type of Christian enthusiast. In art, as well as in life, pilgrims were recognizable from the twelfth century, if not earlier, by their *habitus*, or dress, and the emblems of their special status—their staves and wallets. Crusaders, also visibly distinctive, wore the cross, usually displayed on their outer clothing (frequently on the right shoulder, where Christ had carried it) but sometimes—as we know from the shipwrecked corpses of first-crusaders washed ashore—tattooed on their flesh. Likewise, the Italian flagellants of 1260, barefoot and half-naked, were identifiably penitents.

In contrast, the German flagellants of 1261 wore a kind of uniform like that of monks. Their faces were partially concealed by hoods or cowls, while a long garment covered their lower parts and stretched down to their ankles. This alarmed the clergy. Were these laymen members of some heretical, pseudo-religious order? The revival of the northern Italian *Bianchi* ("the Whites") of 1399, on the other hand, aroused no such suspicions. Indeed, leading clerics enthusiastically joined the processions of this mass movement dedicated to peace and piety. The Bianchi derived their name from "their simple white robes" supposedly enjoined upon them in their foundation legend. During the nine days of their devotional exercises, the Bianchi clothed themselves in them. The color symbolism of pristine innocence is unmistakable. "Their dress is pure," wrote Franco Sacchetti.[11] Behavioral iconography thus conveyed a concentrated message of the essential spirituality of the revival.

Pictorial iconography of the traditional sort was a second means of spiritual shorthand. Every church was an art gallery, but thanks to processional banners embellished with various saints and symbols, Christian art was exhibitable out of doors. A good instance is the peace revival of the *Caputiati* or *Chaperons Blancs* (White Hoods) of late 1182 to circa 1184, so named because of their distinctive white woolen or linen garb. Affixed to a banner or piece of parchment together with an image of the Virgin and Child was the motto that proclaimed their millenarian-pacific ideals: "Lamb of God, who takes away the sins of the world, give us peace." Both the motto of the Caputiati and their image were reputed to have been given to their founder Durand, a carpenter of Le Puy, by Mary or Christ.

The same holds for the *pastores* or Shepherds' Crusade of 1251. By displaying banners of the Lamb and the Cross, traveling bands of armed shepherds asserted both their elect status in the Christian story and their crusading purpose of rescuing the king of France, Louis IX, from Muslim captivity in Egypt. Because the scene of the Annunciation to the Shepherds was regularly sculpted above the portals of Gothic churches, everyone knew that shepherds were uniquely privileged. They were the first to see the Lamb of God, the infant Jesus. The flagellants of 1310, as depicted in a medieval chronicle, show these *disciplinati* marching, lashing their shoulders, exchanging the kiss of peace, all the while gazing at a banner at the head of their procession surmounted by a cross, representing the flagellation of Christ. A more powerful visual encapsulation of the spirituality of their movement cannot be imagined.

Among the most impressive visual displays in medieval revivalism were the immense banners held aloft during the late-fifteenth-century plague processions in the towns and cities of Umbria. Such processional banners or *gonfaloni* were mute prayers to God for forgiveness and pity during times when bubonic plague raged among the helpless citizenry. One of these was the banner or gonfalone painted by Bonfigli in 1464, which shows a large, protective Madonna della Misericordia, Our Lady of Mercy, shielding her city of Perugia from the three arrows of her beardless Son. Under her cloak, as under a fallout shelter, citizens and religious huddle, while in the foreground, through the winding city streets, a *Bianchi* confraternity is solemnly processing. Then at the foot of the gonfalone, amid those fleeing the city and the corpses of plague victims, is as comforting an image as the words of John Donne: "And death shall be no more; death, thou shalt die."[12] Around the Virgin gather the patron saints of the city (including, nearest the viewer, the most recent of them, St. Bernardino of Siena, on the left) and the plague-saint specialist St. Sebastian (pierced by nonfatal arrows representing plague wounds, on the right). The most optimistic sign of all is at the banner's head. One angel (top left) unsheathes his sword: the plague begins. Another angel (top right) sheathes his sword: the plague ceases.

Already remarked upon are the raised voices of medieval enthusiasts as they shouted, cried out, chanted, and sang about their most fervent desires. This was their third expressive mode broadcasting their beliefs. The conciliar outcry of Clermont (1095)—which became the battle cry of the first crusade, *Deus le volt!* ("God wills it!")—has previously been mentioned. But before Clermont came the thunderous acclamations of the late-tenth-, early eleventh-century revival known as the Peace and Truce of God, whose most eloquent chronicler was Rodulfus Glaber (ca. 980–ca. 1046).

In his *Five Books of Histories* (ca. late 1030s) Glaber evokes the intense religious emotions roused by the peace councils—coun-

Fig. 4.5. Agostino di Duccio (1418–1498). St. Bernardino expels the devil. Oratorio di S. Bernardino, Perugia, Italy. Photo: © Scala / Art Resource, N.Y.

cils of the "great, middling, and poor" people—summoned by "the bishops and abbots and other devout men" of Aquitaine and Burgundy following the millennium of Christ's passion in 1033. To these councils, Glaber says, "were borne . . . innumerable caskets of holy relics." Oaths of peace were taken in an atmosphere of miraculous healing. "Such enthusiam was generated that the bishops raised their crosiers to the heavens, and all cried out with one voice to God, their hands extended: *Pax! pax! pax!* ('Peace! peace! peace!'). This was the sign of their perpetual covenant with God."[13]

Another instance is the earliest processions linked to the start of the Children's Crusade of 1212. Here the clerically directed liturgies held at Chartres to gain divine and human support for the endangered Spanish church passed out of clerical control and into the hands of the laity. Led by the French *pueri*, the massed enthusiasts shouted out, "Lord God, exalt Christendom!" "Lord God, return to us the True Cross!"[14] This plea for God to "exalt Christendom" was especially associated with the crusades, something entirely

---

Response to Pope Urban II's Call for the First Crusade, Council of Clermont (1095)

After this speech, those present were very enthusiastic in the cause, and many, thinking that nothing could be more laudable than such an undertaking, at once offered to go and diligently exhort the absent. Among these was the Bishop of Puy, Adhemar by name, who later acting as the Pope's vicegerent prudently and wisely led the whole army of God and vigorously inspired them to accomplish the undertaking. So, when those things which have been mentioned were determined upon in the council and unanimously approved of, and after the papal blessing was given, they withdrew to their homes to make known to those who were not present at the council what had been done. When these tidings were published throughout the provinces, they agreed under oath that the peace which was called the Truce should be kept mutually by all. Finally, then, many persons of every class vowed, after confession, that they were going with a pure intent whither they were ordered to go.

Oh, how fitting and how pleasing to us all to see those crosses, beautiful, whether of silk, or of woven gold, or of any kind of cloth, which these pilgrims, by order of Pope Urban, sewed on the shoulders of their mantles, or cassocks, or tunics, once they had made the vow to go. It was indeed proper that soldiers of God who prepared to fight for His honor should be signed and fortified by this fitting emblem of victory; and, since they thus marked themselves with this symbol under the acknowledgement of faith, finally they very truly obtained the Cross of which they carried the symbol. They adopted the sign that they might follow the reality of the sign.

—Chronicle of Fulcher of Chartres, in *The First Crusade: The Accounts of Eye-Witnesses and Participants*, ed. August C. Krey (Princeton: Princeton University Press, 1921; repr., Gloucester, Mass.: Peter Smith, 1958), 40–41

appropriate in the context of the impending, decisive battle of the Spanish Crusade. Contrariwise, "Lord God, return to us the True Cross!" suggests another locale altogether: the Holy Land, where the True Cross was lost to the Saracens at the battle of Hattin in 1187. When the two chants are juxtaposed, consequently, the direct connection between "exalt Christendom" and the imminent Spanish clash becomes somewhat doubtful. Was it, perhaps, a more generalized, if equally fervent, crusading outcry, denoting all of Christendom in peril, not only Spain, but also, more important, the Holy Land? If so, it could signify a change of direction for the *pueri*—from the crusader West to the crusader East.

Like the acclamations of the *pueri*, those of the flagellants or *disciplinati* of 1260—"Mercy and peace, Lord, give them to us!" "Mercy, Lord, send us peace!"—were probably more transparent to contemporaries than they are to us. Nonetheless, they articulate the miseries of the time and hint at a socioreligious program. What the *disciplinati* were pleading for was an end to the wars between city-states, clan vendettas, and factional violence within cities, as well as an amnesty

Fig. 4.6. Madonna della Misericordia, detail with city of Perugia during the plague by Benedetto Bonfigli (ca. 1420–1496). Cappella Oddi. S. Francesco, Perugia, Italy. Photo: © Scala / Art Resource, NY.

for political prisoners. Acclamations alone, however, did not exhaust the vocal repertoire of the flagellants.

A gifted contemporary chronicler heard their voices:

> And not only by day, but also by night with lighted candles, during a most bitter winter, by hundreds and thousands and tens of thousands, they went from city to city and from church to church, humbly prostrating themselves before the altars, preceded by priests with crosses and banners. They did the same in the villages and small towns, so that plains and mountains alike resounded with their voices crying unto the Lord. Silenced, then, were all musical instruments and love songs. Only the sorrowful songs of the penitents could be heard everywhere, as much in the cities as in the villages, and their doleful rhythms would move hearts of stone, and the eyes of the most obstinate could not contain their tears.[15]

So in addition to their acclamations, there were "the sorrowful songs of the penitents." Other revivalist movements as well—the northern European *pueri* and the Italian Bianchi among them—are known to have raised their voices in song. Would that we possessed the lyrics of all medieval revivals.

In short, what programmatic revivalist crowds give us is an oral epigraphy. As with written inscriptions, their meaning naturally requires decoding. Once deciphered and contextualized, however, acclamations provide the soundtrack for the moving pictures of revivalist behavioral iconography. In addition to communicating their spiritual beliefs, they permitted enthusiasts to proclaim their identity and affirm their solidarity. Shouting together and marching together gave these noninstitutionalized, informal groupings sufficient social cohesion to make their deepest aspirations known.

Programmatic Revivals:
Types, Species, Families

When medieval chroniclers began to understand that revivalism was a recurring phenomenon, they saw it within the framework of specific revivalist families, such as papally authorized crusades, popular crusades, flagellant movements, peace movements, Jubilees, and so on. But any modern attempt to classify medieval revivals runs into difficulties, because many categories intersect and overlap, meaning that any single movement could well find a place in more than one revivalist family. For example, there were medieval revivals like the Children's Crusade of 1212, in which young people were a conspicuous or a leading element. It happens that a good number of these movements were also shrine-directed, that is, pilgrimage revivals, such as the astonishing fourteenth- and fifteenth-century youth movements that converged on the abbey of Mont-St.-Michel in Normandy. These drew young people from northern and southern France, the Low Countries, as well as parts of Germany and Switzerland. Hence medieval revivals were more varied than is usually supposed.

This is particularly true when it comes to the localized urban revivals of the later Middle Ages. Among them was a distinctive subspecies: urban revivals led by preachers, whose centerpiece was a flamboyant religious spectacle, "the burning of the vanities." A collective ritual of purgation and purification leading to civic moral regeneration, it involved laymen and laywomen surrendering their morally dubious valuables to feed the flames in a spectacular public conflagration. How freely such items were given up is debatable. Some evidence exists of direct or indirect social pressure having been applied. But to those whose contributions were wholly voluntary, self-dispossession amounted to a conversionary act. Thus purged and purified, individuals and their city were made new.

First and foremost, "the burning of the vanities" is associated with St. Bernardino of Siena (d. 1444, canonized 1450), an Observant Franciscan and one of the supreme urban revivalists of his age. Bernardin came to Perugia in 1425. On September 23, he preached out of doors in the cathedral square (or piazza) before a congregation that a contemporary Perugian chronicler estimates as "more than 3000 persons." "His preaching was of the Holy Scriptures," says the chronicler, "rebuking the women for painting and plastering their faces, for their false and borrowed hair . . . and likewise the men, for their playing cards, dice, and painted faces, for talismans and charms."

Within fifteen days, Perugia's luxury-loving womenfolk and menfolk had delivered their "false hair, paints and cosmetics" along with their "dice, playing cards, and backgammon sets" to the convent of San Francesco. Then in the same *piazza* Bernardino had "a castle of wood" constructed on which were placed all of their surrendered items together with assorted expensive baubles. The next day, Sunday, October 30, after he finished his sermon, Bernardino had the entire heap of "vanities" set alight. "And so great was the fire that words cannot describe it; and therein were burned things of passing great price."[16]

Bernardino's example was followed by other fifteenth-century urban revivalists, including the Franciscan Brother Richard in Paris and the Dominican Girolamo Savonarola in Florence. But the burning of the vanities was only one of a number of strategies adopted by the medieval preachers of urban revivals who labored for the moral regeneration of town dwellers. In the early thirteenth century, the itinerant French priest Fulk of Neuilly (d. 1202) tried to convert usurers while also endeavoring to reform prostitutes by establishing convents for them or by raising money for dowries to marry them off. Around the same time, a Norman abbot, Eustace de Flay, toured England (1200–1201), preaching Sabbath observance and threatening Sabbath breakers with God's wrath.

If local or regional urban revivals occupied a surprisingly broad category within medieval revivalism, one must not overlook revivalism in the medieval countryside. Notable in this respect were the vast gatherings of country folk who camped out to hear Berthold of Regensberg, the celebrated thirteenth-century German Franciscan revivalist preacher. In sum, the varieties of medieval programmatic revivals were so extensive as almost to defy categorization.

Nonprogrammatic Revivals:
Ecstatic Enigmas

By their nature, nonprogrammatic revivals are more enigmatic. Indeed, it could be argued that far from being "about" nothing, they may simply have been the incipient stage of what later emerged as a full-blown programmatic revival. Thus what is now looked upon as the initial phase of the Lombard Great Hallelujah of 1233 may have actually been a self-sufficient nonprogrammatic revival before the mendicant friars grafted a socioreligious program onto it.

According to Salimbene, it was inspired by a wandering, horn-blowing, oddly costumed, itinerant lay evangelist called Fra Benedetto de Cornetta (Brother Benedict of the Horn). The name "Benedetto" fit his practice of leading the crowd in threefold benedictions—to God the Father, Son, and Holy Spirit, while "de Cornetta" probably derives from the cornet that was his musical accompaniment. Salimbene praises Fra Benedetto as "a simple and unlettered man, but . . . of pure and honorable life." A "second John the Baptist," he calls him, thereby designating him as the precursor of the friars who were to come. "He would go into the churches and the squares [in Parma], preaching and praising God, followed by great multitudes of children." After his praises and benedictions would come "Hallelujah, Hallelujah, Halle-lujah!" Then he would "preach, sounding forth praise to God." Apparently, this was the extent of Fra Benedetto's preaching—blessings, praises, Hallelujahs. Would this, then, be medieval revivalism's "pure" state, that is to say, a simple effusion of religious spirit—ecstatic and joyous—devoid of any agenda, however prayerful? If so, unlike programmatic revivals, it simply *was*, rather than was "about."

More enigmatic and definitely darker in tone than Benedetto's Hallelujah was the revival of the ecstatic dancers (*dansatores, chori-santes*) of 1374. Few revivalist rituals were as extraordinary as theirs. Medieval onlookers were astonished at their spiritual acrobatics. To one clerical chronicler, theirs was a "violent suffering [*passio*] . . . rare and amazing." To another, a "sickness." The group's life span of around five months, from late June to November 1374, was typically brief. Itinerant, hopping (as it were) from shrine to shrine, the chorisantes set off on a pilgrimage that took them through the Rhineland and parts of the Burgundian Low Countries. Their ecstatic performances probably climaxed in and around Liège, where the clergy finally managed to snuff them out. Their dancing was so wild and disorderly that some chroniclers likened it to epilepsy, but the notion of large groups of epileptics having simultaneous ritual seizures is scarcely credible.

With their "loud voices" filling the air, the dancers journeyed from one settlement to another, performing their ecstatic gyrations in front of bemused clergy and laity. They danced and jumped in private houses, in the streets, in the squares of towns, but most notably in churches, where, leaping and dancing before the altars, they aroused the anger of the clergy for disrupting public worship. As with all revivalist rituals, their behavior was imitative. Those who joined the pilgrimage of the chorisantes necessarily were obliged to master intricate behavioral routines before they could perform in public.

To the clergy this was a religious affliction: "many people, men as well as women, irrational folk as well as those oppressed by illness, none of them at peace . . ." Another chronicler affirms: "Usually, between eight and fifteen days they were fully restored to mental and bodily health." Certain that the cause of their illness was demonic possession, the clergy prescribed the traditional cure: exorcism. The chorisantes acquiesced, yet their submission proves nothing, for the clerical explanation was imposed upon them. When asked, they were unable to explain why they did what they did. Whether theirs was a dance of divine affliction or a creative religious performance, the meaning of their ecstatic choreography escapes us.

THE THREE STAGES OF MEDIEVAL REVIVALISM

Quite often there is insufficient historical evidence to reconstruct the beginning, middle, and end of any given medieval revival. Despite this lack of specific evidence, however, to assume that the life cycle of an archetypical or "perfect" revival passed through three distinct phases lets us spot things we might otherwise overlook.

This is particularly true when it comes to the first phase of the model, the mixed religious crowd, already referred to. This initial stage is frequently missing from the chroniclers' reports, which is not surprising. Medieval chroniclers rarely knew anything about a revival's local beginnings, let alone the circumstances of its birth. Large-scale revivals were usually noticed only after they reached their mature, itinerant, second, or "movement" phase, when they had already spread over a wide area. So instead of giving us an account of a revival's historical origins, they supply the foundation legend current among the enthusiasts of the second phase or substitute a picturesque tale of their own invention.

Nevertheless, mixed religious crowds had a formative influence on medieval revivalism. Crowds gathered for a reason; they had a focus (such as a liturgical or popular procession) and a locus (an urban space, a sacred place). Finally, it goes without saying, crowds had to be aroused. Here a preacher's galvanizing rhetoric is the obvious mechanism. The supreme medieval paradigm would seem to be Pope Urban II's powerful speech at Clermont (1095), which summoned the first crusade. This would conform perfectly to the formula—crowd + preacher = religious movement. Nowadays, however, historians prefer to stress the impact of Urban's preaching tour in France, following Clermont—in addition to the cumulative effect of the returning bishops and priests—on subsequent crusade recruitment. Yet there was no doubt on the part of the clerical chroniclers who later reimagined Urban's speech that it was the spark that ignited crusade enthusiasm throughout Latin Christendom. And it is certainly true that revivalistic preaching was conversionary preaching. Such preaching roused crowds, encouraged an atmosphere of the miraculous, opened up a classic route to charismatic leadership, and demanded an immediate response.

The remarkable career of Vitalis of Savigny (d. 1122) is a good illustration of this. Educated cleric, hermit, itinerant preacher of apostolic poverty, and monastic founder, Vitalis, according to a chronicler, "spared neither rich nor poor in his public sermons." "Many multitudes journey[ed] to hear his words. . . . Every rank was mortified by his true allegations, every crowd trembled before him. . . . So . . . he saved many and brought many to his side."[17] Among the "many [brought] to his side" were numerous converts who habitually followed him on his preaching tours. Revivalist preachers like Vitalis regularly attracted groups of especially devoted followers who behaved more like disciples than members of a mixed religious crowd.

But the leaders of revivalist crowds were not necessarily preachers or clerics. They might be laymen like Durand, a carpenter of Le Puy, of the peace army of Caputiati; the shepherd boy Stephen of Cloyes of the Children's Crusade; or Rainero Fasani, who may have inspired the Perugian *disciplinati*. Hermits, like Vitalis of Savigny, or the better-known Peter the Hermit, popular preacher of the first crusade, even if clerics, occupied a quasi-religious status of their own. Medieval hermits had a love affair with crowds, and by no means was

> ### The Difficulty of Sustaining Enthusiasm:
> ### Responses to the Preaching of Fra Robert of Lecce
> ### (Perugia, 1448)
>
> On March 29, which was Good Friday, Friar Roberto resumed preaching in the piazza every day, and on Holy Thursday he preached about communion and invited the public for Good Friday, and at the end of that sermon about the Passion he put on this performance. . . . When it was time to display the Crucifix, Eliseo di Cristofano, a barber in the Porta Sant'Agnolo neighborhood, came out of San Lorenzo in the guise of the naked Christ with the cross on his shoulders and the crown of thorns on his head, and his flesh looked as if it had been beaten and scourged like when the Christ was beaten. A crowd of soldiers led him to be crucified. . . . In the middle of the platform they were met by a woman done up as the Virgin Mary, dressed all in black, weeping and lamenting about what was happening as a mystical likeness of the passion of Jesus Christ. When they had arrived at Friar Roberto's pulpit, he remained there for a while with the cross on his shoulders, and all the people were pouring tears and crying "mercy." Then they set down that cross, and put on it a crucifix that had been there before and arranged it on the cross; and then the wails of the people grew even louder. At the foot of the cross Our Lady began her lament together with St. John and Mary Magdalene and Mary Salome, who recited several verses of the lament for the passion. Then came Nicodemus and Joseph of Arimathea, who unfastened the body of Jesus Christ and laid it on the lap of Our Lady, and then they placed it in the tomb, with all the people wailing loudly the whole time. Many people said that Perugia had never seen a more beautiful and more devout devotion than this one. And on that morning six people became friars, one of whom was the aforementioned Eliseo, who was a foolish young man. . . . When three or four months had passed, this Eliseo di Cristofano of Porta Sant'Agnolo left the friary and went back to being a barber, and he is known as Mr. Lord God; and he later took a wife, and was a bigger scoundrel than he had been before.
>
> —A. Fabretti, "Cronaca della città di Perugia dal 1309 al 1491, nota come Diario del Graziani," in Roberto Rusconi, *Predicazione e vita religiosa nella società italiana da Carlo Magno alla Controriforma* (Turin: Loescher, 1981), 192–93

it an unrequited love. Nor did all medieval religious crowds acquire the momentum of revivals and transmute themselves into religious movements. Crowd enthusiasms could remain isolated, seemingly spontaneous events; at other times they were carefully stage-managed.

Revivalist preachers, who sought to engineer collective enthusiasm as part of fund-raising tours, crusade recruitment campaigns, or moral crusades, became adept practitioners of crowd psychology, a fundamental skill in routinizing revivalism.

After the mixed religious crowd, there appeared the second, itinerant or peregrinatory stage of the revival, the "movement" proper—people in motion. This phase corresponds to the evangelical diffusion of the revival, in which collective enthusiasm gathers pace, makes converts, and sets out to conquer new territory. Most medieval revivals remained local; others gained adherents over a considerable region; only a minority became genuinely European in scope. Following the movement phase, most medieval revivals expired.

But not all. The exceptional revivals that managed to survive went on to achieve relative immortality in a third stage. Institutionalization was the primary route to survival. New religious movements led to the genesis or renewal of religious institutions that in some way preserved—some would say, fossilized—the spiritual impulses originally animating the revival. We have already seen that the hermit and wandering preacher Vitalis of Savigny was accompanied by troops of faithful devotees. Almost like the "groupies" surrounding pop stars, such traveling bands of ardent enthusiasts were by no means unique in the history of medieval revivalism. (For example, the renowned late-fourteenth, early-fifteenth-century Dominican preacher Vincent Ferrer, famous for delivering apocalyptic sermons across half of Christendom, was escorted from town to town by processions of his fervent, self-flagellating supporters.) As for Vitalis, toward the close of his career he founded a monastic house near the village of Savigny. The entourage who joined him on his preaching tours now had a permanent home. Their days of evangelical wandering were over. Apostolic itinerancy was exchanged for monastic stability.

So enthusiasm for the *vita apostolica*, the apostolic life lived in preaching and poverty, resulted in a proliferation of new twelfth-century religious orders. Like Vitalis of Savigny, a number of wandering hermits and apostolic preachers dedicated to the apostolic life, among them Bernard of Tiron, Robert of Arbrissel, and Norbert of Xanten, went on to become monastic founders. All of them came to be venerated as saints. Crusading enthusiasm also laid the foundation for the new military orders, such as the Templars, the Hospitallers, the Teutonic

Knights, and a host of Spanish analogues. During the thirteenth century, there was continuity but also change, because conversionary enthusiasm for preaching and poverty gave birth to a radically new kind of monasticism—the mendicant orders or begging monks. The most influential of these mendicants were the Franciscans and Dominicans. Both developed into highly structured religious organizations indispensable to the papacy.

Putting these new mendicant orders in the framework of medieval popular revivalism is not as paradoxical as it may seem, for here too we see institutionalization as the product of revivalism. First, there emerged a charismatic leader, let us say, Francis the *poverello* or little poor man of Assisi. Disciples were drawn to him as if to a magnet. Francis's initial small fraternity of holy beggars in ragged robes then dispersed and began preaching to mixed crowds in villages, towns, and cities. Conversions to the Franciscans multiplied; the fraternity grew prodigiously, a growth spurt that corresponds to the diffusion or movement phase of a revival. Tighter organizational controls became necessary, and Franciscanism went through an

---

The Flagellants of 1260:
The Chronicle of Salimbene de Adam

The Flagellants came through the whole world; and all men, both small and great, noble knights and men of the people, scourged themselves naked in procession through the cities, with the Bishops and men of Religion at their head; and peace was made in many places, and men restored what they had unlawfully taken away, and they confessed their sins so earnestly that the priests had scarce leisure to eat. And in their mouths sounded words of God and not of man, and their voice was as the voice of a multitude: and men walked in the way of salvation, and composed godly songs of praise in honour of the Lord and the Blessed Virgin: and these they sang as they went and scourged themselves. And on the Monday, which was the Feast of All Saints, all those men came from Modena to Reggio, and the Podesta and the Bishop with the banners of all the Gilds; and they scourged themselves through the whole city, and the greater part passed on to Parma on the Tuesday following. So on the morrow all the men of Reggio made banners for each quarter of the town, and held processions around the city, and the Podesta went likewise scourging himself. And the men of Sassuolo at the beginning of this blessed time took me away with the leave of the Guardian of the convent of the Friars Minor at Modena, where I dwelt at that time, and brought me to Sassuolo, for both men and women loved me well; and afterwards they brought me to Reggio and then to Parma. And when we were come to Parma this Devotion was already there, for it flew as "an eagle flying to the prey," and lasted many days in our city, nor was there any so austere and old but that he scourged himself gladly. Moreover, if any would not scourge himself, he was held worse than the Devil, and all pointed their finger at him as a notorious man and a limb of Satan; and what is more, within a short time he would fall into some mishap, either of death or of grievous sickness.

—G. G. Coulton, *From St. Francis to Dante* (London: Duckworth, 1908), 190–91

institution-building process that at times was painful, although something of the original Franciscan adventure was still preserved.

New lay confraternities were likewise products of popular revivals. They increased significantly during the later Middle Ages, but the impulse to perpetuate a shared religious experience by institutionalizing it was nothing new. Groups of pilgrims returning from a shrine, such as Santiago de Compostela in Spain, would regularly establish local confraternities in honor of St. James. A similar remembrance of things past, as well as a desire on the part of former participants to continue to derive spiritual benefits from an extraordinary religious movement that had once so roused them, explains the remarkable proliferation of *disciplinati* confraternities in the wake of the flagellant movement of 1260, as well as Bianchi confraternities following 1399.

Less commonly than through confraternal institution-building, revivals perpetuated themselves by becoming fixed in collective memory. Here the chroniclers of medieval revivalism—borrowing from one another, adding to and embellishing what little information they disposed of—played an essential part in keeping ephemeral events alive. Even when they diffused half-truths, legends, and myths, as with the Children's Crusade of 1212, they kept obscure, short-lived episodes from disappearing from public consciousness; indeed, they endowed them with centuries of posthumous life. Kurt Vonnegut's best-selling *Slaughterhouse-Five; or, The Children's Crusade: A Duty-Dance with Death* was published in 1969.

OUTCOMES

Institutionalization and cultural memorialization were just two possible outcomes for revivalist movements whose endings were remarkably diverse and unpredictable, varying from successful fund-raising or church-building campaigns to anti-Judaic or anticlerical massacres. Nor can it be forgotten that medieval collective religious enthusiasm, especially when it was not inaugurated by ecclesiastical authority, could be divisive, attracting converts while distracting or repelling others. Furthermore, it is undeniable that certain heretical movements, the early-thirteenth-century, pantheistic Amalricians among

others, were revivalist in their missionary zeal and prophetic fervor. It
is also true that medieval crusading revivals like the first-crusade peasant armies of Peter the Hermit (1096) or the hordes loyal to Jacob, the
Master of Hungary—a prominent leader of the Shepherds' Crusade
of 1251—slaughtered Jews and, in the latter case, priests as well. But
official crusades, which, after all, fused piety and violence, also provoked officially unsanctioned attacks on nearby Jewish communities.
Such violent episodes apart, the overwhelming majority of medieval
revivals were peaceful and orthodox in intent and did not set out to
subvert religious authority. As their name implies, medieval revivals,
on the whole, were aimed at revitalizing rather than overthrowing the
religious structures of Christian society.

The inherently populist nature of medieval revivalism has been
affirmed more than once. The crusade decree of the Council of Clermont (1095) reinforces that point, underscoring the populist character of crusading. Highlighting its intended all-inclusiveness, the decree
began with the word *quicumque*, whosoever, which signifies that the
offer to crusaders of remission from penance was to be made available to anyone who assumed the burden of the cross, every believer
regardless of social status. Crusade revivalism was thus populist from
its inception, in spite of contemporary and subsequent efforts to limit
participation in the crusading host to the military professionals, that
is, the knights.

Christian populism not only figured at the birth of revivals,
as with the mixed religious crowd, but also often featured as an
aspirational outcome. At the same time, contrary to Norman Cohn's
Pursuit of the Millennium, in medieval revivalism there exists very
little evidence of millennial yearnings for an egalitarian Garden of
Eden. On the other hand, the dream of moral crusaders within the
monastic and civic worlds was that of a religious house or city purified and restored to virtue. This ideal was no respecter of status when
it came to individual or collective moral accountability. Perhaps its
best exemplification can be seen in the work of the fifteenth-century
preacher-revivalists, the Observant friars, Franciscans like Bernardino
of Siena, and Dominicans like Girolamo Savonarola. Here we encounter a new Christian populism, a populism at once civic, puritanically
reformist, and theocratic. The key was the reform of civic statutes in

keeping with a puritanical legislative program directed against perceived social evils, such as Perugia's bloodthirsty civic game called the battle of stones, which Bernardino's new civic statutes abolished. The obvious precedent for this was the work of the friars during the Lombard Great Hallelujah of 1233, when they became the moral legislators of communities in disarray. Like revivals themselves, however, such reforms were relatively short-lived. What they do indicate, however, is that an underlying impulse in medieval revivalism was the desire to construct a morally renewed Christian community.

FOR FURTHER READING

Bornstein, Daniel E. *The Bianchi of 1399: Popular Devotion in Late Medieval Italy.* Ithaca, N.Y.: Cornell University Press, 1993.

Cohn, Norman Rufus Colin. *The Pursuit of the Millennium: Revolutionary Millenarians and Mystical Anarchists of the Middle Ages.* Rev. ed. London: Pimlico, 1993.

Cowdrey, H. E. J. *Popes, Monks and Crusaders.* History Series 27. London: Hambledon, 1984.

Dickson, Gary. *Religious Enthusiasm in the Medieval West: Revivals, Crusades, Saints.* Ashgate, U.K.: Aldershot, 2000.

———. "Revivalism as a Medieval Religious Genre." *Journal of Ecclesiastical History* 51 (2000): 473–96.

———. *The Children's Crusade: Medieval History, Modern Mythistory.* New York: Palgrave Macmillan, 2008.

Mayer, Hans Eberhard. *The Crusades.* 2nd ed. Oxford: Oxford University Press, 1988.

Origo, Iris. *The World of San Bernardino.* New York: Harcourt, Brace & World, 1962.

Riley-Smith, Jonathan. *The First Crusade and the Idea of Crusading.* London: Athlone, 1986.

Thompson, Augustine. *Revival Preachers and Politics in Thirteenth-Century Italy: The Great Devotion of 1233.* Oxford: Clarendon, 1992.

Weinstein, Donald. *Savonarola and Florence: Prophecy and Patriotism in the Renaissance.* Princeton: Princeton University Press, 1970.

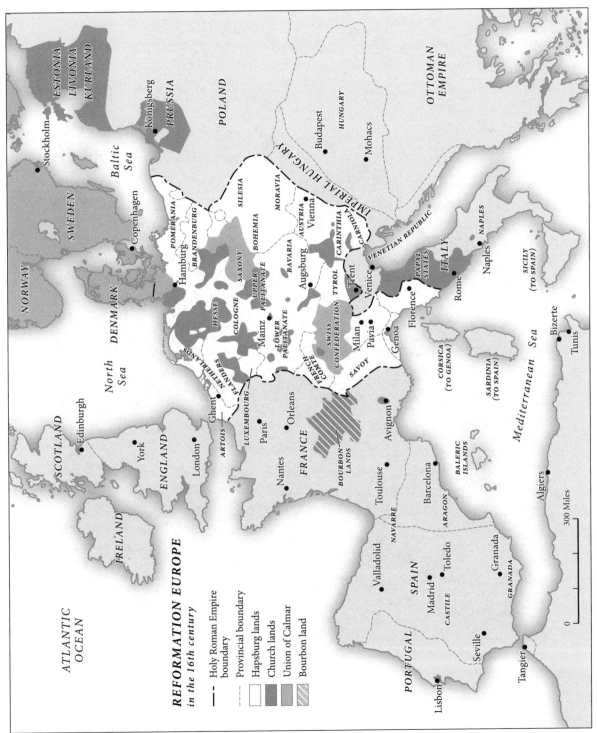

REFORMATION EUROPE
in the 16th century

— · — Holy Roman Empire boundary
— — — Provincial boundary
☐ Hapsburg lands
▨ Church lands
▨ Union of Calmar
▨ Bourbon land

Fig. 5.1. Map by Lucidity Information Design.

Fig. 5.2. Looming high above the town of Eisenach, the Wartburg castle was a refuge for Luther in his time of need. Symboli-cally, it has personified the endangered but defiant "fortress" of the Lutheran faith and Lutheran believers. Yet it was also a prison for those who dissented from that faith. This impressive image from the first part of the twentieth century captures something of that ambivalence. From "Views of Germany," Library of Congress Photochrom print collection, 1905.

REFORMING FROM BELOW

PETER MATHESON

High above the town of Eisenach in Saxony towers the imposing Wartburg castle. With its great halls, its superb museum, and its Renaissance façade, the Wartburg is one of those rare, haunting places a visitor can never forget. It became famous as the refuge of Martin Luther when he was smuggled there after the dramatic gathering of the German princes at Worms in 1521. Luther had already been excommunicated by the papacy. By the time he left Worms, he was also under the ban of the empire. He had had the audacity to defy the assembled might of church and state. He was now the ultimate outsider, both heretic and outlaw. His marvelous hymn "A Mighty Fortress Is Our God," which still inspires people today, recalls this time of crisis and yet confidence. Luther's productivity in the Wartburg was remarkable. Despite the threats he was under and his inner turmoil, he succeeded in translating the New Testament into pulsing, vivid German in the unbelievably short period of eleven weeks. Just imagine it!

This, then, is the familiar, glory side of the Reformation. On the southern tower of the Wartburg, however, one notices a bronze plaque that alerts us to a much darker side. It records the solitary confinement there of Fritz Erbe, a peasant arrested in 1533 for his refusal to have his child baptized. Though by all accounts he had been a gentle, good-living man, the Wittenberg theologians and the Saxon Elector wanted him beheaded for what they regarded as a blasphemous act. The Protestant leader, Landgrave Philip of Hesse, however, hoping that Erbe might still be persuaded to recant, succeeded in commuting his sentence to life imprisonment. At first, Fritz Erbe was imprisoned in the "Stork Tower" in Eisenach, but courageous supporters were able to reach him there and give him some encouragement, so he was transferred to the dark, freezing cold underground dungeon in the South Tower of the Wartburg. He was let down into it by the "terror hole" in the floor, and he remained there until his death in 1548, sixteen years later. He remained firm in his faith to the end, despite the appalling conditions he had to endure and the arguments of the Lutheran preachers who were sent to convince him of the error of his ways.

Martin Luther and Fritz Erbe: Which represents the reality of the Reformation? This latest in a long succession of books about the Reformation has no interest in making either heroes or demons out of Luther and leaders like him, but it will seek to transform the way in which we approach this vast religious upheaval by directing the center of interest away from princes and popes and professors to ordinary people like Fritz Erbe. How did the Reformation, or rather the Reformations—for there were many—affect laypeople, children, the rhythms of day-to-day life? Whose Reformation was it, anyway? Who gave it its momentum? What part did the ordinary urban or village dweller have in shaping it? What about the role of parents or of the great majority of the population that was illiterate or semi-literate? One glance at the table of contents of this book may give some indication of its perspective: it approaches the religious history of the early modern period "from below," in a grounded and down-to-earth way.

A generation ago, the central focus of a volume such as this one would have been on Martin Luther, John Calvin, and other major reformers. It would have traced in detail the controversy about indulgences (certificates of pardon), the rupture with the papacy, and the breakthrough to a new theology—justification by faith and the supremacy of scripture. It would have proceeded to detail the Catholic response to Lutheranism and Calvinism: the great Council of Trent in the middle of the sixteenth century, the emergence of the Jesuits and other new orders, the programs of Catholic reform. The bookends holding the narrative together would have been the prolonged hostilities between the Holy Roman Empire of Charles V and the new nation-states of France, Spain, and England, and the educational and cultural renewal we call the Renaissance.

There remains much, of course, to be said for such an approach. There will always be a need for the history of doctrine and religious concepts, for an account of institutional reform and high politics and the fascinating interplay between them. There will always be a place, too, for grand narrative and for the color and sparkle of towering personalities, with which our period is particularly abundant. It is a dull soul who cannot thrill to that. This book, however, will traverse a different path. Its aim is to alert the reader to quite new streams of research and perspective that are redressing an imbalance—one that has existed for far too long. Academic historians in the past have tended to focus on what is familiar to them: on ideas and political movements and the cultural elite. Moreover, all too often it has been male historians talking about male thinkers, politicians, and clergy. The aim of this book is to open up some new ground, especially for those who have not had the advantage of access to the discussions in learned journals and advanced scholarship, by focusing on the aspirations and frustrations of ordinary folk. How did they react to the religious, social, and cultural upheavals around them? Were they simply swept along, or did they themselves contribute to and modify them?

Fig. 5.3. Here peasants swear an oath of allegiance as they prepare to rise up against their masters. Note the central Christian symbolism of the flag under which they will fight. The woodcut by Pamphilus Gengenbach (c. 1480–1525) dates from 1524.

A NEW DAWN

As we set out on this journey, we have to remember, of course, that the period we are entering was a highly optimistic, utopian one, at an almost infinite remove from our contemporary Western one, with its pluralism and cynicism and disillusionment with all grand narratives and heroic solutions. The literary deposit of this optimism is to be found everywhere, from Thomas More's famous *Utopia* to Campanella's *City of the Sun*, or Martin Bucer's blueprint for a godly society, the *Kingdom of Christ*. Ordinary people, too, had their own fervent dreams of a New Jerusalem, based on stubborn memories as well as ardent hopes. As we will see, many of them had no intention of sitting down passively when they found their rights and freedoms endangered, of letting things take their course. Others did follow the immemorial path of resignation, but what is so distinctive about this age is that a significant minority dared to blaze a new trail.

Indeed, the stirring of spirits was so extraordinary that to make sense of it, people reached back not only to dimly remembered events in their corporate memory but to texts from prophetic and visionary books from the Bible such as Joel and Revelation. The young would again see visions, and the old would dream dreams. Nothing seemed impossible anymore. A new age was dawning, and it was time to lasso the future. The New Jerusalem would come to pass in their own "green and pleasant land." A good and godly society was in its birth pangs.

After all, were not new lands with unheard-of wealth and wondrous plants and animals being discovered? Signs and portents in the sky were eagerly studied for evidence that changes in church and society were imminent. The whole world, it seemed, was to be turned upside down. In this highly charged atmosphere premonitions of doom mingled with hopes for the return of a Golden Age and for liberation from oppression and corruption. It was as if one were eavesdropping on the awesome battles of the legions of angels and devils in the heavens, of the Archangel Michael with Satan, of Christ with Antichrist. As the infidel Turks banged at the eastern door of Europe, as wars and rumors of wars abounded, it seemed that a cosmic battle was about to be joined, one that would be above all a spiritual battle. Therefore, you had better know which side you were on. Woodcuts, vividly colored broadsheets, popular poems, and songs and ballads set these apocalyptic ideas circulating among ordinary people. Sensational preachers such as Savonarola in Florence and still more fantastic rumors swept through homes and marketplaces. Above all, the printing press had put the vernacular Bible into laypeople's hands, and the message of the ancient prophets and apostles, raw and relevant and relentless, was released. It seemed that Jeremiah was knocking at the gates of the cities and the apostle Paul was once again opening up people's minds and hearts to the great themes of the crucified and resurrected Lord. It was a time, then, for great hopes and expectations and for incandescent rage, too.

> What is the evil brew from which all usury, theft and robbery spring but the assumption of our lords and princes that all creatures are their property? The fish in the water, the birds in the air, the plants on the face of the earth—it all has to belong to them. Isaiah 5. To add insult to injury, they have God's commandment proclaimed to the poor: God has commanded that you should not steal. But it avails them nothing. For while they do violence to everyone, flay and fleece the poor farm worker, tradesman and everything that breathes, Micah 3, yet should any of the latter commit the pettiest crime, he must hang. And Doctor Liar [Luther] responds, Amen. It is the lords themselves who make the poor man their enemy. If they refuse to do away with the causes of insurrection how can trouble be avoided in the long run? If saying that makes me an inciter to insurrection, so be it![1]

This quotation is taken from the fiery pamphlet *Vindication and Refutation,* written in 1524 by the preacher Thomas Müntzer. It reminds us that religious enthusiasm could easily slip at this time into social and political radicalism. Those who ministered to the poor on a day-to-day basis saw the oppressive conditions of their lives and could not neatly separate the religious world from the secular one. Müntzer, a conscientious pastor and creative liturgist, wrote, long before Luther, a German Mass for his congregation of tradespeople and peasants in the little town of Allstedt; he went on to play a leading role in the peasant rebellions in Thuringia. Eventually he was to die, after torture, by the sword of the avenging princes. Lutheran and Catholic historians alike have tended to dismiss him in the past as a bloodthirsty terrorist. Yet he was very much part of the whole Reformation movement. He pioneered a mystical theology for ordinary people and sought to open up the scriptures to simple, rough-hewn folk.

THE RADICAL REFORMATION AND THE PEASANTS' WAR

How, then, do we incorporate the whole spectrum of religious concerns into our treatment of the period? How do we free the Reformation from a false intellectualization and spiritualization? Over the past decades there has been a gradual move away from the previous confessional and largely doctrinal and institutional approach. One important step was that from the middle of the twentieth century, historians in the United States in particular began to draw attention to the "left wing" of the Reformation. Mennonites had a special interest in the bitterly persecuted groups of believers who emphasized their simple discipleship of Christ and who became known as the Anabaptists. Up to this time, Lutheran and Calvinist historians from Europe had tended to categorize such radicals either as naive idealists or as bloodthirsty maniacs. Historians such as G. H. Williams, however, have demonstrated that the so-called Radical Reformation needed to be taken seriously as a significant theological and social movement. Williams showed that it embraced a wide variety of groups, from the quietist Anabaptists, who turned their back on all coercion and violence, state-sponsored or not, to the millenarian militants who, for example, attempted to set up a new communal kingdom in the city of Münster in 1534–1535. The emphasis of the radicals on lay leadership and on communal forms of worship and lifestyle commended them to American readers in particular. Their critique of Christendom and their frequent advocacy of tolerance appeared to put them well ahead of their time. Their bravery under persecution also seemed quite inspiring. Though a minority group, they were far from an insignificant one.

Closely associated with this new scholarly appreciation for the Anabaptists and other radicals has been the growing attention paid to the conflagration of the Peasants' War, which spread across most of central Europe in the mid-1520s. Many other peasant revolts preceded it, such as the Peasant Revolt in fourteenth-century England, and many other insurrections were to follow it; nevertheless, until the French and American Revolutions in the eighteenth century, there was to be nothing to rival it in creativity and scope and impact. Marxist historians hailed the Peasants' War as part of the early bourgeois revolution, and their research on its origins and development contributed considerably to our knowledge of it. As with the Radical Reformation, superb editions of new source material became more readily available, and these editions now sit side by side with those on the "official" or "magisterial" Reformation. The crude, smudgy pamphlets of the period have been painstakingly collected and published in readily available microfiche form.

As a result of this work and because of excellent collections of woodcuts and broadsheets, we are now much better equipped to see what the common folk thought and believed—although caution is warranted. By no means, for example, were all the pamphlets attributed to the stereotypical "simple peasant" written by them! While most Western historians in the late twentieth century were unable to accept the historical-materialist analysis of the Marxists, the importance of the Peasants' War was beginning to be recognized. By 1975, the 450th anniversary of the rebellion, serious theologians and church historians were noting its intimate relationship to the Reformation. After all, the peasants and tradesfolk who marched under the rebel flag were often advised, counseled, and led by Christian preachers. Their flags themselves featured Christian symbols such as the rainbow, and the articles they drew up to negotiate with the authorities began with a call for proper preaching, quoted scripture, and were inspired by a thirst for divine justice. They saw Christ as their captain, as the Christ of the poor, and they denounced the oppressive princes, bishops, and magistrates because they had, according to the rebels, acted contrary to "law, honor, and God."

REFORMATIONS, NOT REFORMATION

At the same time, however, as Mennonites and Marxists alerted us to the Radical Reformation and the crucial significance of the Peasants' War, we were also coming to recognize the plurality and diversity of the Reformation movements. From the 1950s, there had been a renaissance of Catholic scholarship that reminded us of the breadth and depth of humanist and Catholic reformers such as Lefèvre in France or the cosmopolitan Erasmus, who had long been offering their own programs of educational reform and creating their own lay networks, wanting to take a very different path from a Luther or a Zwingli.

The guild of twentieth-century historians came to recognize that there was not one Reformation. There were many: humanist, Catholic, communal, Zwinglian, Calvinist, Radical. Few were centered like Luther's on universities such as Wittenberg. While not denying the astonishing brilliance of Martin Luther as translator and interpreter of scripture, as hymn writer and reformer, we began to pay attention to the small army of other reformers and opinion makers, of teachers and city clerks, civic counselors and lawyers. We noted the prevalence of urban sodalities (we would call them book clubs today) and well-staffed professional academies, and the way in which monasteries often harbored alternative opinions.

The reformations were quite varied. Under Cranmer, England went its own distinctive way. François de Sales initiated very attractive and popular forms of Catholic reform in Savoy. In Scotland and the Netherlands grassroots elements worked alongside an insurrectionist nobility. First we began to pay attention to the civic-centered reforms with their focus on the "common weal." Studies appeared on one city after another. But then this was complemented by some remarkable work on rural movements. It became clear that in some areas discontent had been simmering right down to the village level, where new initiatives were being launched to secure resident pastors, their own local church building, and accountable pastoral care. In this "communal reformation," in both town and country, the emphasis was not on the finer points of doctrine or on restructuring the church's institutions but on the rights and liberties of the common folk, based on divine justice.

Some historians suggested that urban reform in southwest Germany and Switzerland had a distinctive "republican" profile. A reformer such as Martin Bucer, for example, in the bustling trading city of Strasbourg had firsthand awareness of laypeople's

---

**Erasmus to Archbishop Warham
1521**

The condition of things is extremely dangerous. I have to steer my own course, so as not to desert the truth of Christ through fear of man, and to avoid unnecessary risks. Luther has been sent into the world by the genius of discord. Every corner of it has been disturbed by him. All admit that the corruptions of the Church required a drastic medicine. But drugs wrongly given make the sick man worse. . . . For myself I am a man of peace, and hate quarrels. Luther's movement was not connected with learning, but it has brought learning into ill-repute, and the lean, and barren dogmatists, who used to be my enemies, have now fastened on Luther, like the Greeks on Hector.[2]

concerns for the "common good," while the wealthier patricians, guild members, and even women such as Katharina Schütz Zell began to make their voice heard. Anticlericalism was another particular focus of research. Its opposition to the channeling of power and wealth to the clergy bound together theological and social concerns, the interests of city leaders and the urban poor, including impoverished clerics. Traditional foci of spirituality, such as monasteries or the revered Franciscan and Dominican friars, found themselves being scrutinized by disenchanted lay eyes and often found wanting. This anticlericalism combined with the apocalyptic excitement we have already noticed to sweep aside centuries-old devotional practices such as pilgrimages and the adoration of the saints. Ritual processions were caricatured in the streets, while in pamphlets long processions of derisory words mocked traditions: worshipers brought to the shrines "bread, wine, beer, along with chicken, goose, and horse"; hoping for healing, they offered wax images "in the shape of your diseased legs, arms, eyes, head, feet, hands, cows, calves, oxen, sheep."[3] This focus on anticlericalism points to the popular roots of the Reformation.

What fired anticlericalism? As important as the sermons or tracts of the new generation of reformers was the sense of injustice and exploitation that they were able to tap into. Reformations need fertile social soil if their proposals are to grow roots. Countless early sermons and pamphlets raised very concrete socioeconomic issues, and since they regarded Holy Scripture as an infallible mirror of God's will for justice, they possessed divine justification for their passionate concern for social justice and at the same time a uniquely authoritative blueprint for a better society.[4] We have to remember, of course, that in this period no one regarded religion as an individual matter. The Christian gospel, a good individual conscience, and social harmony were seen as quite inseparable.

SOCIAL HISTORY

Perhaps the most groundbreaking change in our understanding of the Reformation in recent times has come from the contribution of social historians. Church historians had tended to work within theological faculties. Social historians operated within secular history or economics or sociology departments. While not necessarily unsympathetic to theological and religious issues, they have naturally been much more interested in social dynamics and outcomes than in ideas for their own sake. Their researches, too, were based on very different source materials. Most people in our period could not read—perhaps as few as 5 percent, though literacy could be much higher in the towns. Social historians, therefore, have drawn the obvious conclusion that if we are to do justice to the great majority, we should turn our gaze from theological tomes and sermons and institutional records to humble tax records, wills, domestic accounts, marriage contracts, family chronicles. Since wills were crafted for public effect, they throw light on communal as well as individual concerns.

Thus social historians have given us the tools to get closer to the lifestyles and relationships of the vast majority of the population. They have demonstrated the inadequacy of relying upon the aspirational teachings and literature of the preachers, intellectuals, and theologians, which certainly tell us what the latter believed but give little clue as to how much of this fell on fertile ground. A careful analysis, for example, of the reception of the Reformation in Strasbourg "suggests the social specificity of the various forms of Reformation religion." The upper classes embraced the Lutheran distinction between spiritual and secular freedom; among the tradesfolk, on the other hand, a more radical communitarian Christianity commended itself.[5] It is not just that people accepted or rejected the new teachings according to where they stood in society: they did not even register what was being said unless it spoke to their own situation.

Social historians also introduced a different interpretive grid, which involves asking a variety of questions, sometimes borrowed from the related field of social anthropology. They have asked questions about kinship and social relationships, marriage and family property, patronage, civic and rural pressure groups. English historians have been particularly helpful in pointing to the role of the local parish, for example, in building community and reconciling feuds.

The perspectives of social historians enable us, therefore, to view reality through another lens, to view, for example, bishops or monasteries or their anticlerical opponents in terms of their social role in society as well as their spiritual capacity. We have become conscious that the same theological ideas could be quite differently understood by the aristocracy, the lesser nobility, wealthy townsfolk, guildsmen and artisans in the town, and the destitute. Economic historians have also reminded us that much if not most history is made not by startling cataclysmic events such as Henry VIII's break with the papacy but in long, slow movements of change in agricultural practice or commercial innovation or even in climate. The chapters in this book, therefore, rest on a host of unbelievably patient, qualitative and quantitative studies in regional and national archives across Europe.

CULTURAL HISTORIANS

Cultural history has been another rich vein that has increased in value in recent Reformation studies. Our lives, including our religious lives, are framed and informed much less by formal credos or confessions of faith or by papal or synodical pronouncements than by the songs we sing, the illustrations we hang on our walls, the daily rhythms of our lives, the feasts and festivities we celebrate, and perhaps above all our "rites of passage"—how we mark birth and death, growing up into adulthood, forming lifelong relationships, facing illness and death. How do we celebrate and mourn, how do we distinguish between our private and public life, and how are these practices reflected in the spatial design of our homes and streets and city squares and plazas? These days historians of the Reformation work cheek by jowl with historians of art and music, of architecture and language, not to mention historians of food and costume. Material evidence, such as that provided by architecture, funeral monuments, and inscriptions, has also been paid increasing attention. All these contribute to building up some sense of the texture of the lives of ordinary people.

We have learned, too, from the cultural historian that we may understand a church or a society best when we view it not from the centers of power but from the margins. Accordingly, cultural historians have turned our attention to how urban and rural societies treated their "outsiders": the unclean trades, for example, such as the butchers; nonsedentary groups such as the mercenaries, Gypsies, and wandering players; feared or despised groups such as the Jews and the "witches." The role that the church has played thus appears in a new light.

The quest, of course, for the "ordinary" or average person can be something of a chimera and can sometimes lead to a false dichotomy between popular and elite culture. Rather fringy outsiders, such as the miller Menocchio with his homespun theories of the universe,[6] have sometimes been taken to represent popular religion, while entire swaths of Catholic and Lutheran rural and urban dwellers have been labeled submissive pew-fodder and therefore quite uninteresting.

Unlike today's world, however, the "high culture" in the early modern period was not hermetically separated from the "popular culture" of the majority of the population. With one or two exceptions, such as court and university life, people of all classes mixed quite freely. Gradations, of course, were respected, even to the shape and color of the clothes one was allowed to wear. But everyone attended the same church, went to the feasts and festivals together, mixed and mingled in the street and the marketplace. Shakespeare's dramas remind us how philosophical monologues and buffoonery succeeded and complemented one another.

No small part of the challenge of the religious Reformations, therefore, was that they altered life for everyone, not just for the nuns and the monks who were forced out of their monasteries. The changes impinged on every dimension of life. It is true that many of the fundamental patterns of family relationships, with their intimate connection to property rights, proved remarkably resistant to change, but what is astonishing is how many of the subtle textures of daily life were transformed: the intimate discourse and gestures of divine and human love, the practice of prayer and almsgiving, the central metaphors in which God and Christ, church and spirit, individual and communal life were expressed, were transmuted and transfigured. It was not just the furniture of church buildings that changed but, much more fundamental, the furniture of people's minds and hearts. Where such changes took firm root in the imagination, the Reformation was most profound.

REFORMATION AND WOMEN

At long last, too, historians have come to ask a question so obvious that it was universally ignored: Was there a Reformation for women? Within the last generation or so, we have finally woken up to the fact that 50 percent of the people living, thinking, and working in our period were women. Unsurprisingly, much of this is attributable to the relatively new phenomenon of women historians. It is, however, remarkable how long it has taken to "rediscover" the perspectives and contribution of women in this period, whether as mothers or nuns, wives or single women, and to investigate how they crafted their lives, formed their children, and influenced their menfolk. I can still remember my delight at finding a very useful biographical index at a splendid German library but then my growing mortification as it dawned on me that it listed not a single woman.

The role women have played, however, is only one issue. Interest has moved well beyond casting them as either heroine or victim. As scholars have reviewed gender perspectives, they have discovered that virtually all our previous presuppositions about piety and worship, the fashioning of theology, the reading of scripture, the life of children, the realities of home and public life need to be comprehensively revisited. Issues of male honor, for example, impinged hugely on how women were regarded and treated. Historians are beginning, therefore, to look at understandings of masculinity, and as this is addressed, it has become quite clear that the way in which men viewed themselves varied greatly from one region to another and from one time to another. Once the questions were posed, it all seemed so obvious, but why has it taken us so long to get there?

> **Argula von Grumbach challenging the Ingolstadt theologians to a debate:**
>
> I do not flinch from appearing before you, from listening to you, from discussing with you. For by the grace of God I, too, can ask questions, hear answers and read in German. There are of course German Bibles which Martin [Luther] has not translated. You yourselves have one which was printed forty-one years ago, when Luther's was never even thought of. . . .
>
> God grant that I may speak with you in the presence of our three princes and of the whole community. It is my desire to be instructed by everyone. . . .
>
> I have no Latin; but you have German, being born and brought up in this tongue. What I have written to you is no woman's chit-chat, but the word of God; and [I write] as a member of the Christian Church, against which the gates of Hell cannot prevail.[7]

HOTLY DEBATED ISSUES

Many issues remain wide open as this book goes to press. That is good, because it illustrates that there has never been such an exciting time to study Reformation history as now. At virtually every gathering of early modern historians, for example, there is a debate about periodization: How should we carve up the course of Christian history? This is far from being just a typical academic infight. If, for example, we set a starting point around 1520, this suggests a view of the Reformation as an abrupt break from the past, which begins and ends with Luther. It has become increasingly clear, however, as we work through a whole raft of issues—from popular piety to biblical interpretation to institutional reform—that there is substantial continuity with the late medieval period. If, on the other hand, we were to see the Reformation or Reformations as a subset of a much wider Renaissance movement, that could set the starting point far back in the fifteenth century or even earlier. There are economic, social, political, and cultural arguments for a whole host of different positions. In this volume we are opting for the "long sixteenth century" option, which assumes that the early modern period stretches back into the medieval period and extends well into the seventeenth. Again there are unmistakable signs of a revolt against a narrowly European view of this period, recognizing that the new religious movements were already beginning to have an impact on North and South America and Asia.

Another highly controversial area is that of confessionalization. To what extent should we see this whole period as one in which the real motor and determiner of events was the early modern state, with its agendas of centralized control, standardization, and repression of dissenting views? Were theological and religious considerations at best secondary to state propaganda and indoctrination, especially as religious conflict became identified with political rivalry and military confrontation between nation-states? What degree of popular or personal support did the various Reformations really enjoy? This is, of course, a crucial question for a book such as this one, which focuses on the views of the ordinary person.

Ultimately, the answer given may be dependent not only on the evidence available but on the historian's understanding of what constitutes human nature and human society. As the carefully choreographed Catholic processions wound their way through the streets, however, it is hard to doubt that most people must have felt a heightened sense of solidarity with the earthly community as well as the heavenly community that the processions were prefiguring. On the other hand, the plurality of religious options and the trend toward interiorization of the faith encouraged what the irenic Catholic theologian George Cassander (1513–1566) called "a sort of third type of people," who found good and bad in both sides and longed for a mediating position. Should we assume, from a patronizing position in the present, that communal identity and personal freedom are necessarily opposed to one another? Recent research has certainly shown that the old distinction between a bourgeois, republicanizing Protestantism and a submissive, politically absolutist Catholicism can no longer be maintained.

Finally, how are we to do justice to the "cross-pollination" that took place in people's hearts and minds as well as in institutions at this time? How can we represent appropriately the interplay of biblical themes with social unrest, of theological motifs with cultural or nationalist considerations, of personal inclinations with the whole matrix of economic and social determinants? If the traditional style of doing church history sometimes suggested that nothing mattered except ideas and institutions, doctrine and churchmanship, the new can go to the other extreme, with an overwhelming preponderance of social or gender analysis. There has been, of late, something of a revolt against too analytical and determinist readings of this period. It has been suggested that we have permitted the intrusion of anachronistic categories. Do modern political terms such as "liberal," "conservative," "radical," and "reactionary" really help us to understand this period?

It has been emphasized, therefore, that it would be good to treat the language and values of sixteenth-century men and women with the utmost seriousness and not to read them from our perspectives. We need to avoid using "shopworn" modern categories for the time and place we are studying and "patiently seek conceptions better suited to bring out [their] character."[8] We have to guard against assuming that common folk were only interested in social outcomes and were not passionately engaged with faith in God and love of their neighbor. Countless men and women, after all, risked the loss of property, security, and lifelong friendships, put witnessing to their faith above family or marriage, bought forbidden books, harbored fugitive preachers, and stood firm under all manner of threats. Women faced the risk of being shut away for life. Many believers died a ghastly death by beheading or by drowning or at the stake. It seems inappropriate not to take this seriously.

There are undeniable problems of interpretation here. We can never wholly escape from our own vantage point. The task of fusing the horizons of early modern people with our own will always be a challenging one. At the very least, however, their language and thought, their spirituality, their courage and timorousness have to be allowed to appear in their own alien forms. The great sobering corrective for all of us historians is that we are driven back again and again to the sources, social as well as personal. Analysis and smooth synthesis must always be held to ransom by the discordant testimony of the evidence, textual and nontextual. We have to attempt to create from that testimony and the questions of other historians a rich, textured picture of what faith, discipleship, martyrdom meant for ordinary people. We always have to remember that, as Robert Scribner put it, "the ways in which they sought to relate their religious and secular aspects were more varied and complicated than the neat compartmentalizations 'religious' and 'social' imply."[10]

Behind the simplest hymn or prayer or action or protest lies a whole raft of factors, associations, hopes, and visions that no individual or team of people can hope to uncover or recover. The past is in the past, and it is forever lost to us. Yet its allure and challenge remain. As in all human relationships, we may need both to preserve the courtesies and to move beyond them. A respect or even reverence for the people of the past can spur us to stretch our imaginations, to deploy a comprehensive palette

> **Wilhelm Rem's Augsburg Chronicle of 1524**
>
> Then on 15 September the Council had two weavers beheaded furtively; the alarm bells were not rung. The first was called Speiser, a good follower of the Gospel with a good reputation. When they struck off his leg-irons and brought him to the front of the Council Chambers he asked where they were taking him, and they said to him, they intended to execute him. . . . He said, the Council was dealing with him unjustly and violently. . . . It was because of the word of God that he had to die, and he was quite ready to die. He had a good reputation and was a God-fearing man. Then they chopped his head off on the marketplace. . . . They imprisoned many women and men here because of what they were saying, putting them to torture, and expelling many from the city.[9]

that will do justice to their ideas ("the flowing, curative waters of Wittenberg," as one pamphlet described them) as well as to social and cultural factors, and to trace the way in which groups and individuals tuned in and tuned out of the messages they heard, developed their own idiosyncratic "take" on issues, and spoke out bravely or prudently kept their peace.

I would argue for an approach that respects but does not absolutize the role of ideas, spiritualities, and theologies—which can be valued as genial articulations and responses to the issues generated by the socioeconomic and cultural matrix—but gives equal emphasis to how communities and individuals wove such credos into the warp of their own particular lives. Most communities, after all, expressed their deepest beliefs not in propositional form but in song and ceremony, whether in Catholic processions and pilgrimages or Protestant celebrations of the Lord's Supper or days of fasting and penitence.

DID ANYTHING REALLY CHANGE?

The jury is still out on the question of the "success" of the religious Reformations. Many would argue that they brought about little significant social or cultural change, pointing quite correctly to the reemergence of clericalism, to the censorship of ideas and books, and to the enforced uniformity of the confessional era. Others note the stubborn resistance of rural communities to reforms that looked all too much like impositions from the city slickers. In my own view, the impact and memory of the Reformations, stumbling and compromised as they often were, remained a motor for highly significant change in the mental outlook and actual lives of so-called ordinary people. The audacious expectation of a comprehensive "Reformation," the symbolic language of a new dawn, a new age of light, freedom, truth, and justice, kept recurring in different forms: Puritanism, Jansenism, Neoprotestantism. Even liberation theology, it has been suggested, owes much to its Reformation heritage.

The era's contributions to the Western world we know today are incalculable. New centers of pilgrimage like Wittenberg and Geneva as well as the countless Catholic sites were established. Histories,

Fig. 5.4. Woodcuts depicting daily peasant life from a fourteenth-century calendar. Augsburg Johann Schobsser, "Kalendar" (June 1488) in Adam von Bartsch, *The Illustrated Bartsch: German Book Illustration before 1500*, Vol. 86: Part VII, Walter L. Strauss and Carol Schuler, eds. (New York: Abaris Books, 1984), 310–12.

martyrologies, hymnbooks, and "display cabinets," listing eminent men and women, kept fresh the memories of the new saints, scholars, and confessors for future generations. The Counter-Reformation's massive building programs, educational initiatives, and networks of care for the sick and the poor left a legacy for the future that cannot be gainsaid.

All the Reformations really posed the same question: What is the church, actually? By the variety of their answers, their stern challenge to tradition and authority, and the consequent polarization of opinion, new discursive fields were created. The resources of word, song, and literature opened up endless options for the interior life and for communal experiments of all kinds. The dream of a church in the prophetic mold was not to be forgotten.

An die versamlung gemayner Pawer-
schafft/so in Hochteütscher Nation/vnd vil ande
rer ort/mit empörung vñ auffrür entstandē. ꝛc.

ob jr empörung billicher oder vnpillicher ge
stalt geschehe/ vnd was sie der Oberkait
schuldig oder nicht schuldig seind. ꝛc.

gegründet auß der heyligen Göt-
lichen geschrifft / von Oberlen-
dischen mitbrüdern gütter
maynung aufgangen
vnd beschriben. ꝛc.

Hie ist des Glückradts stund vnd zeyt
Gott wayst wer der oberist bleybt.

Hie pawrßman   Hie Romanisten
güt Christen.   vnd Sophisten.

Wer meret Schwytz   Der herren gytz.

Fig. 6.1. Title page from *To the Assembly of Common Peasantry*. The pope is depicted with his tiara on a wheel of fortune, being turned from a group described as "Romanists and Sophists" onto the waiting lances of "peasants, good Christians." Beneath the picture is the rhyme "Who makes Switzerland grow? The greed of the lords." Image from Horst Buszello, *Der deutsche Bauernkrieg von 1525 als politische Bewegung* (Berlin: Colloquium 1969), 152.

THE DREAM
OF A JUST SOCIETY

JAMES M. STAYER

CHAPTER SIX

JUSTICE DIVINE AND HUMAN

In his lectures on Galatians (1516), Martin Luther set forth a central belief that sustained him in his struggle for a trusting relationship with God: justice is faith in Jesus Christ. So conceived, "justice" is not something that human beings, great or small, can struggle for; rather, it is something freely bestowed to them by their all-powerful God. Also referred to as *iustitia dei* (divine justice), this was a major concept promoted by the Reformation. Nevertheless, the Christianity of the Reformation, which made divinely bestowed justification by faith its watchword, was troubled by the obvious fact that, for whatever reason, justice was not equitably distributed among human beings. Hence, at the beginning of the Reformation, there was a struggle for divine justice, understood as *social justice.*

This struggle for justice only lasted two decades. It was correctly observed by traditional historians that the Reformation could only succeed in institutionalizing itself with the support of established political powers. These powers knew that the struggle for equitable justice was extremely disruptive. In describing the struggle for justice among Reformation Christians, I will try to combine three perspectives that are often thought to be antithetical. The first is the insistence of East German Marxist historians that, although the European Reformation as a whole cannot be labeled "revolutionary," the first stages of the Reformation in Germanic Europe did contain revolutionary elements.[1] The second is Heiko A. Oberman's conception of a "gospel of social unrest," which antedated the Wittenberg Reformation

135

and must be distinguished from it but was nevertheless undoubtedly of a religious character.[2] The third perspective is that of the historians of "confessionalization," such as Heinz Schilling:[3] in the later sixteenth century, magistracies of all major forms of Western Christianity undertook to direct and elevate the lives of their subjects by a process of "social disciplining."

Reformation Christianity burst forth in two waves—the first beginning about 1520 and affecting Germanic Europe, the second beginning about 1550 and affecting the Dutch Republic, France, England, Scotland, and Eastern Europe. This chapter concerns itself with the first wave only. The Reformation in Germanic Europe initially enjoyed broad social support from aristocrats and commoners, townspeople and villagers. After the echoes of the German Peasants' War became muted, certainly by the end of the 1530s, the support of rural commoners for the Reformation diminished, but the Reformation continued its territorial advance with the support of some rulers and a significant minority of aristocrats and townspeople. Expressing the values of superior estates, aristocrats, and townspeople, rulers imposed social discipline and thus replaced initiatives to secure social justice by unprivileged commoners, particularly villagers. What follows will be devoted to presenting this interpretation. It is also my impression that the situation that prevailed in the Germanic Reformation from the 1540s onward applied to the second wave of the Reformation generally. This interpretation is disputed by some historians of the Scottish Reformation, who point to the national reconstruction programs of the Books of Discipline of 1560 and 1578 as having a definite appeal to ordinary people.[4]

Minimizing the connection of the German Peasants' War and the Reformation, Günther Franz has stressed that the slogans of the laced peasant boot and "divine justice" antedated the Reformation, indeed that they had roots in the Lollard and Hussite heresies of earlier centuries. These same points have been made by Heiko Oberman and Tom

---

> **Martin Luther on Galatians 2:16 (1516)**
>
> A wonderful new definition of righteousness! This is usually described thus: "Righteousness is a virtue which renders to each man according to his due" (*iustitia est virtus reddens unicuique quod suum est*). But here it says: "Righteousness is faith in Jesus Christ" (*fides Jhesu Christi*)!
>
> —Quoted in Alister E. McGrath, *Luther's Theology of the Cross: Martin Luther's Theological Breakthrough* (Oxford: Basil Blackwell 1983), 112.

Scott, and they cannot be ignored. The heresies of the late Middle Ages did not enjoy the success of Protestant established churches precisely because they combined religious and social radicalism. Moreover, Franz and Peter Blickle, the outstanding Peasants' War historians of the past century, have stressed that, aside from its religious appeal, "divine justice" was a slogan made to order for the legitimation of peasant revolt. It freed the peasantry from the problematic nature of the appeal to traditional custom that they otherwise had to use against the exploitation of landlords, priests, and rulers. Rural traditions were always specific to a limited territory and its subjects, but when divine justice was the rallying cry, rebels could be recruited everywhere without regard to the many small jurisdictions into which the medieval world was divided.

THE HAPSBURG FEAR OF SWISS AND *BUNDSCHUH*

The battle for "divine justice" began in southwest Germany in the aftermath of the Hapsburg emperor Maximilian I's disastrous failure to provide masters for the "peasant Swiss" in the unsuccessful war he waged against them in 1499. The outcome of this war prompted Basel to join the Swiss Confederation in 1501, continuing a process of unrelenting Swiss expansion into the Holy Roman Empire of the German Nation that had been going on for two centuries and was expected to continue. That same year, the young serf Joβ Fritz began a conspiracy centered in one of the ecclesiastical territories, the Bishopric of Speyer. His banner, designed in Basel, displayed a *Bundschuh*, the traditional laced boot of the peasantry, together with the slogan, "Nothing but divine justice," placed over the image of the crucified Christ. He tried to recruit not only peasants but "Landsknecht" mercenary soldiers unemployed from the recent war. It was no accident that the conspiracy began in an ecclesiastical territory seething with economic anticlericalism; its other slogan was "We cannot rid ourselves of the plague of priests." Its radical aims were to get rid of all intermediate authorities between peasants and the empire (as the Swiss had supposedly done), abolish all temporal and ecclesiastical taxes, and restore common use of waters, forests, and meadows to the peasantry.

Contemporary chroniclers claimed that Fritz had twenty thousand followers in the territories of Speyer before his plans were betrayed.

The semi-legendary Fritz escaped in 1502, to plot two further *Bundschuh* uprisings: in Lehen in Breisgau in 1513 and on both the Alsatian and Baden banks of the Upper Rhine in 1517. The chroniclers give discordant descriptions of these conspiracies, both of which were discovered before anyone acted upon them, just as was the case in 1502. The paucity of sources makes the extent of the plots' support difficult to reckon. The Breisgau scheme was for a relatively moderate program including religious objectives, but the 1517 plot aimed at only temporal (no religious) goals and was spread about by wandering beggars, jugglers, patent medicine quacks, and other "highway people" without fixed abode. A good dose of skepticism is needed for conspiracies that were never carried out and for fascinating conspirators like Joβ Fritz; all we have to go on are crackdowns by nervous rulers and chronicle accounts that depict Fritz's numerous changes of tactics and invariable escapes. In 1525, Fritz was certainly no major player; we are told that he made a curtain call in the Hegau, on the borders of Switzerland, as a man with "an old gray beard," "who would not die before the *Bundschuh* ran its course."[5]

However, the years 1510–1513 saw widespread unrest against urban oligarchies, as Heiko Oberman says, "from Deventer to Regensburg and from Swabia to Saxony."[6] The actions against the *Bundschuh* in the German southwest were probably, as Thomas Brady argues, due to a justified fear by the Hapsburgs and their allies that the unprivileged commoners in towns and villages were looking to Switzerland both for aid and as a model for their aspirations. But the calls upon "divine justice" in the rural areas were probably, as Oberman thinks, patterned on the "civic righteousness" of the towns that had for a century or more connected *iustitia coram deo* with *iustitia coram hominibus* (that is—in opposition to the later tenets of Luther's theology—there is an intrinsic connection between "justice before God" and "justice before human beings"). The chartered towns of the empire saw themselves as each "a church in miniature"—*corpus christianum* in microcosm. Therefore they provided preacherships and morals legislation for their citizens and secured a degree of administrative control over their church institutions that would hobble the bishops in their later attempts to reassert their administrative control against the Reformation.

THE KNIGHTS' REVOLT

Thus, before Martin Luther's theology burst upon the awareness of the Germanys, a "gospel of social unrest" was already in the field—in the German southwest but elsewhere as well—that had an entirely different notion from Luther's about the relation between the gospel of Jesus Christ and the human struggle for justice. The cross-pollination of Luther's theology and the struggle for justice in Germany set in only subsequent to Luther's appearance before the emperor and the princes at the Diet of Worms in April 1521. Before that, the Luther issue was a strictly theological controversy. But during the period that Luther was in hiding in the Wartburg, from May 1521 to March 1522, the implementation of the Reformation became a topical issue. In general, princes and town councils tried to avoid committing themselves to support of or opposition to Luther's theology—this applied even to his protector Frederick the Wise, Elector of Saxony. The first open choices for the Reformation were made by the lesser nobility, especially imperial knights subject to no one but the emperor. Not all of them supported the Reformation, but some of them did and, further, pledged themselves to protect it.

This brings us to the case of Franz von Sickingen, lord of the Ebernburg in the Rhineland and one of the most famous imperial knights in Germany. Franz had mobilized his troops to support the election of Charles V in 1519. It was the special claim of the knightly estate to seek justice for the oppressed by direct military action through the "feud." The feud was of doubtful legality since the imperial reforms of 1495 had declared an end to private warfare and established a supreme court—the Imperial Chamber Court—to settle disputes. However, it was well known that the great princes, whose judges dominated the Imperial Chamber Court, would not submit their own disputes to its decisions. Feuds continued; in many respects the Peasants' War can best be understood as a series of feuds by the peasantry, seeking direct justice from their overlords. In July 1519, Sickingen declared a feud in defense of the humanist Hebraist Johannes Reuchlin against the German Dominicans, who were oppressing him by legal action in the Roman curia. The next year, in the same spirit he offered Luther protection at the Ebernburg and actually gave it to Johannes Oecolampadius and Martin Bucer, the future reformers of Basel and Strasbourg, respectively.

There can be no doubt of Sickingen's sincere commitment to the Reformation, although he was not a trained theologian and did not understand all of Luther's ideas. Some thirty pro-Reformation pamphlets were published at the Ebernburg, advocating the use of German in worship and communion in both bread and wine for the laity, opposing prayers to the saints, and championing the word of God against papal customs.[7] In August 1522, Sickingen organized six hundred knights of the Upper Rhine into a "Christian Confederation" that attacked the powerful ecclesiastical territories of Trier, Würzburg, and Bamberg on behalf of the Reformation. The confederates declared that these ecclesiastical lands, which were ruled by clerics, had been extorted from their ancestors by trickery and false religion. Once these lands had been repossessed, there would be enough for all estates, even the peasantry. Some of the prince bishops, particularly the archbishop of Trier, turned out to be effective warriors. They mobilized the Swabian League, the Hapsburgs' instrument for maintaining peace and order in the German southwest. Princes, whether Lutheran or anti-Lutheran in religion, refused to permit imperial knights to dispossess their fellow princes. The fortunes of war turned against Sickingen and the knights, and he was killed defending one of his castles. Whatever Luther's viewpoint in 1520, by 1523 and the collapse of the Knights' Revolt, he had made it clear that he regarded the territorial rulers, the princes, as the proper authorities to maintain law and order in Germany.

TITHE RESISTANCE

However strange to contemporary notions of class conflict this may appear, the Knights' Revolt acted as a prelude to the Peasants' War. The notion among imperial knights that church lands and revenues, particularly monastic lands and revenues, had been procured through fraud from their ancestors spread in 1523 to the other rural estate, the peasantry. There was widespread refusal to pay the customary ecclesiastical tithe, particularly when it had become the property of cathedral chapters and monasteries. These tithe refusals occurred in the Franconian and Rhenish territories that were the locale of the Knights' Revolt, as well as in rural villages subject to centers of the early Reformation, such as Nuremberg and Zurich. The ecclesiastical corporations that had enriched themselves by appropriating village tithes assumed the responsibility for seeing that Mass was performed in dependent villages. This system, even when diligently applied, was ill suited to providing pastoral care for new centers of rural population, and it was even less workable for evangelical villages, where the preaching of the gospel replaced the reading of the Mass. Hence tithe resistance was a genuinely religious—and at the same time a social and financial—issue.

Like Sickingen's feud against the ecclesiastical territories, village resistance to tithes was accompanied by a pamphlet campaign. Ulrich von Hutten wrote on behalf of the knights and was a protector of Otto Brunfels, who wrote the tract *On Ecclesiastical Tithes* in 1524. Brunfels stressed that the ecclesiastical tithe was not commanded by Christ in the New Testament. It was an alms that properly belonged to the poor, to preachers of the Word, and to the community as a whole for useful public works. Evangelical governments would not tolerate peasant villagers taking this matter into their own hands, creating, in one particular case, a source of friction between the Zurich government and future Anabaptists. Nevertheless, the campaign against monasteries and cathedral chapters that misappropriated the tithe led in one of two directions. Either town governments confiscated these institutions for their own programs of education and poor relief in the spirit of the Reformation, or the monasteries became the first objects of plundering and sacking at the beginning of the Peasants' War. The "recommunalization of the tithe" became the theme of the second article of the *Twelve Articles*, the most widely circulated summary of the insurgents' demands.

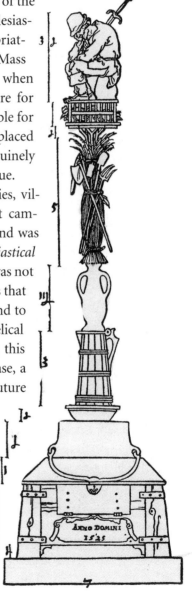

Fig. 6.2. Albrecht Dürer, satirical sketch of a memorial column for the Peasants' War, from Dürer's *Unterweysung der Messung* (Nuremberg, 1525), 164. Image made available by Hans-Jürgen Goertz.

RADICAL PASTORS: MÜNTZER AND HUBMAIER

The diverse theological emphases and reform agendas of major preachers leading the Reformation in the Germanys had a great impact on the Peasants' War. Nowhere was this clearer than in the relation between Martin Luther and Thomas Müntzer. Attending lectures in Wittenberg in 1517–1519, Müntzer was appointed to a pastorate in Zwickau with Luther's support. While there, he developed a style of prophetic biblicism that began a gradual estrangement between him and the Wittenberg theologians.[8] Luther seems to have regarded the prophetic writings in the Old Testament as the outcome of prophets such as Isaiah and Jeremiah devoting themselves to theological study of Moses; by 1521, in a manifesto he published in Prague, Müntzer denounced theologians who claimed to find the Word of God through mere scriptural study and called upon the church not to worship a mute God but a living and speaking one.

> **The *Twelve Articles*: Article 2**
>
> Second, although the obligation to pay a just tithe prescribed in the Old Testament is fulfilled in the New, yet we will gladly pay the large tithe on grain—but only in just measure. Since the tithe should be given to God and distributed among his servants, so the pastor who preaches the word of God deserves to receive it. . . . The remainder should be distributed to the village's own poor, again with the community's consent and according to need. What then remains should be kept in case some need to be called up to defend the country; and then the costs can be met from this reserve, so that no general territorial tax will be laid upon the poor folk.
>
> —From Peter Blickle, *The Revolution of 1525: The German Peasants' War from a New Perspective*, trans. Thomas A. Brady Jr. and H. C. Erik Midelfort (Baltimore: Johns Hopkins University Press, 1981), 196–97.

These differences intensified when Müntzer became pastor of the isolated Electoral Saxon territory of Allstedt from April 1523 to August 1524. Attracting the peasants of surrounding Catholic lands to his new German liturgy in Allstedt, Müntzer had to concern himself with defending his growing flock against imprisonment and exile by their overlords. This was his motive in delivering a sermon at the Allstedt castle in July 1524 to the two Saxon princes, John and John Frederick, calling on them to take up arms in support of the Reformation. That same month, Luther wrote a letter to the Saxon princes denouncing Müntzer's tendency to resort to force. The chain of events that followed led to Müntzer's flight from Allstedt in August and to his securing a role in the ongoing Reformation of the Thuringian imperial city of Mühlhausen. In his sermon in July, Müntzer had warned the Saxon princes that if they did not do their duty to defend the Reformation, their power would be taken from them and handed over to the common people. But Müntzer's enemies at Allstedt were also the princely protectors of the militarily weak imperial city of Mühlhausen. They threatened his new position, so he must have regarded the uprising of the Thuringian peasantry in April 1525 as a heaven-sent deliverance.

A rather different path into the Peasants' War was taken by Balthasar Hubmaier, the pastor of Waldshut and future Anabaptist leader. In December 1523, the government of Austrian territories in the Black Forest and Alsace noted with alarm that he had become a partisan of the Reformation, with strong connections to Zwingli in Zurich. The council of Waldshut rejected efforts to arrest Hubmaier, saying that he proclaimed the Word of God purely and clearly. Some radical supporters of the Zurich Reformation, with connections to the future Anabaptist movement, garrisoned Waldshut in 1524. Zurich would gladly have extended its military and religious influence over Waldshut but avoided a direct confrontation with Austria. What most protected evangelical Waldshut was the uprising in the summer of 1524 of Black Forest peasants, who refused feudal dues and services. A band that combined the traits of a strike and a public demonstration marched around the area under the leadership of a former mercenary, Hans Müller from Bulgenbach. Waldshut was one of their assembly points.

Hubmaier, who thought that he had an agreement with Zwingli that "children should not be baptized before they were of age," was distressed by the rupture between Zwingli and the first Anabaptists in January 1525. He used the disorder of the Peasants' War in April 1525 to introduce believers' baptism in Waldshut with broad congregational support. He also became the most eloquent and theologically schooled defender of believers' baptism against infant baptism

> **Thomas Müntzer, A Protestation concerning the Situation in Bohemia**
>
> Anyone who does not hear from the mouth of God the real living word of God, and the distinction between Bible and Babel, is a dead thing and nothing else. But God's word, which courses through heart, brain, skin, hair, bone, marrow, sap, might and strength surely has the right to canter along in a quite different way from the fairy tales told by our clownish, testicled doctors. Otherwise no one can be saved; otherwise no one can be found.
>
> —From *The Collected Works of Thomas Müntzer*, trans. and ed. Peter Matheson (Edinburgh: T & T Clark, 1988), 368.

Figs. 6.3 and 6.4.
Parallel maps of the incidence of Anabaptism in Central Europe, 1550, and of the spread of the German Peasants' War, 1524–1525, showing that the two movements touched some, but not all, of the same regions. Maps by Lucidity Information Design. Maps from *The German Peasant War of 1525: New Viewpoints*, ed. Bob Scribner and Gerhard Benecke, adapted by permission of Unwin Hyman Ltd., and by Jan Gleysteen in *An Introduction to Mennonite History*, ed. C. J. Dyck, adapted by permission of Herald Press, Scottdale, Pennsylvania.

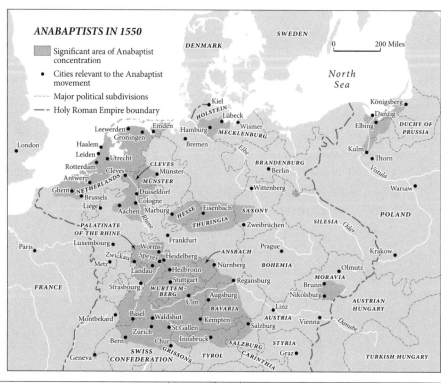

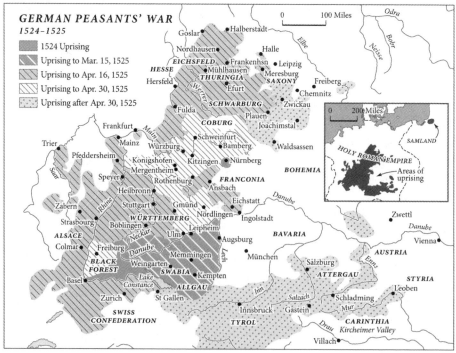

in an exchange of polemics with Zwingli. The collapse of the Peasants' War caused Hubmaier to flee Waldshut just before the arrival of Austrian troops in December 1525. Arriving with the occupiers was Johannes Faber, humanist vicar general of the bishop of Constance and a major enemy of the Reformation. He found in Hubmaier's abandoned papers two pro-peasant declarations: the Constitutional Draft and the Letter of Articles. According to Faber, Hubmaier edited the Constitutional Draft, which justified the deposing of established rulers and outlined a procedure for their replacement. We know of the Constitutional Draft only through Faber, but there is independent authentication of the Letter of Articles, which was used by the Black Forest band.

The Letter of Articles, apparently composed by Hubmaier, imposed a boycott patterned on ecclesiastical excommunication on opponents of the creation of a Swiss-type confederation in the Black Forest. This new government would remove the financial and legal burdens resting on the towns and villages of the region "without any fighting or bloodshed." Castles and monasteries were to be boycotted immediately; their owners could escape the boycott if they withdrew from their strongholds and permitted them to be disarmed or dismantled. Otherwise, the commoners' weapon against their feudal superiors was total social and economic ostracism. Hubmaier's contribution to the peasant resistance was partly opportunistic, making use of the protection it extended to the Waldshut Reformation, and aimed at nonviolent achievement of justice for Waldhut's rural allies. Nevertheless, his entanglement with the Peasants' War in the Black Forest was the main justification the Austrians used for hunting him down in his Moravian refuge and executing him in 1528.

> ### The Letter of Articles of the Black Forest Peasants, Before May 8, 1525
>
> All those who are in this Christian union shall, by the honor and highest obligations which they have undertaken, hold and practice no communion of any kind with those who refuse and oppose admittance to this Christian union and the furthering of the common Christian weal, to wit, by eating, drinking, bathing, milling, baking, ploughing, reaping, or by supplying or letting others supply them with food, grain, drink, wood, meat, salt, etc., or by buying from or selling to them. In those matters which do not promote, but rather retard, the common Christian weal and public peace, they shall be treated as severed and dead limbs.
>
> —From *The German Peasants' War: A History in Documents*, trans. and ed. Tom Scott and Bob Scribner (Atlantic Highlands, N.J.: Humanities, 1991), 136.

CHRISTOPH SCHAPPELER AND DIVINE JUSTICE

The primary outbreak of the Peasants' War occurred in the first months of 1525 in Upper Swabia, leading to the assembly of the leaders of the Baltringen, Allgäu, and Lake Constance bands in the first week in March in the imperial city of Memmingen.[9] The Baltringen leader Ulrich Schmid declared that "divine justice" legitimated peasant demands, and he involved the evangelical leaders Sebastian Lotzer and Christoph Schappeler in drawing up the program of the Upper Swabian peasantry. They became the most important spokesmen of the Peasants' War as the presumed drafters of the *Twelve Articles*, which received the endorsement of all rebel bands except those of northern Switzerland and the Alpine territories of Tirol and Salzburg. Lotzer was a layman, a citizen of Memmingen, literate in the vernacular, a furrier who had been writing pamphlets endorsing Lutheranism from the spring of 1523. Schappeler, Swiss by birth and education, had been a priest in Memmingen since 1513. From 1521, he was a supporter of the Reformation; he participated in the Reformation disputations in Zurich, and in 1524 he became an outspoken opponent of the tithe.

Lotzer was chosen by Ulrich Schmid as secretary of the Baltringen band and is generally thought by Peasants' War scholars to have edited three hundred grievances from the region into the famous *Twelve Articles*. Assuming Lotzer as author of the *Twelve Articles*, scholars sometimes credited Schappeler with being the source of the biblical legitimation of the articles, appearing in the margins of the printed edition.[10] If only one of the two drew up the *Twelve Articles* and the *Federal Ordinance,* the case for Schappeler now appears better, because of the strong presumption that he was the anonymous author of the pamphlet *To the Assembly of Common Peasantry*. Lotzer would not have been able to supply the numerous classical allusions that are sprinkled throughout that pamphlet.

A major reason for the popularity of the *Twelve Articles* was that it was regarded as part of the Reformation's own programmatic literature. The prologue defended the new evangelical teaching against the accusation of its enemies that it undermined spiritual and temporal authority. It declared that all demands of the peasantry were based on the aspiration "to hear the gospel and live accordingly."

Since the gospel taught Christ and peace, any violence and disorder that accompanied the peasant movement was the fault of ecclesiastical and temporal lords who denied justice to their subjects. The first two articles of the twelve gave villagers the right to choose and dismiss their pastors, and adopted the program of tithe resisters that the tithe should be reserved for local purposes, support of the pastor, alms for the poor, and defense of the land. The uncustomary small tithe on meat products was to be totally abolished. Article 12 established the Bible as the standard for all the others; any article shown to be inconsistent with the Bible would be withdrawn, but new demands could be advanced as the commoners' insight into the Bible became greater.

The organization of the *Articles* illustrates the belief of Schmid, Lotzer, and Schappeler that the concerns of the Upper Swabian commoners were in harmony with the Reformation. Articles 1, 2, and 12 were seen as validating the social, economic, and legal demands of the other nine articles. Article 3 rejected serfdom, arguing that it was unseemly for people to hold other people as property, since Christ had died for people in all estates from the most humble shepherd to the greatest lord. Articles 4, 5, and 10 protested against the peasants not having free access to the common resources of the village, forests, waterways, and meadows. Here we have the very general grievance of the peasantry about being excluded by aggressive landlords and officials from sources which had traditionally supplemented the income from their crops—wood and game from the forests, fish and irrigation from water sources, as well as grazing space for their cattle. Articles 6, 7, 8, 9, and 11 brought together labor services, rents, and dues, as well as legal penalties that the commoners regarded as untraditional, unjust, and infringing upon their livelihood.[11] These demands tended especially to reflect the interests of the upper strata of the villages, peasants with lifetime or hereditary leases, who made up the

> ## The *Twelve Articles*: Article 3
>
> Third, it has until now been the custom of the lords to own us as their property. This is deplorable, for Christ redeemed and bought us all with his precious blood, the lowliest shepherd as well as the greatest lord, with no exceptions. Thus the Bible proves that we are free and want to be free. Not that we want to be utterly free and subject to no authority at all; God does not teach us that. We ought to live according to the commandments, not according to the lusts of the flesh. But we should love God, recognize him as our Lord in our neighbor, and willingly do all things God commanded us at his Last Supper.
>
> —From Blickle,
> *Revolution of 1525*, 197.

local authorities supervising the common agricultural life. It appears that in the Peasants' War these village leaders defined the "common good" and controlled the attitudes of their poorer neighbors who did not have farms, the cottagers, landless laborers, and servants.

If the *Twelve Articles* reflected the problems and aspirations of villagers at the local level, the Upper Swabian program for common governance, which Peter Blickle describes quite reasonably as "republican," emerges in the *Federal Ordinance.* This second major document of the Peasants' War, printed in early March 1525 in Memmingen, was probably also drawn up by Christoph Schappeler. This document aimed at creating a "Christian union and league," "for the praise and honor of the almighty, eternal God, to call upon the holy Gospel and the word of God, and to protect justice and the divine law."[12] Its goal was to transform Upper Swabia into a permanent Swiss-type confederation of "towns, villages, and rural regions." Had this plan been realized it would have created a smaller Swiss-type confederation bordering the greater one. Just twenty-five years previously, the Swiss victory over the Austrians in the Swabian War had led to the annexation of a similar confederation, Graubünden. In 1525, the expansion of Switzerland appeared as an inexorable historical process. The Swiss recognized the Holy Roman emperor as a shadowy overlord, which in no way interfered with their practical independence. This Swiss connection lends special interest to the contention of Peter Blickle and other prominent Peasants' War historians that Swiss-born Christoph Schappeler was the author of a third important printed pamphlet of the Peasants' War, *To the Assembly of Common Peasantry*, published in Nuremberg in May.[13]

If we assume Schappeler's authorship, *To the Assembly of Common Peasantry* provides the key to the precarious balance between nonviolent resistance and self-defense that has puzzled interpreters of the *Twelve Articles* and the *Federal Ordinance.* It must have been written in late March or early April, when it became evident that the army of the Swabian League under the Upper Swabian landlord George of Waldburg had opted for a military solution of the dispute with the peasantry. The substance of the pamphlet concerned the source of rulers' legitimacy, how rulers can lose their legitimacy, how to get rid of an illegitimate ruler, and with whom to replace him. It amounted to a rationale for resistance to tyranny and an argument for replacing hereditary lords with republican authorities directly responsible to the emperor, in the manner of imperial cities, as the pamphlet explicitly stated.

The author wrote in an Upper Swabian dialect, laced with Swiss expressions, and made various allusions to the republican experience of the Romans and of the Swiss when they were oppressed by tyrants. The substance and the phraseology of the *Twelve Articles* and the *Federal Ordinance* recur throughout the pamphlet, particularly the insistence upon "freedom," so that common people could not "be sold like cattle." Its content suggests a close acquaintance with the theology of Zwingli. Luther's doctrine of two kingdoms, from his *On Temporal Power* (1523), was explicitly rejected: "Again and again people speak of two commands: the divine, which concern the soul, and the political, which concern the common good. But God knows these commands cannot be divided, for the political commands which genuinely promote the common good are also divine." On the title page is an illustration that identifies the peasants as "loyal Christians" in opposition to "Romanists and sophists," as well as the jingle "*Wer meret Schwyz, Der herren gytz*" (Who makes Switzerland grow? The greed of the lords). The connection of the Upper Swabian Peasants' War with the Swiss traditions of resistance to tyranny—indeed, to the theme of southwest Germany "turning Swiss"—could hardly be more explicit.[14]

After the Peasants' War, Lotzer disappeared, and Schappeler took refuge in his native Saint Gall, where he served as a Reformed pastor until his death in 1551. In his later reassessments, Schappeler concluded that the struggle began as a religiously motivated effort at liberation but that the peasants' violence and greed ended by turning south Germany into a Sodom and Gomorrah. "We pray for forgiveness and ask that we who started because of faith will not perish without it."[15] Luther's total rejection of Schappeler's notions of justice appeared in print in *Admonition to Peace: A Reply to the Twelve Articles of the Peasants*, before the publication of *To the Assembly of Common Peasantry*.

> **Christoph Schappeler, To the Assembly of Common Peasantry**
>
> And to say nothing of the old histories: what great and ineffable deeds have so often been performed by that poor little band of peasants, your neighbors the Swiss? . . . The majority of their enemies have been put to flight, and king, emperor, princes and lords held up to mockery, the more powerful and the greater the armed might that was used against them. And as often as the aforesaid Swiss fought for themselves, for their country, their wives and children, and had to defend themselves against arrogant powers, they have mostly been victorious against the odds and earned great honor. All that without doubt occurred through the power and providence of God.
>
> —From Scott and Scribner, *German Peasants' War*, 275.

THE NEW ORDERS OF GAISMAIR AND MÜNTZER

The moderate conceptions of evangelical justice voiced by Hubmaier or Schappeler pale when compared to the aspirations of Michael Gaismair or Thomas Müntzer. In May 1525, when the peasant bands were being suppressed elsewhere, Gaismair shocked the Tirol by seizing the treasure of the archbishop of Brixen, hiring mercenaries, and mounting a temporarily effective resistance against the Hapsburgs. During the leisure afforded by his refuge in Switzerland in early 1526, he imagined the constitution for a liberated Tirol, a semi-utopian version of the struggle for justice in the Peasants' War. Gaismair's Tirol was to be a Reformation territory with the Mass outlawed, images destroyed, books of scholastic philosophy and canon law burned, the scriptures the sole basis of university instruction, and the Word of God preached everywhere. All privileges, whether those of aristocrats, townspeople, or merchants, were to be abolished. The mines that distinguished the Tirolian economy were to be expropriated from the big south German companies (denounced as "monopolies") and used to finance the Tirolian government. This would have been a land on the Swiss model, purged of lordship—far more radically egalitarian than Switzerland was in reality.

In Müntzer's case, the extent of his aspirations is more difficult to determine. In his final interrogation he said that Mühlhausen aimed to secure itself from the neighboring princes by controlling a territory of fifty-mile radius around the city. He had obviously given up hope of just rule from any princes, whether or not they presented themselves as supporters of the Reformation. His oft-quoted watchword was: "The people will become free,

---

Michael Gaismair's Territorial Constitution for the Tirol, Composed Early in 1526

You should root out and expunge all godless men who persecute the word of God, burden the common man, and hinder the common good. You will spare no effort to establish a wholly Christian constitution, which is founded in all things on the word of God alone, and live wholly according to it. All privileges shall be abolished, for they are contrary to the word of God and pervert justice, so that no one will have advantage over another. All fortifications around towns and all castles and fortresses should be demolished so that henceforth there should be no more towns, but only villages, in order that all distinctions between men will be abolished, from which disruption, pride and disturbance may arise in the land, but rather there will be a complete equality in the land. All images, wayside shrines and chapels which are not parish churches should be abolished throughout the entire land, along with the mass, for it is an abomination before God and wholly unchristian.

—From Scott and Scribner, *German Peasants' War*, 265–66.

and it is the will of God that he alone shall be their lord." This statement has been interpreted by Hans-Jürgen Goertz as at once democratic and theocratic, but what does it mean? There is a consensus among contemporary scholars that, unlike Luther, Müntzer did not expect an imminent end of the world or an immediate second coming of Christ. He was a prophetic revolutionary, presenting himself in the personae of Gideon, Elijah, or John the Baptist. The value he placed on the prophetic "church" of the Old Testament weighs his theocratic democracy toward theocracy. He seems to have seen his time as experiencing a new Pentecost, initiating a Spirit-led Reformation church in succession to the Old Testament prophets and the church of the apostles—a veritable third age of the church. This was to have been the dawn of a new world, not the end of the world. Ultimately, like Schappeler, Müntzer rejected the material objectives of the peasant bands and concluded that they were not cut out for the high mission he had imagined for them.[16]

> **Confession under Torture of Thomas Müntzer (May 1525)**
>
> The articles which they held and sought to put into practice were: All things are to be held in common and distribution should be to each according to his need, as occasion arises. Any prince, count or gentleman who refused to do this should first be given a warning, but then one should cut off his head or hang him. . . . If things had turned out as he had hoped and planned he had meant—and that had been common knowledge among all the members of his covenant—to appropriate all the land within a forty-six mile radius of Mühlhausen and the land in Hesse, and to deal with the princes and gentry as described above.
>
> —From *Collected Works of Thomas Müntzer*, 437.

THE ESTABLISHED CHURCHES AND THE ANABAPTIST PROTEST

The aftermath of the Peasants' War was that the princes and theologians grew to disdain the rural majority of the Germanic lands. In the pre-1525 pro-Reformation pamphlets a typical spokesman was Karsthans, "the evangelical peasant," who understood the gospel better than the monks and the scholastic university professors.[17] After 1525, Karsthans disappeared. It is hard to know how deeply the pro-Reformation message of a Hubmaier or a Schappeler, or even a Gaismair or a Müntzer, was absorbed into the consciousness of the rural people. But certainly the interest of the villagers who flocked to Allstedt to experience Müntzer's new German ritual was not an isolated occurrence. Peter Blickle writes of the post–Peasants' War

Germany: "Now the princes had to take over the Reformation. Only if they could bring it under political control could revolt be eliminated root and branch."[18] That was surely the meaning of the decision of the Imperial Diet of Speyer in 1526 that from henceforth the individual estates should regulate religion as their consciences dictated, recognizing that they would have to justify what they did to God and the emperor. The consequence of this was Luther's approval (with whatever mental reservations) of the Saxon Visitation of 1528, which organized the territorial church as a branch of the government. This became the model for the organization of the churches that followed the Lutheran Augsburg Confession. From now on godly princes, devout burghers, and aristocrats became the mainstay of the evangelical faith and the support of the new pastorate that imposed their version of "social disciplining" on the rural populace.

What remained of a bottom-up struggle for justice in the Reformation after 1525 expressed itself in the nonconformist sects, the Anabaptists, and, more equivocally, the "civic righteousness" of some of the German and Swiss towns. Socially, the Anabaptists were in the majority persons from villages and small towns, but a strong minority lived in cities in Switzerland and south Germany and in the Netherlands and Hanseatic north Germany. In the first two or three years, they were led by highly educated humanist laypeople, but as these first leaders were eliminated by persecution, urban and rural artisans became the characteristic Anabaptist leaders. Vernacular literacy rather than Latinity shaped an anti-elitist notion of justice among these sectarians. Later, in the seventeenth century, doctors became the first trained professionals to assume leadership roles among Dutch Mennonites.

The Anabaptist sects, which began to appear in 1525, were in some cases led by men who had been able to spread their message under the protection of the peasants' uprising, as we have noted of Hubmaier, or, like Hans Hut and Melchior Rinck, had an earlier close association with Müntzer. More general than their leaders' association with the Peasants' War, however, was their preoccupation with the community of goods ascribed to the early church in Acts 2, 4, and 5. Felix Mantz, a major leader of the earliest Anabaptists in Zurich, stated that, immediately after he baptized people, he "taught them further about love and unity and community of all things, as in Acts 2." Although an early Swiss Anabaptist congregational ordinance prescribes the community of goods, this principle was assumed to be compatible with the maintenance of separate household economies and amounted in practice to generous sharing with needy brothers and sisters in the congregations. The Swiss Anabaptists, particularly, disapproved of people living from invested property. Everyone, they believed, should support himself from his own work, and anyone who had more than he needed had a Christian obligation to put it to the use of the poor.

Within the Anabaptist groups that arose from onetime followers of Thomas Müntzer the stress was on *Gelassenheit*, a mystical breaking free from material attachments. When heavy persecution in 1528–1529 drove many Anabaptists from Switzerland and south Germany to take refuge on the estates of tolerant aristocrats in Moravia, sectarian disputes about the community of goods became a major issue. These quarrels were exacerbated by the tensions between Anabaptists in the settled Moravian population and indigent refugees. The years 1534–1536 became a crisis for the Anabaptist community of goods for several reasons. In Münster in Westphalia, an Anabaptist congregation came into control of the city and adopted an apocalyptic militancy. In the course of a sixteen-month siege of the city by Catholic and Protestant princes, the Münster Anabaptists set up a "Davidic" kingdom that aspired to world domination, pending the return of Christ, and practiced polygamy and the community of goods (the community of goods was more theoretical than real, given drastic inequalities of condition during the siege). At the same time, King Ferdinand prevailed upon the Moravian aristocracy to expel the Anabaptists.

The only Anabaptist sect that was able to maintain itself through the Moravian persecution was the Hutterite group, which in later years systematized the community of goods in large multifamily dwellings, living from the profits of

> **Swiss Anabaptist Congregational Ordinance (1527)**
>
> Of all the brothers and sisters of this congregation none shall have anything of his own, but rather, as the Christians in the time of the apostles held all in common, and especially stored up a common fund, from which aid can be given to the poor, according as each will have need, and as in the apostles' time permit no brother to be in need.
>
> —From *The Legacy of Michael Sattler*, ed. and trans. John H. Yoder (Scottdale, Pa.: Herald Press, 1973), 45.

craftsmanship and controlled in all details of their lives by a rigid hierarchy of elders. In the aftermath of the crisis in Münster and Moravia, most Anabaptist leaders, like Menno Simons and Pilgram Marpeck, abandoned the early church of Acts 2, 4, and 5 as a norm. They instead regarded the New Testament church as compatible with the holding of private property and insisted only that Anabaptists should assist each other generously with mutual aid. This general abandonment of the community of goods, along with internal Anabaptist revulsion against the excesses of the Anabaptist rule in Münster, marked a decline of the radical hostility of the Anabaptists to the surrounding persecuting society. The Anabaptists put their stress on personal holiness of life, an emphasis of the movement from the beginning, and achieved the status of tolerated nonconformists later in the sixteenth century, a situation that continued until the Thirty Years' War in Moravia and permanently in the Dutch Republic.[19]

CIVIC RIGHTEOUSNESS

Mass support for Lutheranism continued in north Germany into the 1530s. It did result in a democratizing expansion of the ruling group in some Hanseatic cities such as Hamburg, as burgher committees supervised, and eventually amalgamated with, the established councils.[20] In southwest Germany and Switzerland medieval traditions of "civic righteousness" continued the Reformation aspirations for communal justice, and the ideal of a godly life held some balance over against Lutheran justification by faith alone. For instance, Zurich's Reformation ordinance on alms for the poor was in the tradition of essentially medieval ideals of morality, piety, and social hierarchy and conformity. The poor were to be assisted only if they behaved worthily and deferentially and if they were authentic residents of Zurich. Poor relief was connected with the dismantling of the ostentatious cult of the old church. The images that had previously decorated the churches were "images of man," while the poor were a "true image of God."

Zwingli came to the Reformation from Erasmian biblical humanism, and there were deep-seated differences between him and Luther.

After Zwingli's death in 1531, however, Martin Bucer's diplomatic facility negotiated a merger for the south Germans, uniting them with the Lutherans in the Wittenberg Concord of 1536. Pastors in Basel and Bern gave their support to the Wittenberg Concord, but they lost out in their struggles with Heinrich Bullinger, who soldiered on as leader of a doctrinally distinct Reformed Protestantism in Zurich. The jump of the Reformation over the linguistic frontier between German- and French-speaking Europe did not work to the benefit of Lutheranism.[21] Calvinism became the primary vehicle for the spread of the Reformation to France, the Netherlands, England, Scotland, and Eastern Europe. In this way a Swiss republican model added a tincture of anti-tyrannical "freedom," in the tradition of William Tell, to the further history of the Reformation. But it was the freedom of an elite of burgers and aristocrats who conceived of themselves as God's elect. In some respects the struggle for justice among people continued in the later Reformation of northern and western Europe and made its way across the ocean to the Americas, but it subsisted on a slighter social foundation than Hubmaier, Schappeler, Gaismair, and Müntzer had hoped for in the early months of 1525.[22]

FOR FURTHER READING

Blickle, Peter. *The Revolution of 1525: The German Peasants' War from a New Perspective.* Translated by Thomas A. Brady Jr. and H. C. Erik Midelfort. Baltimore: Johns Hopkins University Press, 1981.

Matheson, Peter, translator and editor. *The Collected Works of Thomas Müntzer.* Edinburgh: T & T Clark, 1988.

Scott, Tom, and Bob Scribner, translators and editors. *The German Peasants' War: A History in Documents.* Atlantic Highlands, N.J.: Humanities, 1991.

Scribner, Bob, and Gerhard Benecke. *The German Peasant War of 1525: New Viewpoints.* London: Allen & Unwin, 1979.

Stayer, James M. *The German Peasants' War and Anabaptist Community of Goods.* Montreal: McGill-Queen's University Press, 1991.

EXPANSION AND CHANGE

AMANDA PORTERFIELD

CHAPTER SEVEN

After 1600, new technologies and forms of industry revolutionized the lives of people around the world. Emerging nation-states, international commerce, modern warfare, and growing demands for democracy led to new forms of social organization affecting people's relationships to one another and to the material world. New ideas about the spiritual world, and new ways to engage its forces, explained these relationships and helped people manage them. Volume 6 of A People's History of Christianity explores the beliefs and practices of Christian people during the tumultuous period of modern transformation prior to 1900. Focusing on the expanding reach of Christian cosmologies, on Christianity as a vehicle of modern individualism, and on Christian missionaries as catalysts of social criticism and reform, the volume examines some of the ways that Christian beliefs and practices mediated changes in the lives of ordinary people.

The meaning of the term "modernization" has often been discussed and its implications for religion hotly debated.[1] This introduction defines modernization broadly as enthusiasm for rational explanations of life that privilege individualism, nationalism, scientific enterprise, and strategic planning. While modernization played out differently in different parts of the world, people everywhere utilized religious beliefs and practices to define and shape it. And while modernization posed many challenges for religious belief and traditional forms of religious practice, people often turned to religion (especially Christianity) to work through these challenges. In Europe, where the driving forces of modern social change first took hold, Christian beliefs and practices figured prominently in people's efforts to negotiate the revolutionary social changes associated with individualism, nationalism, scientific enterprise, and other aspects of modernization. As Europeans moved deeper into other parts of the world, more and more people took up Christianity, sometimes in bits and pieces, and always in the context of their own situations. In many different places around the world, Christian symbols, stories, and practices helped people negotiate the forces of modernization.

Modern conversions to Christianity differed in important respects from earlier conversions. During the first centuries of Christian expansion, the political and economic power of the Roman Empire waned, and local customs often engulfed imperial interpretations of Christianity. Although subversive interpretations of Christianity as a religion of the poor never disappeared, traditions of skeptical inquiry and secular reasoning associated with Greek culture declined as Christianity expanded in ancient and early medieval worlds. For all the maiming and killing associated with conversion after Christianity became the established religion of the Roman Empire in the fourth century, conversion left familiar assumptions about the nature of spiritual forces and their relation to the material world unquestioned. In the modern era, by contrast, the spread of Christianity coincided both with the expanding power of Western political and economic influence and with an upsurge in new questions about divine reality and new ways of conceptualizing spiritual authority. Many people took hold of Christian beliefs and practices in modern efforts to maintain or reconstruct their worlds.

As Christians from Europe reached into the Americas, Asia, and Africa in the seventeenth and eighteenth centuries, people indigenous to those regions encountered Christianity, in many cases, through its connections to imperial power. Representatives of Spanish, Portuguese, British, French, Dutch, and German princes invoked the authority of Christ to assert the divine right of their princes to rule over new people and new land, or at least pacify them for purposes of trade and extraction of natural resources. People in the Americas, Asia, and Africa also encountered Christianity through strategic missionary operations designed to spread the gospel and offer the blessings of salvation to those perceived to need them.

Catholic religious orders sent some of their most talented members to foreign fields to support the work of European expansion and bring Christianity to native peoples. Catholic missionaries reintroduced Christianity to parts of India, Persia, and China where it had died out, and brought it to the Americas and to places in Asia and Africa where it had never been. Beginning in the seventeenth century, English, Scottish, German, Dutch, and Danish Protestants also established mission societies, and in the course of the nineteenth century, commitment to foreign missions became a hallmark of evangelical religion in Europe, Britain, and the United States. Through these extensive missionary efforts, and through the expansion of Western influence more generally, people outside of Western Christendom encountered the Christian God, along with the ships, weapons, tools, costumes, manners, books, food and drink, gender roles, sexual habits, and diseases of Westerners who viewed Christianity and Western culture as coextensive and interdependent.

People outside of Europe also had to come to terms with some of the revolutionary changes rocking Western Christendom, revolutionary changes that were destabilizing Western cultures even as those cultures expanded their borders. These changes included challenges to the divine rights of Christian princes, the union of church and state, the legitimacy of monarchical rule, the truth of religious beliefs, and the efficacy of traditional religious practices. The destabilization of traditional cosmologies began inside of Western Christendom and moved outward from there to many parts of the world. Beginning in the reformation movements of the sixteenth century, Protestant attacks on superstition carried devastating messages about the impotence of saints, sacraments, priests, relics, and icons. As Christianity expanded throughout the world, the destabilization of traditional cosmologies spread to other peoples, upsetting traditional family structures, economic patterns, and religious beliefs about authority.

Challenges to religious authority, and defenses of that authority, became increasingly far reaching in their social implications. In North America, English Protestants justified their desire for independence from British rule by refusing to accept the divine right of George III (or any other king) to rule over them. Extending a line of thought that can be traced back through Puritan revolutionaries in seventeenth-century England, American revolutionaries in the eighteenth century portrayed their right to political independence as a logical extension of Protestant refusal to accept the authority of Rome. In January 1766, a corset maker named Thomas Paine made this connection clear in *Common Sense*, the pamphlet that galvanized popular support for the American Revolution. "For monarchy in every instance is the Popery of government," Paine announced in *Common Sense*. Appealing to the supreme authority of God, he exclaimed, "But where says some is the King of America? I'll tell you Friend, he reigns above...."[2]

Such revolutionary appeals to God did not go undisputed. In America, Paine's reputation plummeted as evangelicals sought to rein in democratic claims to reason and natural rights and to define Christianity in terms of emotional experiences of new birth. Partly in reaction against the revolutionary philosophy and violence of the French Revolution, American culture became more conservative. When Paine defended the French Revolution in *The Age of Reason* (1797) and attacked the belief in miracles associated with Christianity, evangelicals tarred him as an atheist.

Revolutionary tendencies and backlashes against them reached people in Asia, Africa, and the Americas, compounding other unsettling aspects of Western intrusion. Christianity provided language for new and revolutionary demands for political freedom in many parts of the world, as well as language that called for return to social order. Christianity was often the language of democracy; it was also a language of social control, manifest in systems of belief and practice that channeled people's feelings and exploited their labor more rationally, efficiently, and systematically than ever before.

Appealing to the Bible to Denounce Monarchy

Government by kings was first introduced into the world by the Heathens, from whom the children of Israel copied the custom. It was the most prosperous invention the Devil ever set on foot for the promotion of idolatry. The Heathens paid divine honors to their deceased kings, and the Christian world hath improved on the plan by doing the same to their living ones. How impious is the title of *sacred majesty* applied to a worm, who in the midst of his splendor is crumbling into dust.

As the exalting one man so greatly above the rest cannot be justified on the equal rights of nature, so neither can it be defended on the authority of scripture; for the will of the Almighty, as declared by Gideon and the prophet Samuel, expressly disapproves of government by kings.

—Thomas Paine, *Common Sense* (1776; New York: Penguin, 1976), 71–72.

COSMOLOGY

As millions of people outside of Europe became acquainted with Christian beliefs and practices and Christians in the West became acquainted with non-European peoples, the stories in the Bible offered an overarching schema to accommodate people's expanding awareness of human diversity. Stories from Genesis traced the origin of all human beings to a first set of parents, Adam and Eve, whose disobedience of God's law led to their expulsion from paradise and transmission of sinfulness to all their progeny. With humanity plagued by sin and in dire need of assistance, God sent his Son to earth as the redeemer. Through his perfect life and sacrificial death, Christ atoned for the sins of people who placed faith in his power to save them from death, sin, and hell.

The biblical story of fall and redemption was not new; Christians had been telling much the same story for centuries. But after 1600, when Christianity was expanding and people everywhere were constructing new forms of social organization, the biblical story of fall and redemption provided a narrative framework that encompassed all the people in the world and suggested explanations for the expansion of Christianity and Western culture in the modern era. As far as many Christians in the West were concerned, the Bible supported their conquest of the earth's people and resources and explained their apparent superiority over other people as deriving from their knowledge of God and the Bible. While some cited the Bible as inspiration for building a new era of civilized tolerance and human equality, others cited it to justify extensive systems of social differentiation that included slavery. But even as they disagreed about the implications of biblical teaching with respect to the organization of modern life, and about how equal God intended people to be, modern Christians drew inspiration from the biblical story of fall and redemption to promote new plans for the reorganization of human society, new technologies of communication, and new forms of industry and commerce.

Especially among Protestants in the Calvinist tradition who felt part of God's initiative going forward in history and transforming the world, confidence in God's transcendent oversight coincided with religious ideas about Christian stewardship of the earth, in which true Christians lived righteously in the world, managing its resources peaceably and in conformity with God's will. Protestants often reached out to others to explain the rational order of nature, the providential history of human civilization, and the need to live in a right relationship with God. As champions of literacy and education, they established schools all over the world and produced many translations of the Bible and many books, magazines, and pamphlets to promote their points of view. At the same time, however, literacy and education also stimulated new interpretations of the Bible, new constructions of history, and new religious movements over which Western Protestants had little control.

As part of their rejection of the authority of the Roman Catholic Church, Protestants laid great emphasis on the Bible as a dynamic source of social criticism and reform, downplaying the clergy's role in administering salvation, and challenging some of the traditions that had accrued to Christianity over the centuries. In their appeals to the Bible as the ultimate authority, and in their shift away from priestly authority and church tradition, Protestants looked backward to the primitive origins of Christianity described in the Bible and often tried to align their lives with the primitive church. Many believed that God's plan for redemption was finally unfolding in their own day and that Christian life was awakening after the long dark ages of medieval oppression. Protestant emphasis on the activist message of the Bible helped stimulate expectations of change that justified and even helped propel innovations in technology, commerce, and economic production.

While Protestants were often at the forefront of modern social change between 1600 and 1900, people involved with other branches of Christianity were also modernizing. Catholic adventurers, soldiers, and merchants from Spain, Portugal, and France established colonies, extracted resources, utilized labor, and introduced Western beliefs and practices to many people around the world. The spread of Catholicism in the modern era not only amplified the meaning of Catholic universalism but also encouraged more systematic efforts on the part of the church authorities in Rome to regulate Catholic devotions and Catholic teaching, centralize church government, and elevate papal authority. In strategic forms of outreach, Catholic missionaries acquainted millions in Asia, Africa, and the Americas with modern Christianity through their work as educators, nurses, representatives of papal authority, and priests. Generally more tolerant of indigenous religious practices than Protestant missionaries, and more willing to allow non-Western beliefs about the spirit world into Christianity, Catholic missionaries contributed significantly to the growth, vitality, and indigenization of Christianity.

In North America, some native peoples incorporated biblical symbols and stories into their own cosmologies while resisting conversion. In more than a few cases, Natives employed Christian symbols in banding together to oppose colonial and American aggression. In eastern North America in the eighteenth and early nineteenth centuries, for example, Natives allied with the Delaware chief Pontiac invoked their knowledge of biblical stories against British interpretations, claiming that God intended Indians to retain rightful sovereignty over American land. Later in the nineteenth century, in western North America, Native American Ghost Dancers led by the Paiute

Fig. 7.1. Native Americans (Modoc or Ottawa) at the Quapaw Mission, Indian Territory, Oklahoma, 1870.

prophet Wovoka incorporated Christian ideas about the restoration of paradise and the resurrection of the dead into an indigenous movement based on visions of the purification of their land and the expulsion of white people.[3]

INDIVIDUALISM

The globalization of Christianity in the modern era often involved new expectations of individual self-discipline that diminished the authority of traditional rites of social consensus and communal discipline. In the city of Urmiyah in nineteenth-century Persia, for example, American Protestant missionaries subjected Nestorian children to frightening experiences of isolation and self-recrimination that missionaries found conducive to repentance and conversion. At the school for Nestorian girls in Urmiyah, the missionaries insisted that each child spend time alone in a closet praying about her sins, thinking about hell, and begging God for forgiveness. Unused to such forced solitude—especially when it came to religious life, which in traditional Nestorian culture was more communal than private—the children became terrified of God and of their own sinfulness. The missionaries regarded this terror as a good thing. Most of the girls at the school accepted the missionary regimen, not only because their parents had sent them there, but also because of their learning to read and write, important advantages linked to new forms of individualized piety and to new economic opportunities developed through missionary contacts.[4]

The emotional distress associated with modern conversion derived partly from the breakdown of familiar forms of solidarity and from the anxieties associated with expectations of personal autonomy. In many cases, the personal trauma of conversion involved a disconcerting sense that an old world of miracles and signs from heaven could not be taken for granted and a new and more impersonal world of evidence, power, and industry was arising. Claims about miraculous events did not disappear, however. In many cases, Christians were more insistent than ever about supernatural reality as highly personalized experiences of Christ and other superhuman entities flourished against a background of growing skepticism, rationalism, and modern political and economic change.

Christians in the modern era often believed that individual religious expression was conducive to social order. The evangelical movement, with which most Protestant missionaries identified, was defined by the belief that social order was best achieved through internalized self-discipline and the personal transformation of new birth, and not through the imposition of religious conformity by clerics acting on high. While evangelicals disagreed on questions about the nature of free will and sanctification, the role of education in conversion, and the meaning of the gospel with respect to race and gender, underlying commitments to personal transformation and self-discipline defined evangelicalism as a broad movement within modern Protestant Christianity.

One of the early formulators of modern evangelicalism, the Anglican pastor and preacher John Wesley, developed "methods" for facilitating conversion and holiness. Designed to enhance the individual's internal sensitivity to feelings of remorse, forgiveness, and love, these methods of nurturing piety encouraged individuals to build virtuous lives anchored around such feelings. In highlighting the importance of personal piety and individual religious experience, evangelicals promoted strict standards for virtuous behavior that emphasized personal discipline and close emotional ties between husbands and wives, and between parents and children, that supported the construction of cohesive middle-class cultures. Although it did encourage experimentation and diversity in many cases, evangelical pietism could be a means to social conformity, particularly when linked to clear-cut rules of feeling and behavior.

Nagging problems of hypocrisy moved to the fore as a consequence of Christian investment in religious subjectivity. Hypocrisy was not a new issue for Christians, but it became more subjectivized as ordinary Christians worried that they might not have received saving grace after all. While medieval Christians had also voiced concerns about salvation and hypocrisy, their concerns often revolved around episodes of bad behavior. Distress about behavior did not disappear, but signs of internal anxiety about the paradoxical nature of religious assurance and the slipperiness of Christian humility became increasingly widespread. The profound uncertainty that many modern Christians felt about their spiritual status reflected anxieties associated with feelings of lost innocence and alienation from traditional communities. Pervasive doubt also stimulated growing demands for new sources of religious certainty.

For many Catholics, belief in the objective presence of Christ in the sacraments held fear of hypocrisy and uneasiness about religious authenticity at bay, and the Roman Catholic Church did its best to regularize the sacraments and bolster the authority of the priests who celebrated them. But Catholics had to deal with complaints about the hypocrisy of the church and its priests, as well as with the cultural diversity of Catholic expression that, in many regions, was outpacing priestly efforts to regularize the faith. Despite top-down efforts to impose religious uniformity, converts to Catholicism in many different regions of the world fused their enthusiasm for the sacraments and saints with adherence to native traditions. In many instances, the indigenization of Christian belief and practice contributed to the revitalization of native traditions and communities. In more than a few cases, indigenous people embraced Christian ideas and symbols only

Fig. 7.2. According to the note written by a missionary on the back of the photo, Chief Black Horse is pictured here promising a missionary "that Navajo will not lie and steal any more."

to set themselves apart from European Christians and from missionaries, who were not infrequently perceived as wolves in sheep's clothing.

As European Christians claimed dominion over other lands and people, they often found their claims to moral superiority challenged and even in some cases their identity as Christians questioned. In seventeenth-century North America, for example, more than a few Huron and Iroquois people suspected Jesuit missionaries of causing deadly epidemics through witchcraft. In the eighteenth and nineteenth centuries, Native prophets emerged claiming that God had created both Indians and whites and that Indians could find happiness in the afterlife if they avoided the white man's ways and found their own path to salvation. While many converted and brought beliefs about the presence of spirits in the mountains, winds, waters, and seasons with them into Christianity, other Native Americans incorporated Christian beliefs about resurrection and the restoration of paradise into Nativist movements of religious and political resistance separate from Christianity.

The high-handed and inhumane treatment often dispensed by demanding Christians helped to fuel modern preoccupations with Christian hypocrisy. Critics of established churches and external forms of religious authority focused on the disparity between Christian idealism and the behavior of people who called themselves Christian, and complained about their hypocrisy, as the Puritan writer Roger Williams did in 1643 when he compared the spiritual status of English people in the Puritan colony of Massachusetts Bay to that of Native Americans. The natural gifts God bestowed on Adam and Eve could be found in every land and tribe, Williams believed. So could the taint of Adam and Eve's original sin. Indian and English stood on the same precarious moral footing; if anything, English people were worse off since they had often heard but not always heeded the gospel message.

As founder and president of the colony of Rhode Island, Williams established religious freedom and secular government for Christian reasons, arguing that Christ had established a new covenant of grace with individual saints and that God no longer worked his will through nations as he had in ancient times through the nation of Israel. Williams challenged the idea that kings had any divine right permitting them to take over Indian lands or to act in other ways that presumed God stood behind their political authority. Resisting the notion that Christianity could be connected to any nation or government, Williams argued that Christians were scattered throughout the nations of the world. Citing the parable of wheat and tares, he maintained that God intended Christians to live hidden among others until the judgment day.

A century and a half after Williams declared religious freedom in Rhode Island, the First Amendment to the United States Constitution guaranteed religious liberty to all citizens and prohibited the federal government from singling out any religion for official recognition or taxpayer support. The principal author of the amendment, James Madison, argued that people should worship the Creator as directed by individual conscience, that entanglement in politics corrupted Christianity, and that people who chose Christianity freely were less passive and more sincere in their religious lives than people who had religion imposed upon them. Like Williams, Madison understood secular government to be a logical and necessary corollary of religious freedom, and religious freedom to be an equally logical and necessary corollary of Christian humility.

A Christian Warning against Ethnic Pride

Boast not proud *English*, of thy birth & blood.
Thy brother *Indian* is by birth as Good.
Of one blood God made Him, and Thee & All
As wise, as faire, as strong, as personall.

By nature wrath's his portion, thine no more
Till Grace *his* soule and *thine* in Christ restore.
Make sure thy second birth, else thou shalt see
Heaven ope to *Indians* wild, but shut to thee.

—Roger Williams, in *A Key into the Language of America*, ed. John J. Teunissen and Evelyn J. Hinz (1643; Detroit: Wayne State University Press, 1973), 135.

Although the transformation of Christian life from an enveloping world to an available choice was halting and often incomplete, it affected people almost everywhere and coincided with the development of secular realms of commerce, government, and science. Many Christians embraced burgeoning market economies, greater separation between church and state, and the freedom to pursue scientific investigations, presuming that they did so under the ultimate supervision of a creator who predestined everything or, alternatively, allowed human beings to work out their destinies in this world and learn from their own mistakes and sinfulness. Expanding realms of secular enterprise free of institutional religious oversight provided arenas for people of different, conflicting, and even no religious faiths to interact productively, complementing the widespread tendency to define religious faith more privately and individualistically.

Christianity mediated a worldwide transformation after 1600, a transformation that brought different peoples and cultures into contact with one another in unprecedented ways. The geographical spread of Christian ideas and symbols to China, India, Africa, and the Americas coincided with the expansion of market economies; new industrial technologies; more systematic exploitation of natural resources, including human labor; and new forms of transportation and communication that brought people and goods together across distances more frequently than before, disrupting the stability of traditional societies based on face-to-face consensus. In the hands of new interpreters, Christian ideas, symbols, and stories played a major role in carrying forward this global process of modernization, contributing to the criticism of established social structures and forms of religious authority, to the creation of new institutions and forms of social authority, and to increasing communication between different groups within particular societies as well across cultures around the world.

SOCIAL CRITICISM AND REFORM

Christian missionaries contributed to new religious movements as people around the world incorporated elements of the missionaries' worldview into their own cosmologies, revising some aspects of their own traditions to accommodate change, or resisting its incursions. Beginning with their encounters with Catholic missionaries, people outside of Europe appropriated Christian language and behavior as means of constructing new relationships between their local cultures and the modernizing and universalizing forces of Western expansion.

Important as the connection between Christianity and modernization has been, however, the relationship between the two was never seamless or uncomplicated, with Christianity functioning simply as a means of support for modern individualism, economic development, or political reform. As a medium for negotiating change in the modern era, Christianity was not simply a reflection of larger forces of social change but a collection of beliefs, stories, symbols, and practices that people used in many different ways to construct their feelings, thoughts, and behaviors. As a multidimensional cosmology and flexible medium of response to the world, Christianity inspired revolutionary fervor in some situations, new forms of allegiance to traditional authority in others, and tolerance, open-mindedness, and honest self-appraisal in still others. Because people interpreted Christianity in their own terms, missionaries and converts did not always understand one another or agree about what Christianity meant. And because the spread of Christianity after 1600 coincided with the spread of modernization, people turned to Christianity to resist and control modernization as well as to embrace it. Christians were often outspoken in criticizing aspects of modernization that seemed to undermine their moral values and ideals. Catholics were especially sensitive to the problems involved in linking Christianity to nationalism, religious liberty, and free markets, and often suggested that Protestants had forsaken Christianity for the modern world.

Protestants also worried about the problems that nationalism, religious liberty, and free markets posed for human existence and found themselves struggling to rein in forces of modernization that they had helped set in motion. Protestants encouraged doubts about miracles and challenges to religious authority that stimulated avalanches of popular doubt and resistance to authority that extended far beyond what the architects of Protestant faith had intended. The rapid growth of Protestant Christianity in many parts of the world coincided with full-scale industrial development in the West and with strategic exploitation by Western businesses of mineral, agricultural, and labor resources in less developed parts of the world. Protestant missionaries challenged the most egregious forms of economic and political exploitation, often taking the part of natives against harsh policies that removed people from tribal lands and transformed them into a modern underclass of poor and dispossessed workers. While challenging the worst brutalities associated with these aspects of modernization, missionaries also engaged in modern forms of social interaction and modern ways of conceptualizing human society that changed the fabric of life almost everywhere.

In the Middle East, Protestant missionaries established Christianity as an agent of modernization prior to 1900 by promoting Western education, female literacy, and new standards of personal piety among Christian minorities. Muslims in the Ottoman Empire generally tolerated Christians as minority peoples who recognized God, but relegated them to second-class status because of their perceived impurity and religious ignorance with respect to Islam. As Protestant missionaries from Europe and North America worked to educate Eastern Christians to become missionaries to their Muslim neighbors, these efforts exacerbated tensions between Eastern Christians and Muslims and gave Muslims the impression that Western Christians and their Eastern allies meant to conquer the Islamic world, an impression that contributed to the resentment of Western culture evident in much of the Muslim world today.

In southern Africa prior to 1900, American Protestant missionaries worked not only to convert Africans to Christianity but also to bring them into the modern world as educated property owners. To that end, missionaries from North America and Europe established schools, created industrial farms for growing and processing sugar cane, and developed plans for African land ownership, entrepreneurial business, and political participation. Nineteenth-century missionaries often found themselves at odds with the British colonial government, which thwarted many of these plans through laws and policies deliberately aimed at excluding Africans from land and business ownership and from political participation.

Few of the efforts missionaries made to orchestrate Christian modernization in southern Africa worked out as missionaries hoped. Africans experienced the worst effects of modernization, and for all their good intentions, missionaries contributed directly to those negative outcomes. Intending to better women's lot, missionaries attacked polygamy, marriage customs linking exchanges of women and cattle, and women's responsibility for manual labor, all of which missionaries found offensive. But efforts to elevate the status of women disrupted the kinship structures, sexual customs, and traditional gender roles in terms of which people understood their social responsibilities and derived respect from one another. The breakdown of tribal structures, erosion of traditional forms of sociability, and transition to an urban industrial economy left many women more isolated, impoverished, and subject to abuse than before.

In nineteenth-century India, missionaries also worked to improve the living conditions of people, and these efforts often met with greater success than those in southern Africa but were not necessarily accompanied by conversion. Protestant missionaries challenged the Hindu caste structure, in some instances forcing converts from higher castes to share in the Lord's Supper with converts from lower castes in violation of ritual prohibitions designed to prevent members of high castes from being polluted by contact with inferior people. Criticism of the caste system was not new—Buddhism emerged in sixth-century BCE India as an alternative to the caste system and its priestly establishment—but the arrival of Protestant Christianity in nineteenth-century India coincided with the influence of modern Western theories of government and individual rights. Partly in conjunction with Christian evangelicalism, liberal political theories taken up by Indian reformers from writings by John Locke and John Stuart Mill challenged hierarchical divisions of society based on status at birth.

If Christianity mediated democracy in India, it did so more through Christianity's association with Western education and political theory than by demonstrations of egalitarian behavior on the part of missionaries. In many cases, British and American missionaries honored a double standard, challenging certain aspects of the caste system while addressing themselves to members of the priestly, educated Brahmin caste and considering Christians to be members of a spiritual elite. To the extent they presented conversion to Christianity as an initiation into an elect corps of spiritually purified beings, Protestant missionaries also followed in the path of the early seventeenth-century Italian Jesuit missionary in India, Roberto Nobili, who dressed and ate like a Brahmin and used language from the Vedic scriptures read by Brahmins to offer salvation in Christ. The special efforts missionaries made to establish good relationships with Brahmins often dovetailed with British colonial rule and with the class system to which British missionaries themselves belonged. In their self-identification as leaders of an elite religious class superior to Brahmins, nineteenth-century Protestant missionaries could also be compared to Christians in south India who traced their religious ancestry to the apostle Thomas, believed to have arrived on the Malabar coast of the Indian peninsula in the first century CE. Thomas Christians in India took pride in their high caste status, patronized Hindu temples, and held to standards of ritual purity that separated them from people in lower castes.

In nineteenth-century India, despite strenuous efforts on the part of missionaries to bring Brahmins into the Christian fold, Christianity appealed more to people of lower castes than to Brahmins, and mass conversions among low caste groups during the later decades of the century significantly increased the number of Christians in Asia. Contributing in many instances to the dignity and empowerment of

Fig. 7.3. Missionary view of Christian instruction in Burma, ca. 1850. © CORBIS.

poor people, evangelical Christianity encouraged experiences of being saved and loved by God that carried over into growing consciousness of the injustice of the caste system and more egalitarian ideas about social order. In addition, European and American pietism dovetailed with some of the mystical aspects of Hindu devotionalism, contributing to popular forms of mystical piety in both India and the West.

Meanwhile, others in India embraced democratic ideas associated with liberal British and American political thought but found it unnecessary, and even unreasonable, to convert to Christianity. In the eastern region of Maharashtra, Hindu reformers borrowed ideas about women's education and social welfare from Christian missionaries working in the region. In the northwest city of Calcutta, Hindus educated in British-run schools called for a transformation in Indian society and spoke out against religious superstition, the caste system, and the practice of *suttee*, or widow burning, which seemed to them, as it did to Protestant missionaries, to epitomize the denigration of women in traditional religion. The social reform movements led by religious Hindus in Maharashtra and by more secular intellectuals around Calcutta laid important groundwork for the political movement for independence from British colonial government in the twentieth century and for the establishment of India as a democratic nation.

In the complex history of Christianity's direct and indirect impact in India, Protestant missionaries played a crucial role. But the social changes they helped to ignite passed quickly out of their control. More often than not, the response to the Christianity that missionaries represented and taught was not what missionaries intended. In the region around Bombay, devotees of Krishna embraced Jesus as a form of their god and sang kirtans, or hymns, based on Bible stories about Jesus and delighted in Jesus as a new avatar of Krishna. In addition to revealing Christian influence within Hinduism, these kirtans reflected the power of Hindu religiosity to absorb that influence in new, hybrid expressions of belief and practice.

In India as elsewhere, people interpreted Christian ideas, symbols, and stories in the context of their own cultures, drawing their own conclusions about the identity of Jesus and the implications of Christian virtue and salvation and taking aspects of missionary teaching in directions missionaries did not anticipate. At the same time, the universalizing thrust of Christianity created new pathways of interchange among people of different cultures and new ways of thinking about human society. In India, the universalizing elements of Christian missionary ideas contributed to new linkages between India and the West and to new ways of thinking about India as a modern society in which people of different regions and religious backgrounds might live together as a politically independent, democratic nation.

In nineteenth-century China, the impact of modern Christianity was narrower but no less revolutionary. Although Christians had lived in China for centuries, their biggest impact on Chinese culture occurred in the context of modernization. In ancient times, Nestorian Christians traveled the Silk Road as traders, physicians, and missionaries, and in 638 CE the T'ang emperor paid for the construction of a Christian church in the capital city of Chang'an, the most populous city in the world at the time. Franciscan missionaries arrived in the thirteenth century and oversaw the building of the first Catholic church. But when Jesuit missionaries entered China in the sixteenth century, they found no sign of any remaining Christians. In the eighteenth and nineteenth centuries, in the context of growing demand for trade with China in the West and military efforts to force China to open its ports, first Catholic and then Protestant missionaries encountered considerable suspicion and regulation. When Protestant missionaries pressed for admittance in the early nineteenth century, the government assigned them to designated areas, restricted their travel, and confined their efforts to narrow corridors of activity.

In 1832, the first Chinese Protestant, Liang Afa, published an account of creation and God's rule over the world in which he explained Noah's ark, the covenant between God and Israel, the life of Jesus, and John's vision of the coming kingdom of God in the book of Revelation. Liang distributed his tract outside the gates of the Canton, where young men from the surrounding region passed by on their way into the city to take qualifying exams for civil service. In 1836, Liang's book passed into the hands of Hong Xiuquan, a candidate for civil service who had just failed his qualifying exams for the second time. Inspired with a new vision of his destiny as a result of reading Liang's description of biblical history, Hong proclaimed himself the younger brother of Jesus, baptized many followers, and preached abut his Father's coming kingdom. Combining Christian ideas with resistance against both the oppression of the dynastic feudalism of the Chinese government and the intrusion of modern Western capitalism and military force, Hong promoted biblical images of apocalyptic warfare in his drive to bring the heavenly kingdom to earth. He also preached about Jesus' love of the poor and his warnings against wealth, proclaiming this gospel message as a mandate for a new social order in which all families formed one family of God.

Amid the destabilization of the Qing Dynasty after the Opium War ended in 1842, Hong's religion of God Worshippers mushroomed into a mass movement that dominated central and southern China over the next decade. Hong established the Taiping Kingdom, based on a fusion of Christian, Confucian, and socialist principles. When the imperial troops representing Manchu rulers destroyed the Taiping capital in 1864 and ended the God Worshippers' reign, forty million people had died during the revolution as victims of combat, execution, and starvation.

Hong's effort to bring about a new social order based on religious equality reflected modern ideas about the politics of religion derived from Protestant Christianity, recast in a distinctively Chinese mode. Although Hong's God Worshippers were crushed by the Manchu army, echoes of their ideas persist into the present; as many historians argue, Hong's movement laid some of the groundwork for the development of the revolutionary political ideology that came to expression in Chinese communism.

Protestant and Catholic missionaries founded numerous churches in China, some of which still exist today. American Protestants also invested heavily in women's education in China and in the establishment of hospitals and medical and nursing schools. In the late nineteenth century, Protestants opened the first hospitals and medical schools in many provinces and also established nursing schools that altered the practice of medicine in China and created new opportunities for women's education and professional development. The Chinese incorporated Western medicine on their own terms, however, disregarding American beliefs that Protestant Christianity and scientific medicine were more or less coextensive, and dashing missionary hopes that doctors and nurses would draw Chinese people to Christ. Accepting Western medicine as one among a variety of complementary arts, the Chinese found it relatively easy to take Western medicine without Christianity. When Christianity was outlawed during the Communist Revolution, the Communists took over many of the medical and nursing facilities founded by Protestant missionaries as a part of a pluralistic system of health care that included traditional forms of Chinese medicine as well as scientific medicine imported from the West.[5]

Although the conversion of Chinese people did not succeed as missionaries hoped, Christian missionary efforts contributed significantly to modernization in China. With an infrastructure of rational bureaucracy and political art already in place, and predating modern

Western influence by many centuries, modern Western ideas about education, science, and social reform stimulated new interest in democratic ideas, along with an expansion of bureaucratic institutions and further systematization of knowledge. If the Chinese rejected the individualism and capitalism of the West, and relatively few people converted, the ideas and activities of Christians nevertheless contributed to the development of modern political thought in China as well as to the development of modern science and technology.

FOR FURTHER READING

Chidester, David. *Christianity: A Global History.* New York: HarperCollins, 2000.

Porterfield, Amanda. *Healing in the History of Christianity.* New York: Oxford University Press, 2005.

———. *Mary Lyon and the Mount Holyoke Missionaries.* New York: Oxford University Press, 1997.

Robert, Dana L. *American Women in Mission: A Social History of Their Thought and Practice.* Macon: Mercer University Press, 1997.

Saler, Michael. "Modernity and Enchantment: A Historiographic Overview." *The American Historical Review* 111, no. 3 (June 2006): 692–716.

Walls, Andrew. *The Missionary Movement in Christian History.* Maryknoll, N.Y.: Orbis Books, 1996.

NEW WAYS
OF CONFRONTING DEATH

CARLOS EIRE

> Logically, beliefs could exist without rituals; rituals, however, could not exist without beliefs.
>
> —Edward Shills[1]

That death demands rituals and beliefs became very evident in the period 1600–1900 as skepticism and doubt increased in those societies that had once made up Christendom. The reason for this is quite simple. Up until the seventeenth century, Christian beliefs and rituals were part and parcel of the civic culture of Europe and its colonies, where unbelief and heresy were seldom tolerated. This meant that Christian burial rites were required for everyone and that the beliefs expressed through these rites were unquestionable. Even in cases of those who were barred from Christian burial, such as heretics or suicides, the exclusion from ritual was itself a ritual and an affirmation of belief for the society at large. As the questioners and skeptics grew in number after 1600, and as the choice of *not* having a Christian burial became possible, the nature and meaning of Christian burials became ever more significant among believers, for the mere existence of an "other"—especially one with diametrically opposed beliefs—necessarily sharpens all identities. Moreover, the very fact that the unbelievers continued to have rites of some sort made it clearly evident to everyone, including the unbelievers themselves, that death rituals are a social necessity and that all such rituals—even those that mock Christian beliefs—always express attitudes and beliefs, by necessity.

When it comes to attitudes toward death, the period 1600–1900 could easily be called an age of questioning, or, as some French historians like to say, a period of de-Christianization. At the beginning of this era, around 1600, Christians everywhere were still caught up in the violent disagreements of the Reformation era and, in addition, were beginning to feel the ascendancy of rational skepticism and science, all of which cast doubt in one way or another, either from within the Christian religion itself because of theological differences, or from outside of it because of new ways of thinking and discoveries that seemed to contradict long-held assumptions. Over the next three centuries, the challenges to Christianity multiplied at a very fast pace. By the end of the nineteenth century, the Christian religion had lost its hegemony over Western culture, thanks to the secularizing effects of the doubt and skepticism that had first begun to take hold around 1600, and thanks also to the scientific and industrial revolutions.

To understand fully how Christians dealt with death during this period, one must go back to the cataclysmic events of the sixteenth century, for the process of change unleashed in that period was still very much in progress by 1600, as part of what is now called "the long Reformation" or "the second Reformation" or "early modern Catholicism." One must also go back further to the Middle Ages, and even to ancient times, for what the Protestants rejected in their Reformation is as important as what they affirmed, and much of what they rejected had to do with ancient or medieval rituals they deemed to be of pagan origin.

The Protestant Reformation began in 1517 over the issue of death rituals. The flash point was the doctrine of purgatory and the practice of performing certain rituals to alleviate the suffering of the dead in the afterlife. It could be argued, then, that differing attitudes toward death are a crucial difference between Protestants and Catholics and a key to the battles they were still waging against one another around 1600.

Atheism as a Modern Option

What reason do atheists have to say that one cannot rise from the dead? Which is more difficult, to be born or to be reborn? That that which has never existed should exist, or that that which has existed should exist again? . . . Custom makes the one seem easy, absence of custom makes the other seem impossible: a vulgar way of judging!

—Blaise Pascal, "Pensees," in *The Oxford Book of Death*, ed. D. J. Enright (New York: Oxford University Press, 1987), 156–57.

DEATH IN CHRISTIAN TRADITION

The practice of praying for the dead and of offering masses for them had ancient origins. By the fourth century, it was already so widespread that Saint Augustine (354–430) not only accepted it without question but also promoted it. By the sixth century it was also commonplace to believe that purgation, or a painful cleansing of the soul, could take place in the afterlife and that the living on earth could alleviate the suffering of those souls. As Pope Saint Gregory the Great (540–604) put it: "Each one will be presented to the Judge exactly as he was when he departed this life. Yet, there must be a cleansing fire before judgment, because of some minor faults that may remain to be purged away." It matters very little that Gregory spoke of purgatory as a fire, or condition, or state, rather than as a specific place, or locus: this was the doctrine of purgatory, plain and simple. Purgatory provided a realm of spiritual activity for the dead, a realm into which the church extended and on which the living could have an impact. Equally important was the way in which Gregory promoted the redemptive power of the Eucharist over this realm, as when he says, "The holy sacrifice of Christ, our saving Victim, brings great benefits to souls even after death, provided their sins can be pardoned in the life to come. For this reason, the souls of the dead sometimes beg to have Masses offered for them."[2] Here, in a nutshell, was the rationale behind saying masses for the dead. Gregory went even further, providing a formula for salvation that would become immensely popular throughout Western Christendom: thirty masses said for a soul over a span of thirty days, one each day, guaranteed release from purgatory for that soul. This cycle of masses, which came to be known as a trental, or as "the masses of St. Gregory," became immensely popular in the Middle Ages and would later become an emblem of Catholic identity in the period 1600–1900, in defiance of the Protestant challenge, thanks to its promotion by the Council of Trent.

Medieval Catholics would hold firm to five basic beliefs, all neatly summarized by Gregory. After 1517, Martin Luther and all Protestants would reject much of this as un-Christian, and Catholics would embrace all of it with even greater fervor in response. In due course, greater skeptics would later ridicule all of these beliefs as unreasonable: (1) that the human person is made up of two basic components:

body and soul; (2) that the soul separates from the body at death and is immediately judged at that moment; (3) that the soul is then immediately sent to one of three destinations: heaven, purgatory, or hell; (4) that purgatory is a temporary destination where the soul is cleansed and where it can be aided by the sacrifice of the Mass offered by the living through the church; (5) and that there will be a final judgment at the end of history, when purgatory will be abolished and all souls will be reunited with resurrected bodies for eternity, some to enjoy eternal bliss and others to endure eternal torments. All five of these tenets were neatly summarized in the Latin adage *Salus hominis in fine consistit*, which loosely translated means "One's eternal fate is decided at the moment of death." Within this theological framework, each soul's eternal destiny depended on its behavior—on performing good works and avoiding sin—and also on whether or not the church had forgiven its sins. Furthermore, each soul's fate in the afterlife depended on its state at the moment of death, which meant that if one wanted to avoid hell, one needed to die a "good death." By far the most important element of a "good death" was the presence of a priest who could administer the sacraments of penance, Eucharist, and extreme unction. Medieval Christians believed that confessing one's sins and receiving absolution, communion, and the last rites were so essential that they looked upon sudden, unexpected death as one of the most awful things in the world or, worse, as a clear sign of God's wrath.

Fig. 8.1. *Allegory of Death* (*In Ictu Oculi*) by Juan de Valdes Leal (1622–1690). Hopital de la Caridad, Seville, Spain. Photo: Scala/Art Resource, NY.

One more set of medieval beliefs and practices that developed after Gregory's time looms large over the Reformation and the entire early modern period. In its official teaching, the medieval church made it clear that while all sins were forgiven by its sacrament of penance, what one gained from priestly absolution was not a totally clean slate but rather a commuted sentence, a reduction of eternal penalties into temporal ones. This is why the priest always imposed *penances*, so one could make *satisfaction*: prayers, fasts, pilgrimages, almsgiving, and other such good works that ostensibly made up for one's failings. If one sinned very infrequently, like the saints, then penances were manageable and one could ostensibly go straight to heaven at death. But if one sinned with regularity, like most people, then penances could never be made up before one died. And this meant that the penances had to be completed in the afterlife. This is why ending up in purgatory was the best outcome that most Christians could hope for, and why purgatory was always so crowded.

One of the most salient characteristics of the late medieval Western church—reaffirmed and strengthened by early modern Catholicism—was the way in which its living members constantly acted as intercessors for the dead. This means that by the late Middle Ages, masses were always being offered for the dead, everywhere, at all times, on a much larger scale than ever before, with the support of a highly sophisticated theology. One significant component of this theology gave rise to yet another link between the living and the dead, and between the church and the afterlife, a link that made purgatory ever closer to earth: the issuing of indulgences.

An indulgence was a favor, or privilege, granted by the church that remitted the punishment one still owed God for sin after being absolved in the sacrament of penance. Indulgences came into widespread use in the eleventh century, in connection with the Crusades, when Pope Urban II granted all warriors who would fight to regain the Holy Land a plenary indulgence; eventually, they would be extended to the souls in purgatory, whose fate became the responsibility of the living. In the long run, this concern with the dead would become the proverbial straw that broke the camel's back, for it was because of one priest's bad sermon on indulgences and another priest's response to it that the papacy lost its hegemony in Europe and that the unity of the Western church was forever undone. Exposing a yawning abyss between official theology and popular piety, and dredging up nearly every guilt-inducing, pocket-picking pitch through which he could hawk indulgences to an anxious laity, Johann Tetzel unleashed the Protestant Reformation by preaching these words to many a Saxon crowd in 1517, on behalf of Pope Leo X and his new Basilica of St. Peter in Rome:

> Listen now, God and St. Peter call *you*. Consider the salvation of *your* souls and those of *your loved ones* departed. . . . Listen to the voices of *your dead relatives* and friends, beseeching *you* and saying, 'Pity us, pity us. We are in dire torment from which *you* can redeem us for a pittance.' Do *you* not wish to? Open *your* ears. . . . Remember *you* are able to release them, for *as soon as the coin in the coffer rings, the soul from purgatory springs*. Will *you* not then for a quarter of a florin receive these letters of indulgence through which *you* are able to lead a divine and immortal soul into the fatherland of paradise?[3]

PROTESTANT ATTACKS ON TRADITION

When Martin Luther challenged Tetzel with ninety-five theses in which he questioned the theology behind indulgences, Pope Leo X dismissed the controversy as a "monkish squabble," not realizing the true magnitude of the struggle that would follow. Between 1517 and 1521, Luther's challenge would evolve very rapidly into a wholesale rejection of the pope and his church and of much of Catholic theology and piety. Luther's attack on the medieval Catholic Church was best summarized in his two battle cries: *sola scriptura* (by scripture alone) and *sola fide* (by faith alone). The *sola scriptura* principle allowed Luther to scrutinize all theology and piety according to his interpretation of the Bible and to reject anything he judged as nonbiblical, such as the doctrine of purgatory. The *sola fide* principle, which Luther claimed was the true, biblically centered way of understanding how Christ saves from sin and death, was complex and paradoxical, but reduced to its simplest elements, it boiled down to this: salvation is never earned; it is simply and freely granted by God to those who have faith in the saving sacrifice of Jesus Christ. As Luther saw it, largely through his interpretation of Paul's theology in the New Testament, sin is totally inescapable. One is saved not by one's own good works, or by penances, but rather by Christ's sacrifice on the cross, through which God chose to overlook the sins of the human race. This meant that the Catholic Church was dead wrong in asserting that individuals could not go to heaven until their souls were spotless, for sinlessness was impossible to attain and they could never hope to make satisfaction to God for their sins. It also meant that purgatory was not only an unbiblical invention but also totally unnecessary, along with masses and prayers for the dead.

In one fell swoop, Luther did away with purgatory and severed the connection between the living and the dead. "The Scriptures forbid and condemn communication with the spirits of the dead," he argued, citing Deuteronomy 18:10-11 ("No one shall be found among you who . . . consults ghosts or spirits, or who seeks oracles from the dead"). Moreover, Luther also demonized all of the medieval apparition tales that undergirded belief in purgatory, saying, "Whatever spirits go about, making a noise, screaming, complaining, or seeking help, are truly the work of the devil."[4] Masses for the dead, then, were nothing but demonically inspired sorcery and necromancy.

The essence of Protestantism was the conviction that the medieval church was corrupt and that piety had become intolerably unbiblical. Martin Luther had sparked a revolution with that insight, but his attempt to purify church and society according to scriptural guidelines was somewhat limited in comparison with those of other Protestant reformers such as Andreas Bodenstein von Karlstadt (1480–1541) and Ulrich Zwingli (1483–1531). Luther was never too worried about idolatry or pagan holdovers as he was about "works righteousness," that is, the idea that one's acts can gain God's favor. When he drove the iconoclasts out of Wittenberg, he did so because they thought that destroying the idols would please God, not because of their hatred of idolatry. Changes in attitudes mattered much more to Luther than

> ### The Endurance of Ghosts
> Anno 1670, not far from Cyrencester, was an Apparition: Being demanded, whether a good Spirit, or a bad? Returned no answer, but disappeared with a curious Perfume and most melodious Twang.
>
> —John Aubrey, "Miscellanies," in *The Oxford Book of Death*, ed. D. J. Enright (New York: Oxford University Press, 1987), 208.

changes in ritual; idolatry is in the heart of the worshiper, he insisted, not in the worship itself. Consequently, his reform of ritual was somewhat moderate, and Lutheran funeral practices retained some of the external trappings of Catholic ritual, such as the singing of hymns and the tolling of bells. Among those Protestants who came to be known as Reformed, the heirs of Karlstadt and Zwingli, however, much more of medieval funeral piety was rejected as idolatry and superstition.

It would be up to John Calvin (1509–1564), a second-generation reformer, to articulate and widely disseminate this aggressive war against the "idols" of medieval popular religion. Calvin thought in binary terms, seeing a great dichotomy between "true" and "false" religion and finding the source of all falsehoods deep within the human heart, where idolatry was a basic instinct. As he once said, "Every one of us is, even from his mother's womb, a master craftsman of idols."[5] Over and against such instincts stood the "true" revealed religion of the Bible, made manifest by well-trained and correctly inspired clergymen like himself. The Catholic clergy were liars and thieves, he claimed, not just for teaching false doctrine and encouraging idolatry, but also for saying useless masses for the dead. Scolding a former friend who had become a Catholic bishop, Calvin thundered, "You do not own a single piece of land that has not been placed in your hands by purgatory."[6] Nowhere did his disgust with idolatry shine through more clearly than in his contempt for the Catholic ritual of the Eucharist and its role in the cult of the dead:

> Satan has attempted to adulterate and envelop the sacred Supper of Christ as with thick darkness, that its purity might not be preserved in the Church. But the head of this horrid abomination was, when he raised a sign by which it was not only obscured and perverted, but altogether obliterated and abolished, vanished away and disappeared from the memory of man; namely, when, with most pestilential error, he blinded almost the whole world into the belief that the Mass was a sacrifice and oblation for obtaining the remission of sins . . . for the living and the dead.[7]

The social and cultural repercussions of this redefinition of death and the afterlife were immense but have never been the subject of much sustained study. Only very recently has it been proposed that this severing of the bond between the living and the dead should be viewed as a major change in the daily lives of Christian Europeans. On a personal and social level, the shift from a communally shared responsibility for each death to a very personal and private one signified a turn toward individualism—a turn that has been identified as the key to "modernity." This individualistic turn was perhaps most intense for Protestants at the moment of death, and Martin Luther was well aware of it:

> The summons of death comes to us all, and no one can die for another. Every one must fight his own battle with death by himself, alone. We can shout into each other's ears, but everyone must himself be prepared for the time of death: I will not be with you then, nor you with me.[8]

The psychological and cultural impact of this individualism has yet to be adequately analyzed by historians. Suddenly, death and the afterlife stopped being a communal experience. Barred from aiding the poor souls in purgatory, and also from praying to the saints in heaven and from seeking the suffrages of their relatives and neighbors, Protestants now faced the divine tribunal and their eternal destiny alone, at the end of *this* life. Gone was the communion of saints, and gone too was the chance to earn salvation in the world to come. *This* life and *this* world, then, became the sole focus of religion. In his classic study *The Protestant Ethic and the Spirit of Capitalism*, Max Weber argued that Protestants gained an economic edge over Catholics because they shifted their attention away from the hereafter to the here and now, developing a piety he dubbed "this-worldly asceticism." Though he did not focus on death rituals per se in order to defend his thesis, perhaps he should have, for the economic repercussions of this individualistic, "this-worldly" turn were profound and very easy to discern. Societies that had previously invested heavily in the cult of the dead suddenly redirected a substantial amount of money and resources to other ends. The significance of this major difference between Protestant and Catholic cultures seems even larger when one takes into account that the Catholic Church responded to the

Protestant rejection of purgatory by stressing the value of masses for the dead more than ever before, and that Catholics everywhere intensified their investment in the afterlife.

By 1650, the difference between Protestant and Catholic investment in death was immense. One example alone speaks volumes about the place of the dead in a Catholic economy. In Spain, in the cities of Madrid and Cuenca, investments in funerals and especially in masses for the dead spiraled upward between 1560 and 1650, at a time when the price of a mass continually increased, along with the price of everything else, because of the inflation caused by the so-called price revolution of that period. This meant that the residents of Madrid and Cuenca not only requested more and more masses with each passing year but also spent more and more for each of them. Since most masses were paid for by gifts of land to the church or by rents to be collected on land, this meant that the church accumulated more and more real estate as the demand for masses increased. The end result was the same in Madrid and Cuenca—and it is safe to assume also in most Spanish towns: by 1750, the church had become the chief landlord in the realm. In Cuenca, for instance, the church owned over half of the city's properties and nearly half of all of the surrounding land. It also employed about two-fifths of the total population. In stark contrast, in Protestant societies such as those of England, the Netherlands, Scandinavia, and Germany, the church had been stripped of most of its real estate and all of its income from masses for the dead during the earliest days of the Reformation. Historians need to ask, how was that capital redirected in Protestant societies, and what difference did it make?

Placing a higher value on masses for the dead was only one of the ways in which Catholics reacted to the Protestant challenge. We have plenty of evidence that in France, Italy, and Spain, Catholics also began to stage larger and ever more elaborate funerals, a trend that peaked around the middle of the seventeenth century. In addition, the Catholic Church did all it could to renew interest in every aspect of the cult of the dead that had been rejected by Protestants. What we find, then, is a renewed emphasis on prayer to the saints and veneration of their relics, on the establishment of shrines with wonder-working relics and holy corpses that do not decompose, on the use of traditional *ars moriendi* ("art of dying") texts, and on sermons focused on Catholic eschatology.

In addition, of course, we find the continuation of many traditional practices, such as the celebration of anniversary masses, the ringing of bells, the use of votive lights, and the holding of memorial banquets. We also find a strengthening of the role of confraternities, those lay associations that had developed in the Middle Ages to engage in many different kinds of charitable and devotional activities. Above all, confraternities that focused on funeral devotions enjoyed a great resurgence among Catholics. To ensure the right kind of preparation for the last rites and the moment of death and also to ensure a good funeral, Catholics joined confraternities that aided the dying and buried the dead. Belonging to a confraternity was a lot like taking out spiritual life insurance: it was a pooling of resources that eventually would benefit each member. Confraternity membership enabled one to prepare for one's own death, through repeated visits to other's deathbeds and burials, and when one's turn came to die, one was then assured the presence and intercession of one's confraternity at one's own deathbed and funeral. If one did not belong to any such confraternity, one could still be summoned, for a fee. In some cases, the dying became members on their deathbeds. By the end of the Middle Ages, such confraternities numbered in the tens of thousands all over Europe. In the sixteenth and seventeenth centuries, Catholics would throng to them.

In contrast, what we find among Protestants of all types is an all-out assault on the Catholic cult of the dead and the Catholic idea of the communion of saints and anything that smacked of "popish" idolatry or superstition, such as elaborate ceremonies, the use of bells and candles, the presence of confraternities, or even the use of traditional funeral vestments by the clergy. Whether or not those who lived through this immense change adjusted quickly remains a matter of debate. There is certainly plenty of evidence that in places such as Sweden and England, where Protestantism was imposed from above on everyone by the monarch, resistance flared up. In Durham, England, Bishop James Pilkington found it hard to break his flock's attachment to the dead, issuing many a reprimand between 1561 and 1576, such as the one contained in his rules for funerals. In one brief paragraph, Bishop Pilkington neatly catalogued all of the Catholic rituals that the faithful continued to observe. His list gives us a clear picture of the differences between a Catholic and a Protestant funeral:

> . . . that no superstition should be committed in them, wherein the papists infinitely offend, as in masses, dirges, trentals, singing, ringing, holy water, hallowed places, years's days and month-minds, crosses, pardon letters to be buried with them, mourners de profundis [psalms] by every lad that could say it, dealing of money solemnly for the dead, watching of the corpse, bell and banner, with many more that I could reckon.[9]

But there is also plenty of evidence that some gave up their ancient customs willingly, or at least without resistance. One story alone, from a remote corner of England, illustrates the process of change vividly. During the reign of Henry VIII (1491–1547), a priest serving a farming community that was barely beyond subsistence level needed new funeral vestments, so he spent years and years collecting funds for this purpose, penny by measly penny. Finally, after begging and scrimping for twenty long years, he purchased the much-needed black vestments. Then, less than a month later, he received a royal order to stop using such vestments and to surrender them to the king's agents. He recorded this without a hint of emotion in his churchwarden's diary and surrendered to the crown his vestments and everything else that went with them: the images, the lights, the altars, the rituals. He continued to minister to his flock and to bury the dead with no less dedication, though in ways unfamiliar to him and to them. He saw his sources of income dry up and vanish and saw the parish brought to financial ruin, since the change in rituals also meant an end to the funding that made them possible.

COMMON CONCERNS

Another dramatic change wrought by the religious turmoil of the early modern age was an increase in violence and the sudden resurgence of martyrdom, as Catholics and Protestants both struggled to obliterate each other and to crush all heretics in their midst. Catholics, of course, gathered new relics from their newly minted martyrs and enshrined them grandly whenever possible. Although Protestants rejected the cult of relics, they still found a way to enshrine and revere their martyrs, in texts that recounted their faith and heroism. Two of the most popular books of the early modern age were John Foxe's *The Acts and Monuments of the Christian Church,* also known as the *Book of Martyrs*, and Jean Crespin's *History of the Martyrs*, both of which went through numerous editions and translations and served for generations as companion volumes to the Bible in many a Protestant home. Both texts also made an effort to trace the persecution of the "true" church from Roman times down to their own day in order to legitimize the Protestant Reformation. Among the Anabaptists, who were persecuted by both Catholics and Protestants, martyrdom was elevated to an even higher theological status as one of the marks of the true church.

Martyrdom was not the only thing shared by Catholics and Protestants. As one might expect, many other beliefs and customs continued to be shared, despite obvious differences. In general, most of the similarities had to do with ethics, which, given the Ten Commandments, is not too surprising. This sharing of a common ethical code has led some historians to argue that Protestantism and Catholicism were much more alike than different and that the early modern period is best understood as a time when religion became a tool in the hands of the elite, a means to strengthen the process of state building. Some historians see this era as one when the social and church elites worked hand in hand to promote a more vigorous Christian identity among the lesser folk. Some historians speak of this as *confessionalization* or *social disciplining*. Among Protestants it is also spoken of as the Second Reformation or the Long Reformation. Some historians have gone so far as to argue that both the Catholic and Protestant Reformations need to be seen as attempts to really *Christianize* Europe, which up until then had only had a really thin Christian veneer.

If one searches for similarities between Catholics and Protestants, one can indeed find them. When it came to funeral customs, Catholics and Protestants continued to practice burial rather than cremation, and they carried it out in hallowed ground, either in the church or in an adjacent or nearby cemetery. As one would expect, funeral rites could vary tremendously, not just between the different churches, but also according to class and status. On the whole, Protestants aimed at a greater simplicity, though this could also be true of Catholics, within limits. Their different approaches to prayer and ritual always made Catholic funerals quite unlike Protestant ones, even the simplest of ones, and the Catholic linking of death to the Mass continued to be one of the more striking differences. For some clergy on both sides, excess pomp on the part of the rich and mighty became a constant source of irritation and something they often railed against. Despite their theological differences, Protestant and Catholic clergy shared another trait in common. This was their common emphasis on the ever-present danger of death and of the need to be ready for it. It is no surprise, then, that *ars moriendi* treatises remained popular among the laity of both religious camps, especially throughout the seventeenth century. On the surface, the emphasis on a "good death" was remarkably similar. These words written by a Protestant would have made perfect sense to a Catholic: "It is the art of all arts, and science of all sciences, to learn to die."[10] As one might expect, of course, that is as far as the similarities extended: Catholic and Protestant *ars moriendi* texts were very different in content. Whereas Protestants were encouraged to face God alone by placing their faith in Christ, without any purgatory on the horizon, Catholics were instructed to rely on every kind of intercession and sacrament they could find, with purgatory in mind as the most likely entry point into the afterlife.

Yet another similarity between Protestants and Catholics was their clergy's apparent fascination with hell, especially in the seventeenth century, when highly detailed meditations on the subject flourished. Apparently, many among the laity liked the subject too, for devotional texts focusing on death and the afterlife in which hell figured prominently were a popular, best-selling genre. Hellfire sermons rang out in both Protestant and Catholic churches. The warning was always clear: sin leads directly to hell. As one Spanish Jesuit put it: "Watch your step. Why do you mock eternity, why don't you fear the eternal death, why do you love this temporal life so much? You are on the wrong track; change your life."[11] If such warnings were not enough, graphic descriptions of hell might do the trick:

> I wish you could open a window through which you would view what happens in hell, and see the torments inflicted on the rich who live in ease and have no compassion for the poor. Oh, if you could see how their flesh is boiled in those cauldrons and how they are baked in those inexorable flames, where every single devil will sear them with firebrands. . . . And it will be very good to imagine how those who can't stand the summer heat outside of their roomy cellars will suffer in the blaze of the eternal fire.[12]

According to some historians, literature and sermons on hell proliferated in this period, principally as part of the common processes of "confessionalization," "social disciplining," and "state building" shared by Protestants and Catholics. Scaring the hell out of people, literally, was a strategy of the early modern state, say many historians: it was a way of creating a more fearful and law-abiding citizenry, with the help of the church.[13] Whether or not this reductionist interpretation of the place of hell in the early modern mentality will stand the test of time remains to be seen.

SKEPTICISM

In the long run, it was religion itself that fell victim to all the violence and the hellish imagery, for the higher the human cost of religious warfare, and the more intense the scare tactics on the part of the clergy, the more urgent it became for Europeans to question their ultimate values. Moreover, the more Christians battled each other in print, developing ever-sharper arguments with which to demolish one another's positions, casting doubt ever more skillfully, the easier it became to take the next logical step toward skepticism, and the more acceptable unbelief became. So in the same way that Protestants rejected purgatory and much of Catholic eschatology in the sixteenth century, skeptics cast doubt on the afterlife and all of religion in the following two centuries. The change was one in scale and intensity rather than one of doubt suddenly appearing. Unbelief had been there all along, even in the most fervently religious societies: the files of the Inquisition and Calvinist consistories prove that skeptics existed and that the ruling elites had a way of silencing them or forcing them into hiding. In sixteenth- and seventeenth-century Spain, the Inquisition handled hundreds of cases of individuals who denied the existence of heaven and hell, and even of God, and who ended up as martyrs for their unbelief. Simple agnosticism was probably more widespread than church authorities would have liked. François Rabelais (1494–1553), a contemporary of Martin Luther, Ignatius Loyola, and John Calvin, may have given voice to a fairly common attitude when he joked on his deathbed, "I go to seek a great Perhaps."[14]

Critiques of religion and of Christianity in particular grew in intensity throughout the seventeenth and eighteenth centuries, gaining ever more ground among educated elites who trusted reason rather than faith and considered themselves "enlightened." First came the dismantling of the traditional cosmos, in which heaven and hell were not other dimensions but physical locations. In that cosmos, the earth was at the center of the universe, surrounded by seven heavenly spheres: the heaven where God and the blessed souls dwelled was the highest place of all, the empyrean or seventh heaven; hell was the lowest place of all, inside at the center of the earth. Thanks to the astronomical discoveries of Nicholas Copernicus (1473–1543) and Galileo Galilei (1564–1642), the traditional geography of the cosmos and the afterlife was blown away, and questioning increased. If the new invention of the telescope and new mathematical calculations could prove that the Bible was mistaken about the visible universe, why not also doubt its accuracy about an unseen cosmos, the afterlife? Among the first to take issue with Christian notions of the afterlife were thinkers heavily influenced by the new science, such as John Locke (1632–1704), John Toland (1670–1722), and Isaac Newton (1642–1727) in the British Isles, Pierre Bayle (1647–1706) in France, and Gottfried Wilhelm Leibniz (1646–1716) in Germany. What their critiques shared in common was the assumption that reason alone should govern all thinking. Arguing that reason is superior to revelation, then, many began to deny the existence of hell, principally because the idea of a just and merciful God tormenting his creatures for eternity seemed thoroughly contradictory and unreasonable. Though many of these early critics of hell thought that it was a useful teaching for the simpler folk, who might become even more immoral without the fear of hell, some nonetheless began to deny hell openly and aggressively.

Denying hell and the afterlife was also one step closer to denying the existence of the soul and even the existence of God. It is no surprise, then, that by the mid-eighteenth century full-fledged atheists were not too hard to find, at least among the educated elites. In 1747, for instance, Julien Offroy de la Mettrie published a treatise entitled *L'homme machine* ("Man the Machine"), in which he argued that it was impossible to prove through reason the existence of anything beyond the material universe, and that God and the soul were irrational concepts. We human beings are nothing more than our bodies, he argued, and nothing more than an organic apparatus. The same is true of the entire universe, which is devoid of spirit and is merely one vast machine. After midcentury, atheism became à la mode in the brightest circles of the "enlightened," and hostility toward Christianity and religion became popular as did hostility toward Christianity and religion in general. For instance, in 1761, Paul Heinrich Dietrich, the Baron D'Holbach, a good friend of Benjamin Franklin, published a book entitled *Le Christianisme dévoilé* ("Christianity Unveiled"), in which he denounced Christianity as contrary to reason and nature. In 1770, he issued an even more popular attack, *Systeme de la nature* ("The System of Nature"), in which

> ### Hell as an Unacceptable Idea
> Heaven and hell suppose two distinct species of men, the good and the bad. But the greatest part of mankind float betwixt vice and virtue. Were one to go round the world with an intention of giving a good supper to the righteous and a sound drubbing to the wicked, he would frequently be embarrassed in his choice. . . . The chief source of moral ideas is the reflection on the interests of human society. Ought these interests, so short, so frivolous, to be guarded by punishments, eternal and infinite? The damnation of one man is an infinitely greater evil in the universe, than the subversion of a thousand millions of kingdoms.
> —David Hume, "Of the Immortality of the Soul," in *The Oxford Book of Death*, ed. D. J. Enright (New York: Oxford University Press, 1987), 201.

he not only denied the existence of God but denounced the Judeo-Christian concept of a bloodthirsty, capricious, and vengeful deity as the source of humankind's worst ills. Writing in 1794, the American revolutionary Thomas Paine summarized an entire century of anti-Christian polemic:

Of all the systems of religion that ever were invented, there is none more derogatory to the Almighty, more unedifying to man, more repugnant to reason, and more contradictory in itself, than this thing called Christianity. Too absurd for belief, too impossible to convince, and too inconsistent for practice, it renders the heart torpid, or produces only atheists and fanatics. As an engine of power, it serves the purpose of despotism; and as a means of wealth, the avarice of priests; but so far as respects the good of man in general, it leads to nothing here or hereafter.[15]

Committed to replacing religion with rational "enlightment," men like Paine found themselves facing the age-old question of how societies can motivate their members to act ethically without any notion of reward or punishment in an afterlife. Without the fear of hell, what is there besides brute force to prevent wrongdoing? The great *philosophe* Voltaire (1694–1778) was skeptical enough of reason to say that "if God did not exist, it would be necessary for men to invent him." Governments, he concluded, always needed God and hell: "I do not believe that there is in the world a mayor or any official power . . . who does not realize that it is necessary to put a god into their mouths to serve as a bit and bridle." Voltaire's friend Denis Diderot (1713–1784), the editor of the venerable *Encyclopedia*, was less cynical and more representative of the optimism shared by many Enlightenment thinkers. For Diderot, reason itself seemed enough. "Philosophy makes men more honorable than sufficient or efficacious grace," he argued. Seeing no need for God or hell, he replaced them with a vague yet powerful entity:

Posterity is for the philosopher what the next world is for the religious man. . . . O posterity, O holy and sacred support of the oppressed and the unhappy, you who are just, you who are incorruptible, you who will revenge the good man and unmask the hypocrite, consoling and certain ideal, do not abandon me.[16]

Needless to say, as such views gained an ever-larger following, particularly in Western Europe and the Americas, centuries-old attitudes toward death and the afterlife began to change at a relatively quick pace.

THE SECULARIZATION OF DEATH

Overall, the greatest change was the increasing secularization of death. One of the first signs of this development was the detachment of cemeteries from churches. Partly for reasons of public health, but also partly because of secularizing pressures, graveyards began a gradual migration from the vaults beneath churches or churchyards to lots no longer adjacent to the churches, and eventually to much larger areas outside cities and towns. By the time Thomas Paine wrote his *Age of Reason,* the migration of the cemeteries to neutral space was well under way, and so was the development of the nonreligious funeral. A century later, the process was irreversible almost everywhere in the Christian world.

Another change that can be measured in last wills and testaments is the gradual decline and disappearance of any mention of the soul in these legal documents. In Protestant societies, where it had become illegal to offer masses for the dead, the change is subtler, but in Catholic societies, where masses for the dead dwindle and disappear, the shift in attitudes is so immense that some scholars view it as conclusive proof of the "de-Christianization" of Europe.

French historians who speak of "de-Christianization" usually have the French Revolution in mind, of course, when that specific term had a very concrete meaning as part of the revolutionary vocabulary. "De-Christianization" referred quite specifically to the dismantling of the church and the replacement of Christianity by the ideals of the Revolution. This bloody upheaval, the first in human history to industrialize killing on a mass scale with its guillotines, could not help but focus on death, for, as everyone quickly discovered, a counterreligion needed its own inverted ceremonies. First, the brand-new

Fig. **8.2**. The guillotine, a modern instrument of death used in the French Revolution to behead agents of monarchy. Photo: © Bridgeman-Giraudon / Art Resource, NY.

church of Saint Geneviéve in Paris was turned into a mausoleum for the great heroes of the new republic; renamed the Panthéon, after the ancient Roman temple that ostensibly served all the gods, this monument to *enlightened men* underscored the Revolution's triumph over religion and superstition. In 1791, the great cynic Voltaire's remains were transferred there and interred with a surplus of Revolutionary pomp and ritual. Not much later, in 1792, active de-Christianization began in earnest with the killing of priests. In Angers, for instance, clerics were bound in pairs, packed into leaking boats, and set adrift to sink and drown. Mocking baptism, the revolutionaries boasted of this "de-Christianization by immersion." In total, it is esti-

Fig. 8.3. Interior view of Panthéon, Paris (1764), by Jacques Germain Soufflot (1713–1780). Photo: © Bridgeman-Giraudon / Art Resource, NY.

mated that about twenty thousand priests agreed to voluntarily "de-Christian-ize" themselves by simply abjuring their posts and their faith, but thousands of others refused and were slaughtered. During this time, naturally, death rituals were transformed through a hypersecular-ization that reversed the sacred and the profane. In addition to vandalizing and destroying churches, or turning them into "temples of reason," revo-lutionary mobs desecrated cemeteries and did all they could to ritually dishonor the remains of their dead enemies. Those brought to the guillotine were humili-ated first by ritual insults and then by having their decapitated remains disposed of as trash or carrion, with ritual disrespect. At the abbey church of Saint Denis, which housed the tombs of the royal family, the corpses of kings and queens were dug up and ravaged. Rumor had it that some of the well-preserved remains, such as the heart of King Louis XIV, were actually eaten. Conversely, the heart of the revolutionary Jean Paul Marat (1743–1793), who had been assassinated in his bathtub, was enshrined in a reliquary. Immediately, a cult of the great Marat developed, encouraged by the ever-changing Revolutionary leadership.

RESURGENT CHRISTIAN FERVOR

All of these excesses, which were well publicized around the world, could not help but have their effect. Once the terror subsided and order was restored, nothing could be the same, either in France or in the rest of the Christian world. A great rift had opened in Western culture: unbelief seemed poised to gain the upper hand. Yet as secularization increased, so did Christian fervor. In Europe and the Americas, the age of Enlightenment and revolutions was also a period marked by renewed, intense devotion to the beliefs that were being challenged. One need only turn to the many apparitions and divine messages that Catholics embraced as genuine during this period, which gave rise to immensely popular devotions, such as that to the Sacred Hearts of Jesus and Mary in the seventeenth to eighteenth centuries and to the Miraculous Medal in the nineteenth century. One of these devotions, the wearing of the scapular of Our Lady of Mount Carmel, better known as the Brown Scapular, had to do with death. According to pious tradition dating back to the thirteenth century, the Virgin Mary had promised in an apparition that anyone who died while wearing this small piece of cloth around their neck would not "suffer everlasting fire." In other words, simply wearing this scapular could earn even the worst sinner an entrance into purgatory rather than hell—a promise undoubtedly anchored in the ancient Catholic belief that monastic garb could guarantee salvation, since the scapular was a small replica of the outermost part of the monastic habit. In the middle of the seventeenth century, thanks to the efforts of the Carmelite order, devotion to this scapular blossomed throughout the Catholic world, and the lure of its promises became so attractive that between 1650 and 1900, fourteen other scapulars associated with other religious orders and confraternities would be approved by Rome, each related to some apparition and some large promise. At the very same time, throughout the world, many Catholics continued to be buried in monastic habits purchased from religious orders for the express purpose of dressing the corpse.

Among Protestants, there was plenty of fervor too, and some of it very traditionalist. In Germany, Pietism led to a religious revival that transcended political and national borders. Eventually, this renewed fervor would give rise to even grander revivals, as charismatic preachers took the Christian message to the world at large, beyond church walls. In North America, the Great Awakening would take place alongside the Enlightenment, and the Second Great Awakening alongside the Industrial Revolution. Belief in heaven and hell did not vanish but intensified among the thousands who heard Jonathan Edwards (1703–1758), John Wesley (1703–1791), and George Whitefield (1714–1770) preach, or who sang the inspiring hymns of Charles Wesley (1707–1778). Keeping in mind that Jonathan Edwards was a well-educated Yale graduate and a contemporary of hell-deniers such as D'Holbach, Voltaire, Diderot, Franklin, and Paine, one can only be amazed at the dissonant challenge offered by his sermon "Sinners in the Hands of an Angry God," which terrified many who heard it in 1741, leading them to fits of despair and sudden conversions:

> The God that holds you over the pit of hell, much as one holds a spider, or some loathsome insect over the fire, abhors you, and is dreadfully provoked: his wrath towards you burns like fire; he looks upon you as worthy of nothing else, but to be cast into the fire. . . . It is nothing but his hand that holds you from falling into the fire every moment. . . . Yea, there is nothing else that is to be given as a reason why you do not this very moment drop down into hell. . . . O sinner! Consider the fearful danger you are in: it is a great furnace of wrath, a wide and bottomless pit, full of the fire of wrath, that you are held over in the hand of that God, whose wrath is provoked and incensed as much against you, as

against many of the damned in hell. You hang by a slender thread, with the flames of divine wrath flashing about it, and ready every moment to singe it, and burn it asunder.[17]

Great revivals could not stop secularizing trends from increasing in the nineteenth century, however, as industrialization and urbanization changed much of the Christian world. On an intellectual and spiritual level, doubt and unbelief intensified in the nineteenth century, not just among the intelligentsia, but also among the new working class, and especially among those who embraced socialist and materialist ideology, which tended to view all religion as a means of oppression by the elite. On a very basic practical level, burying the dead became a business like any other. As society grew more complex, it was only natural that the handling of the dead be turned over to professional morticians who gradually took over many of the tasks previously handled by families and their clergy. Along with the morticians came their funeral homes, which also transferred much of the ritual that had previously taken place at the home of the deceased or at the church, further severing the ties that bound the dead to their families and their churches.

At the very same time, as cemeteries moved beyond the crowded cities, their landscaping evolved in new directions, changing the relationship between the dead and the living. Unfettered by space limitations, great necropolises sprang up all over the Christian world, where individuals and families now had the chance to erect the kinds of memorials that had once been reserved for nobility and royalty. In great cities such as Paris, the dead suddenly had their own suburbs, replete with mausoleums great and small, festooned with sculptures, crosses, obelisks, epitaphs, and plaques, all in a parklike setting: an enduring image and symbol of the world of the living, where the social hierarchy was reified most permanently in stone. Some of these nineteenth-century suburbs of the dead aimed at closeness with nature and were designed as parks rather than cities, with carefully planned landscapes that offered tranquil, scenic views. Many of these new cemeteries were open to all who could buy space within, regardless of religion, but the practice of maintaining specific cemeteries for each church or religious group endured and even expanded in the nineteenth century. In death, as in life, the poor ended up in the equivalent of slums, segregated from the paying clientele, often in mass graves or unmarked plots. Most of the urban areas of Europe and the Americas are dotted with these necropolises, which were swallowed up by expanding cities and are now not only very crowded, or totally full, but also smack-dab in the middle of densely congested areas. Smaller cities and towns also followed suit, and by the end of the nineteenth century, the world where most Christians lived was one in which the dead and the living were segregated, and one in which the cemetery became the focal point of all piety for the dead.[18]

SPIRITUALISM

Beautiful cemeteries were not the only place to commune with the dead, however. As secularization intensified and traditional Christianity lost its once-dominant place in Western culture, ancient occult

Fig. 8.4. Mount Auburn Cemetery, Cambridge, Massachusetts, nineteenth-century engraving. From W. H. Bartlett, *Bartlett's Classical Illustrations of America: All 121 Engravings from American Scenery, 1840* (Mineola, N.Y.: Dover, 2000), plate 115.

beliefs and practices began to resurface in the nineteenth century, under new guises, as if to fill the vacuum created by unbelief. Ghosts began to reappear with a vengeance, as did people who believed they could communicate with the dead, when an immensely popular phenomenon known as "spiritualism" quickly gained public attention and won many adherents. Freewheeling and prone to contention—despite the existence of professional associations such as the Society for Psychical Research—it was very far from a cohesive movement. At bottom, spiritualism was a great resurgence of belief in the existence of the soul and in its immortality, for all "spiritualists" believed or hoped that the spirits of the dead lingered on earth and that they could communicate with the living. Ghosts and hauntings had long been part of popular culture, even though Protestant and Catholic clergy alike had tried to suppress such beliefs. Many historians often refer to belief in ghosts as one of those enduring bits of "popular religion" that the elites could never erase. Chances are that the afterlife described by the ghost of Hamlet's father in Shakespeare's play bring us closer to popular beliefs than nearly anything else, and what we find him describing to a Protestant Elizabethan audience is a perfect blend of very *wrong* un-Christian folklore and Catholic beliefs about purgatory:

> I am thy father's spirit,
> Doomed for a certain term to walk the night;
> And for the day confined to fast in fires,
> Till the foul crimes done in my days of nature
> Are burnt and purged away.[19]

Ghosts had never ceased to exist—nor could they stop talking or complaining about grudges and unfinished business, it seems. But beginning in the mid-nineteenth century, reports of ghosts and haunted places began to proliferate, as did so-called experts, or "mediums," who claimed that they had special knowledge or powers that allowed them to speak to the dead and relay their messages to the living. Most churches condemned these beliefs and practices outright, as they had always done, denouncing them as delusions or, worse, as demonic in origin. While some Christians rejected spiritualism or were ambivalent, some clearly embraced it, turning it into part of their Christian faith. The wall between such beliefs and Christian culture had always been somewhat permeable, so it was not too uncommon to even find Christian clergy—especially outside of the mainline churches—engaging in some sort of spiritualism or acting as mediums.

Among the spiritualist beliefs and practices that took root in the nineteenth century, none was more common than that of the séance, a gathering at which mediums would question the dead and seek replies from them. Mediums could claim all sorts of special powers that had once been the preserve of medieval mystics or of witches and demoniacs, that is, those who were in touch with the spiritual dimension: telepathy, clairvoyance, levitation. Some claimed they could make objects materialize out of thin air or, more commonly, that they could heal the sick.

Fig. 8.5. Spirit photograph, 1872, by Fredrick Hudson. © Wm. B. Becker Collection /American Museum of Photography.

After the invention of photography, other "experts" appeared on the scene who claimed to be able to photograph ghosts, ostensibly giving them scientific credibility. Spiritualism cut across class lines and circled the globe: its appeal seemed universal and as boundless as the public's credulity. None other than Sir Arthur Conan Doyle, the creator of the hyperlogical detective Sherlock Holmes, was a firm believer in spiritualism and toured the world, speaking to sell-out crowds, showing them photographs of ghosts. A lasting survival of the spiritualist craze can be found in almost any toy store nowadays: the Ouija board, a "game" once taken very seriously by spiritualists in which two people act as mediums, deciphering messages from the dead. Spiritualism would peak in popularity in the 1920s and 1930s as millions of distraught families sought to cope with the loss of their young men between 1914 and 1918 in the Great War.

An outgrowth of spiritualism that flourished in the late nineteenth century was *theosophy*, a movement founded by Helena Blavatsky in the 1870s. Under her leadership, the Theosophical Society disseminated a combination of spiritualism, ancient Indian philosophy, Gnostic teachings, and several other occult beliefs and practices. By reintroducing belief in reincarnation to the West and by claiming to provide access to memories of past lives, theosophists had some impact on Christians. As in the case of spiritualism, the fact that all of the mainline churches condemned theosophy did not deter all Christians from believing in some of its teachings, especially in reincarnation and the remembering of past lives.

CONCLUSION

Increased secularization caused a few other changes in Christian attitudes and practices in the course of the nineteenth century, most notably in regard to suicide, cremation, and mourning customs. Until the seventeenth century, suicide was considered a sin, and Christian burial was routinely denied to anyone who died at their own hand. Gradually, Christian attitudes toward suicide began to change, especially among Protestants, as the medical profession grew increasingly aware of the connections between mental illness and despair. By 1900 the balance of opinion had begun to shift in most Christian churches toward compassion and a greater acceptance of the physiological and psychological causes of suicide, among both Protestants and Catholics, although the Catholic Church continued to pronounce it a mortal sin. Similarly, the previously banned practice of cremation gained greater acceptance outside the Catholic Church, among Protestants, as burial space became increasingly difficult to find and burials became ever more costly. Mourning customs, which had always varied widely among Christians but had always been an essential part of dealing with the dead, also began to decline by 1900, especially in the industrialized world, where nonproductive behavior and outward signs of sadness tended to be frowned upon.

Changes such as these were but more recent versions of the adjustment that Christians have always made to their cultural environments. Social, cultural, and political developments, coupled with advances in science, technology, and medicine, began to speed up the process of change so much by 1900 that when the history of nineteenth-century Christian attitudes toward death is viewed in the light of traditions that lasted for centuries, the shifting seems abrupt. But the fact remains that even in situations in which Christians had to make decisions on the basis of opinions that came from the secular environment outside of their faith, or from other religious traditions, those who defined themselves as Christians continued to bring their faith into play. Whether they cremated their dead or buried them in secular cemeteries, or whether they dabbled in spiritualism or not, or whether they prayed for the dead or not, Christians confronted death and the disposal of their remains within an ancient framework of belief in an afterlife and a resurrection. Around 1900, death continued to pose the greatest challenge of all to Christians, as to all people, and within that challenge lay another: how best to Christianize the attitudes and rituals of the secularizing societies in which they lived, where death was becoming an unsightly inconvenience and where the dead were already being shuffled off the face of the earth quickly, with out-of-sight, out-of-mind industrial efficiency, with no apparent care for their immortal souls and no hereafter as their ultimate destination, other than perhaps some Ouija board or a séance.

> **Mourning the Afterlife**
>
> Those—dying then,
> Knew where they went—
> They went to God's Right Hand—
> That Hand is amputated now
> And God cannot be found—
> —Emily Dickinson, "Those—dying then," in *The Oxford Book of Death*, ed. D. J. Enright (New York: Oxford University Press, 1987), 188.

FOR FURTHER READING

Ariès, Philippe. *L'homme devant la mort*. Paris: Seuil, 1977. Translated by Helen Weaver as *The Hour of Our Death* (New York: Knopf, 1981).

Chéroux, Clément, and Andreas Fischer, eds. *The Perfect Medium: Photography and the Occult*. New Haven: Yale University Press, 2005.

Cressy, David. *Birth, Marriage, and Death: Ritual, Religion, and the Life-Cycle in Tudor and Stuart England.* Oxford: Oxford University Press, 1997.

Eire, Carlos. *From Madrid to Purgatory: The Art and Craft of Dying in Sixteenth-Century Spain.* Cambridge Studies in Early Modern History. Pages 28–31. Cambridge: Cambridge University Press, 1995.

Gregory, Brad S. *Salvation at Stake: Christian Martyrdom in Early Modern Europe.* Harvard Historical Studies. Cambridge: Harvard University Press, 1999.

Harding, Vanessa. *The Dead and the Living in Paris and London, 1500–1670.* Cambridge: Cambridge University Press, 2002.

Koslofsky, Craig M. *The Reformation of the Dead: Death and Ritual in Early Modern Germany, 1450–1700.* New York: Palgrave Macmillan, 2000.

Marshall, Peter. *Beliefs and the Dead in Reformation England.* Oxford: Oxford University Press, 2002.

McManners, John. *Death and the Enlightenment: Changing Attitudes to Death among Christians and Unbelievers in Eighteenth-Century France.* Oxford: Oxford University Press, 1981.

Pearsall, Ronald. *Table-Rappers: The Victorians and the Occult.* Stroud, U.K.: Sutton, 2004.

Reinis, Austra. *Reforming the Art of Dying: The* ars moriendi *in the German Reformation (1519–1528).* Burlington: Ashgate, 2007.

Walker, D. P. *The Decline of Hell: Seventeenth-Century Discussions of Eternal Torment.* Chicago: University of Chicago Press, 1964.

MULTIPLICITY AND AMBIGUITY

MARY FARRELL BEDNAROWSKI

CHAPTER NINE

CHRISTIAN HISTORY AS STORY

On the eve of *el dia de los muertos* we are gathered in the crypt of the *parrochia*, the parish church, in the center of San Miguel de Allende in the state of Guanajuato, Mexico. Our guide, Cesar del Rio, points to the tomb of his uncle who committed suicide when Cesar was three years old, not long after his uncle had had an encounter with what he experienced as an evil force or spirit in this same crypt where other ancestors are buried. Cesar acknowledges both the impossibility that this event was "real"—he knows a lot about psychology—and his own inability to disbelieve it completely. He tells us that he is typical of many Mexican people born in the 1960s: of *mestizo* (European and indigenous) heritage; a professional person who holds a law degree; a teacher of history; Roman Catholic by heritage and, at least in part, by belief. He is, he tells us, "superstitious." He participates fully and proudly in an annual procession that begins its winding way down from the mountains behind San Miguel at midnight and culminates in the city at sunrise. He occasionally visits the shrine of Our Lady of Guadalupe with his mother and other relatives. As he looks at the shrine's much-venerated painting, he is powerfully moved because of all she means to the people of Mexico and to people of other Latin American countries, but he asks Our Lady, "Are you real? Do you really help us?"[1]

* * *

The island of Gotland lies in the Baltic Sea where it borders Latvia, Estonia, and Sweden, to which it has belonged since 1645. A short ferry ride to the north is the island of Faro, site of Ingmar Bergman's home and film studios. Only fifty kilometers wide (population approximately 57,600), Gotland is home to more than ninety medieval churches built between 1100 and 1350. Church-building ceased in 1350 after Gotland's fortunes as a major Hanseatic League port declined. The churches were left "frozen in time" according to a pamphlet, "The Key to the Churches in the Diocese of Visby," published for visitors by the Church of Sweden (Lutheran). Although thousands of stained glass windows, wooden statues, and wall paintings were destroyed during and after the Reformation, the churches themselves were not destroyed, most likely because there were not sufficient funds to demolish and rebuild them, as happened in other parts of Sweden. The churches may be frozen in time architecturally, but they are all still in use today, not merely tourist attractions. Congregations are small, between a hundred and three hundred, and attendance is low at the every-other-Sunday services, sometimes not more than ten or twenty. The churches are "in the midst of life" on Gotland, says the Bishop of Visby, concerned not just with church life but with what happens in the community: "Spiritual and secular interests are interlinked. The church on Gotland has accepted the challenge of forming modern church services in medieval church chambers."[2]

* * *

Marika Cico (pronounced "tsitso"), a ninety-five-year-old Albanian Orthodox Christian when writer Jim Forest met her in the early 1990s, tells the story of the first liturgy celebrated in the town of Korca since the communist government closed all the churches in 1967. "Finally," she said, "the Communist time began to end [in 1990]. We were so happy, but all the churches were closed. In response to our request, the government in Korca decided we could have one church back and that we would be permitted to have the liturgy there. The first service we prepared for was Theophany on the 6th of January in 1991. We had been preparing everything, but needed a bell! Then we found the solution, a large brass mortar used for grinding garlic. It rang perfectly." The "time of no churches" was over.[3]

* * *

"When he was in his mid-teens Sadao Watanabe, a well-known Japanese print artist, first visited a Christian church, introduced by a neighbor who was a school teacher. He had lost his father when he was ten years old, and tended to live a closed and isolated life. He described his first impression of Christianity as follows:

"'In the beginning I had a negative reaction to Christianity. The atmosphere was full of 'the smell of butter,' so foreign to the ordinary Japanese.'

"Now in his print work he joyfully depicts the celebration of the holy communion with *sushi*, pickled fish and rice, a typical Japanese dish, served on traditional folk art plates. For him rice is a more natural and a more fitting symbol of daily food than bread which is foreign."[4]

* * *

According to longtime Maryknoll missionaries Joseph Healey and Donald Sybert, there are many concrete African metaphors for the church as "the people of God." One is the fireplace or the hearth:

> In Kenya, the Kikuyu word for "fire" is "mwaki." Traditionally, a small group or community gathered around the fire, fireplace, or hearth. A neighborhood community was called "mwaki" from the way that people made a fire and shared that fire. When the fire had been lit in one home, all the other homes in the neighborhood took their fire from that one place. This sharing of fire helped them to identify themselves as one community. "Mwaki" or "fire" was symbolic of other types of sharing and forms of communion, such as celebrations, performing local ceremonies, and discussing and approving important community issues. The fireplace with a cooking pot is a symbol in Africa for God blessing the people.[5]

* * *

An eighty-year-old Christian man stands guard at his wife's hospital bed in Minneapolis, Minnesota. She has been on life support for several months and is unresponsive. Her doctors are concerned that her body is beginning to deteriorate. Her husband is convinced that he has the moral obligation to keep her alive "until God takes her." Their adult children are divided on how to proceed.

In the neonatal intensive care unit of the same hospital, young parents, members of a social justice–oriented Roman Catholic parish, watch their twin daughters from behind a wall of glass. Born fourteen weeks premature, they are attached to numerous tubes and tiny enough to fit in their father's hand. There is no certainty about what lies ahead for them, physically or mentally. At the very least there will be many surgeries and months in the hospital. The parents have always said to each other that they would never choose—for themselves—to hold on to life at all costs. But what are the most loving, the most Christian decisions to make for their daughters? And what will help them decide? Medical advice? The counsel of clergy? The wisdom of their own hearts?

* * *

The *New Saint Joseph People's Prayer Book*, published by the Catholic Book Publishing Company in 1980 and 1993, is available at any ordinary Roman Catholic religious goods store. Along with "traditional and contemporary prayers for every need and occasion," there is a section of more than eighty pages called "Prayers from Other Religions": Protestant and Orthodox Christians; Jewish religion; religions of the East; and religions of the Americas (Native American prayers). One of the most intriguing prayers, given the history of Christianity's innumerable and often violent disputes over matters of doctrine and ritual, is a "Prayer of Thanksgiving for the Gifts of the Various Christian Churches," with invocations such as the following: "For the *Eastern Orthodox Church*: its secret treasure of mystic experience; its marvelous liturgy; its regard for the collective life and its common will as a source of authority," and "For the power of the *Methodists* to awaken the conscience of Christians to our social evils; and for their emphasis upon the witness of personal experience, and upon the power of the disciplined life."[6] Who would have dreamed in the years before the Second Vatican Council (1962–1965) that such a prayer book, meant for ordinary Catholics, would exist before the end of the twentieth century, if ever?

* * *

So many stories! And such various stories. Religion is story before it is anything else, and it is story after it is everything else. This is the intriguing claim of sociologist, novelist, and Roman Catholic priest Andrew Greeley, one that he has made many times in both scholarly and popular arenas. A people's history of Christianity is, finally, story-history—not analyses of theological abstractions or institutional development and disputes. These are stories about daily life, about emotions and struggles, about transformations and tragedies, about the devotional piety and convictions and doubts, the creation and disruption and re-creation of families, communities, and worldviews. They are not isolated stories, because stories without context and interpretation are merely anecdotes—interesting, often touching or instructive, but not necessarily illuminating about broader issues and patterns. Thus for each of the stories above and for those that will follow in the chapters of this volume, there are back stories, distinctive histories of religious and cultural circumstances.

We find in these twentieth-century stories multiple plotlines that take on powerful significance when we look at them in terms of people's history:

- encounters between intense religious devotion and modern and postmodern consciousness;
- the waning of church membership and attendance and the decline of this institution's cultural relevance—or so it appears at the moment—in many developed countries of the West;
- the repression and then the reemergence of Christianity in the aftermath of totalitarian regimes;
- the several-centuries-long unfolding of religious dynamics related to colonialism, inculturation, and postcolonialism in Africa, Asia, and Latin America;
- the realization that women, while very much present in the church, have been for the most part absent from written history;
- the bewilderment not just of ordinary people but of experts,

both religious and medical, over issues related to the beginning and the end of life;

• the realities associated with increasing religious pluralism and the discovery that "the other," whether Christian or non-Christian, now lives not on another continent or in the neighboring town but next door;

• the discoveries of dimensions of power and wisdom, courage and creativity that figure prominently in the people's stories and that bring new depth to the study of Christianity.

The people's histories of Christianity in the twentieth century differ from continent to continent, country to country, tradition to tradition, and even neighborhood to neighborhood. For that reason the stories and the themes in this most recent period of Christianity are geographically and culturally, chronologically and methodologically, literally and figuratively all over the map. We cannot attempt to cover global Christianity, from the beginning of the twentieth century to its end. There are other volumes available that take this chronological approach.[7] Instead, we offer a range of angles on some of the crises, the opportunities, the challenges, the disillusionments, and the hopeful surprises that Christianity has encountered in the twentieth century: global, regional, communal, and individual. A more modest label for what follows might well be *Some Selected Elements of a People's History of Twentieth- and Twenty-First Century Global Christianity.*

CHRISTIANITY ON EVERY CONTINENT

By the end of the twentieth century Christianity had taken root and shape all over the world and in the consciousness of Christians as a global religion. One of the major issues is the extent to which Christianity has demonstrated its capacity to assume multiple forms and still be recognizable as the religion of Jesus. If the history of the people's Christianity in the twentieth century tells us anything, it lets us know that whatever else it may be—and this it has in common with other world religions—it is a vast arena of human creativity whose symbols, rituals, scriptures, and stories are translatable across multiple cultural and historical boundaries.

The face of Jesus is familiar when it appears in the art of many cultures, no matter how different he looks from the famous and ubiquitous *Head of Christ* by Warner Sallman.[8] The elements of communion are recognizable within the forms of dried fish and rice and in the basic foods of other parts of the world. What is essential, the histories of the people tell us, is the gathering for a meal taken together. The stories of the Bible are translatable, capable of speaking movingly to experiences that cross many kinds of boundaries, although this kind of translating is not merely a process of substituting the words of one language for the words of another. Translation is interpretation is transformation, and the Bible in the "non-biblical world," as Hong Kong scholar Kwok Pui-lan tells us, is not the same "book" that it is in the West.[9] To claim these things is by no means to make the case that the history of the people's Christianity in late modernity is a history of triumphalism, one of Christianity's traditional temptations to excess. It is to say that all these things speak of the people's history of Christianity as the history of the people's creativity: taking the "stuff" of Christianity—its scriptures, symbols, rituals, and moral codes—and making it their own in various parts of the world.

Fig. 9.1. *Head of Christ* by Warner Sallman (1892–1968). © 1941 Warner Press, Inc., Anderson, Ind. Used by permission.

CHRISTENDOM OR CHRISTIANITIES

As many sources tell us, Christianity at the end of the twentieth century remained the largest of the world's religions, although not by as large a percentage of the world's population as was the case in 1900.[10] Much of the recent news about Christianity focused on the extent to which its population centers had moved to the southern hemisphere. Predictions abound about what this means. Will the shift southward bring with it very different forms of Christianity, the likes of which we have not seen before? Or, as some suggest, will it be mostly a premodern Christianity, a supernaturalist Christianity, very familiar to anthropologists and historians of religions?

If the number of Christians is increasing in the southern hemisphere, what is happening in the north? What does the history of Christianity in the West tell us? Is Christianity in the northern hemisphere losing its vitality, its cultural relevance? Is it collapsing into secular culture, becoming so "worldly" that soon its distinctive characteristics will no longer be discernible? Or is it changing its forms in ways that are only barely evident at present, moving away from reliance on church bureaucracies and beginning to revitalize the churches with new forms of community? Some huge urban Roman Catholic parishes in the United States are dividing into "house churches" and at the same time retaining their connection to "the mother church," and popular and scholarly religious journals and books in North America and Great Britain are full of articles about "the emerging church," devoted to suggestions about what the church needs to look like and be like in a pluralist, postmodern world.

FOR FURTHER READING

Bamat, Tomas, and Jean-Paul Wiest, eds. *Popular Catholicism in a World Church: Seven Case Studies in Inculturation.* Maryknoll, N.Y.: Orbis Books, 1999.

Chidester, David. *Christianity: A Global History.* New York: HarperCollins, 2000.

Healey, Joseph, and Donald Sybertz. *Towards an African Narrative Theology.* Maryknoll, N.Y.: Orbis Books, 1996.

Jenkins, Philip. *The New Faces of Christianity: Believing the Bible in the Global South.* New York: Oxford University Press, 2006.

McLeod, Hugh, ed. *World Christianities c.1914–c. 2000.* Cambridge History of Christianity. Cambridge: Cambridge University Press, 2006.

Moore, Rebecca. *Voices of Christianity: A Global Introduction.* Boston: McGraw Hill, 2005.

Thistlethwaite, Susan Brooks, and Mary Potter Engel, eds. *Lift Every Voice: Constructing Christian Theologies from the Underside.* Revised and Expanded Edition. Maryknoll, N.Y.: Orbis Books, 1998.

GENDER AND TWENTIETH-CENTURY CHRISTIANITY

MARGARET BENDROTH

On a cold winter Sunday in 1977, Pauli Murray led Holy Eucharist for the first time, standing in the chapel where her grandmother had once been baptized as a slave. The moment resonated with historical significance. Murray was one of the first women to be ordained by the American Episcopal Church, a veteran of a long and bruising battle for equal rights. That morning she stood behind a lectern engraved with the name of Mary Ruffin Smith, the wealthy white woman who had once owned Murray's grandmother Cornelia and who had built the chapel many years before. The sanctuary overflowed with local and national network media—even Charles Kuralt of the CBS program *On the Road* was on hand to record the event—and a joyous interracial congregation of family, friends, and supporters. At that moment, as Murray recalled in her memoir, *Song in a Weary Throat*, "all the strands of my life had come together.... I was empowered to minister the sacrament of One in whom there is no north or south, no black or white, no male or female—only the spirit of love and reconciliation drawing us all toward the goal of human wholeness."[1]

This small but significant moment of transformation is a good place to begin the story of gender and Christianity in the twentieth century. As she stood in that North Carolina chapel, Pauli Murray metaphorically demolished nearly every social category imaginable, breaking down old barriers of race as well as social class, and two millennia of established Christian custom barring women from the priesthood. Moreover, during the course of the late twentieth century, her act of hope and defiance was repeated many times over around the world, as women stepped into new public roles as pastors, theologians, and church leaders. An age-old pattern of predominantly male leadership in Christian churches appeared to be rapidly nearing its end. By the turn of the century, large ecumenical gatherings brought together women from Africa, Asia, and Europe and across the Western Hemisphere to reconsider Christianity's egalitarian message and its influence on the oldest human divide, the one separating male from female.

In many ways, therefore, Pauli Murray's life is emblematic of the much larger story of religion and gender in the twentieth century. There is no denying that a narrative of liberation makes sense for this subject—the past hundred years have seen many vivid accounts of hope and struggle, achievement and success. Pauli Murray's moment of personal triumph encapsulates a whole host of positive changes brought about in the twentieth century.

Of course she does not stand for all. A people's history of the twentieth century, almost by definition, directs our gaze away from solitary achievements, however dramatic, toward the broad range of human experience. Across the dauntingly diverse world of modern Christianity, most women continued to sit in pews and work in kitchens, as their mothers and grandmothers had done for many years before. With limited opportunities for education or leadership, acceptance into ordained ministry was, for many if not most, neither an option nor a dream.

But Pauli Murray's personal battle does open up a useful line of thinking about the complicated dynamics of gender and the larger structures of human experience that historians and anthropologists have documented across time and geography. In that sense, her long trip to the front altar was not just a confrontation with a particular ecclesiastical power structure, but a struggle against deeply rooted social ideologies about women's proper place. What a given culture considers to be "feminine" or "masculine" varies constantly across time and distance; the simple fact of biological difference admits endless nuance in meaning. Moreover, because of their basic interest in family stability and the ordered transmission of belief across generations, religious communities play a central role in shaping gender expectations. They have at their disposal a range of tools—myth and symbol and proscriptive texts—to enforce boundaries between male and female roles, and as we shall see, to critique existing cultural patterns. In the twentieth century, therefore, the intersection of religion and gender was often a deep tangle.

To begin with, there is no simple way to describe twentieth-century Christianity. Clearly, the events of the past hundred years have baffled the expectations of even the most acute observers. With the resurgence of Pentecostal churches and the rise of Catholic lay movements all around the world, the case for secularization seems thin at best. Modern Christianity never slowed down or disappeared, as an earlier generation of sociologists had once predicted; in Latin America, Africa, and Asia, it continued to grow and gather converts, sometimes in unprecedented, almost unimaginable numbers. In Africa, for example, the percentage of Christians grew from about 9 percent in 1900 (around ten million) to over 45 percent by 2000 and should be close to half the continent by 2025, over 633 million. South Korea, a nation closed to the West until the late nineteenth century, could be nearly 80 percent Christian by 2025. Even in thoroughly modernized societies like the United States, religion of every kind continues to flourish. With a religious adherence rate of over 60 percent, the United States is (statistically at least) one of the most religious nations in the world.[2]

It is more accurate to say that over the past hundred years, Christianity has decentered. Once a predominantly Western church, Christianity has become a truly worldwide faith, with the majority of the world's Christians now living outside the United States, Canada, and Europe. By 1980 the "average" Christian was young, brown, female, and living in the Southern Hemisphere. But demographics do not even begin to tell the story. Over the past century, religion of all types has become more contested, more

> ### Feminists Changing the Churches
>
> Aware of the limitations on the range of options open to women in the past, mainstream Christian feminists—both scholars and ministers—see the church as a significant cultural force in forming the attitudes, self-understandings, and expectations of women—and of men—and of society itself. They are deeply conscious of the damage that the churches have done to women, in the theologies, the language, and the structures that have kept women in a narrowly defined "place." They are determined to change the churches, radically. They refuse to leave. Perhaps they are more revolutionary than those who have given up. They refuse to ignore the liberating, indeed revolutionary, message that the churches bear about the realm of justice, peace, and equality coming in the future but, as the gospel proclaims, even now being born among us.
>
> —Anne E. Carr, *Transforming Grace: Christian Tradition and Women's Experience* (San Francisco: Harper & Row, 1988), 18.

privatized and personal, with an increasingly tenuous hold on the public square. Though the human tendency to doubt is hardly new, public skepticism about religion is no longer checked by social custom or intellectual defense. At the very least, the story of modern Christianity is far more layered and tragic, more triumphant and mysterious than any one-dimensional narrative of progress—or decline—could ever encompass.

Even more daunting is the problem of generalizing about the lives of ordinary believers. Women, for example, form a solid majority of Christian believers: in the United States they have consistently comprised two-thirds of all church members, and in newer areas of Christian expansion their numbers are even higher. In Chinese house churches, Latin American Pentecostal churches, and African indigenous churches, the proportion of women is 70 to 80 percent.[3] Despite the universal themes in Pauli Murray's story, she can hardly speak for the multitude. The average church woman is not behind a pulpit on Sunday morning, but busy in the parish kitchen or in other less visible forms of service. Indeed, in terms of statistical realities, the truth about gender and twentieth-century Christianity is deeply embedded in the regular, often invisible rhythms of local church and parish life.

Generalizations are difficult—but they are not impossible. While there is no single narrative of gender and twentieth-century Christianity, it is not difficult to locate a few common themes. Obviously, for women all over the world the emergence of second-wave feminism in the 1970s and 1980s had a fundamental, permanent effect on church politics; controversies over women's right to ordination have roiled probably every religious body at some point in the last thirty years. In the workplace, home and family life, and countless personal relationships, feminism has deeply altered the expectations of both men and women.

But there are also deeper themes at play, fundamental to second-wave feminism but older and more universal. In a broad sense the history of gender and religion in the twentieth century is about the differential effect of modern individualism. The power to define oneself is, of course, a central motif in the history of Western civilization, easily traceable through the Renaissance and Reformation, the Enlightenment, and the modern era. Even the most overworked undergraduate is probably mercifully unaware of the countless number of books, paintings, and poems that have been devoted to the quest for personal autonomy. In the twentieth-century the discussion became if anything more intense, as scholars and social critics labored to analyze the effects of "expressive individualism," where the old demand for personal freedom is increasingly unhindered by traditional social forms. The debate was much broader than a simple liberal-conservative divide; sometimes it invoked conservative critiques of feminism and warnings about the future of the family, and at others it centered on the future of participatory democracy under the atomizing force of modern technological, political, and economic change.

All too rarely, however, did the debate recognize the added complexities of gender and religion. Certainly most people are aware that even in the most technologically driven societies, women still temper their desire for personal autonomy with the competing demands of home and family, sometimes by choice and sometimes by necessity. And it has become equally clear that, especially for men in modernizing societies, the gift of individual freedom can also be an insupportable burden. The absentee fathers and stressed breadwinners of the late-twentieth century signify a growing crisis around the role of men—to the point that popular pundits and social scientists ask, only half in jest, whether men are even "necessary" to the future of the human race.

The Christian tradition has all too seldom addressed these issues in depth. More typically it has followed dominant cultural models, assigning women the obligation of self-sacrifice and men the power to lead, regardless of the strain this might impose on both. But over the course of the twentieth century, genuine Christian critique of modern individualism, recognizing its

---

The Individual in Modern Times

A half-century ago the family took precedence over the individual; now the individual takes precedence over the family. The individual once was an intrinsic part of his or her family. Private life was secondary, subordinate, and in many cases secret or marginal. Now the relation of individual to family has been reversed. Today, except for maternity, the family is nothing more than a temporary meeting place for its individual members. Each individual lives his or her own life and in so doing expects support from a now informal family. A person who considers his or her family suffocating is free to seek more rewarding contacts elsewhere. Private life used to coincide with family life; now the family is judged by the contribution it makes to the individual private lives of its members.

—Antoine Prost,
"The Family and the Individual,"
in Antoine Prost and Gerard Vincent,
eds., *A History of Private Life.*
Vol. 5, *Riddles of Identity
in Modern Times*
(Cambridge: Belknap, 1991), 84.

vastly differential effects on men's and women's lives, slowly began to emerge. Though the specific contours of male and female roles have changed over time, and vary across geographic and cultural contexts, the questions are broadly similar: Does Christianity liberate women? Can—and should—a Christian woman or man operate as a free, autonomous individual? And what kinds of obligations does Christian faith impose on men? Pauli Murray's moment of public triumph demonstrates the hope—and the reality—of reconciliation across many historic divides. But as this chapter suggests, the debate is far from simple and far from over.

THE FAMILY CLAIM

In the late nineteenth century, the American social reformer Jane Addams coined the term "the family claim" to describe the problem besetting the young women of her generation. Even though opportunities for education and meaningful employment had been growing throughout the post–Civil War era, opting out of marriage and motherhood still took personal courage. "Any attempt that the individual woman formerly made to subordinate or renounce the family claim," Addams observed, "was inevitably construed to mean . . . that she was setting up her own will against that of her family. . . . It was concluded that she could have no larger motive, and her attempt to break away was therefore selfish."[4]

Three-quarters of a century before the emergence of second-wave feminism, the debate over marriage and career was already old and familiar. In the rapidly industrializing, pluralistic world of early twentieth-century American culture, many women were already well-versed in the struggle between personal fulfillment and the demands of family. Enormous cultural tension centered in the fact that though women's domestic responsibilities were lessening, their presence in the home still carried heavy symbolic weight.

If women's role was beset by competing certainties, the role of men seemed disconcertingly vague. The Victorian father was the undisputed head of the family but had no obvious function in the private sphere; by the turn of the century, even his religious obligation to lead in family devotions was falling into disuse. Not surprisingly perhaps, church leaders regularly bemoaned the absence of men at Sunday services and worried about the long hours spent at work away from the arms of wife and children. It hardly seems stretching the point to suggest that a great deal of the social tensions around women's proper place was rooted in deeper anxieties about late nineteenth-century masculinity.

In the late nineteenth century, much of the difficulty stemmed from the widespread cultural assumption that gender differences were fixed, immutable, and primary. Before modern people learned to think of male and female in more physiological terms, as a complex function of genetics, hormones, and social environment, most Western Christians assumed the two categories were fundamentally spiritual, especially in the case of women. A woman was not just someone with a female body or a certain social status but, as one historian has put it, "thoroughly sexed through all the regions of [her] being."[5] Nineteenth-century Victorians read all kinds of psychological, intellectual, and religious implications into the basic fact of biological difference. Indeed, according to influential Protestant theologian Horace Bushnell, men and women were so different in both soul and body "that they are a great deal more like two species, than like two varieties."[6]

As the twentieth century opened, most Western Christians, both Protestant and Catholic, assumed that women's nature was fundamentally domestic and inherently religious. While men's aggressive, dominating temperament pushed them into the public sphere of government, business, and politics, women's gifts of modesty and passivity suited them for the private realm. That division of labor was, to be sure, a middle-class ideal that hardly described the lives of many poor or working-class women; yet it also reflected a significant social reality. By the opening of the twentieth century, opportunities for meaningful, self-supporting employment for women were relatively few, and church work attracted talented, ambitious women in large numbers. Indeed, while male participation lagged, Christian service gradually became the most important means by which women in the industrializing Western world could achieve leadership and expertise, without the appearance of selfish ambition. As Methodist women contemplated forming a missionary society in 1869, one that

Women and Missions

Men have been the gatekeepers of the institutional church and theories about its relation to mission. Women have rather concerned themselves with the personal and ethical aspects of mission. Put another way women's mission theory focused either on personal witnessing or on working toward the reign of God. Church planting and the subsequent relationship between church and mission was rarely part of women's public missiological agenda. Even if women planted mission churches in practice, suitable men took over the pastoral work as soon as possible. . . .Women were innovators in making personal connections with indigenous people for the sake of sharing the gospel—adopting orphans to teach them about Christianity, initiating house to house friendship evangelism among secluded women in zenanas and harems, living two by two in *pueblos jovenes* among the people they went to serve. From Ann Judson befriending the wives of high Burmese officials to Gertrude Howe setting up house to support her Chinese protégés attending American medical school, the interpersonal side of mission work often wore a female face.

—Dana Robert, *American Women in Mission: A Social History of Their Thought and Practice* (Macon, Ga.: Mercer University Press, 1996), 409–10.

in just four decades would boast a budget of over $800,000, they defended their ambitious dream as "God's voice speaking to us—for who can so well do this work as we? Does it not seem as though the responsibility were thus laid directly on us? And shall we shrink from bearing it?"[7]

In fact, even the ecclesiastical differences between Protestant laywomen and Catholic sisters obscured important similarities in women's roles. At the turn of the century, many a Catholic parish depended on the quiet participation of laywomen in devotional rituals and the religious training of children. And they depended as well on the unstinting labors of many thousands of nuns, who provided the regular unpaid service that made brick-and-mortar Catholicism such a long-term success. Indeed, the model Catholic woman, like the model Protestant one, was a willing servant. Her role was fundamentally domestic, either as a mother at home or as a Sister carrying out an equivalent labor in a school or hospital.

In the decades after the Civil War, many American Protestant women learned to negotiate the demands of the family claim and cement their leading role in Christian service by organizing for foreign missions. Barred from preaching in the mission field or from leading roles in denominational missionary agencies, separate women's groups proved a hugely successful alternative. By the early twentieth century, women from a broad range of Protestant denominations in North America and Europe had established national organizations dedicated to training, funding, and supporting independent female missionaries. They staked their claim to an entirely separate mission field, arguing that only women could reach the heart of non-Christian cultures, through the medium of the home. By the turn of the century, "woman's mission to woman" was all but eclipsing earlier efforts led by men and proving itself a powerful (if not deeply ambiguous) means of exporting both Christianity and Western culture to growing missionary fields in Africa and Asia.

This meant that, for women, Christianity expanded out of its historical Western base as both a conservative force and a modernizing one. Arriving inextricably linked to the aggressive agenda of European and American imperialists, it both affirmed women's traditional, subservient domestic role and inexorably undermined it. Female missionaries insisted that true Christianity was inseparable from a clean, well-maintained home and obedient, well-educated children—yet their own busy, independent lives belied that simple formula. Though often couched in pious phrases, their core message was that Christianity liberated women from "heathen degradation" and subservience to men. Firm believers in the superiority of Western ways, and of the Christian faith, they established schools, clinics, and hospitals that both elevated and undercut women's commitment to the home.

Fig. 10.1. Lecture on "Caring for your Baby," Nanking, China. From *Light and Life* 49 (1919).

Not surprisingly perhaps, Western missionaries enjoyed marked success in gaining female converts—even when they tried not to. To use just one fascinating example, among eastern Africa's Maasai people, a so-called church of women arose in spite of the stated preference of Roman Catholic Spiritan fathers for male converts. Reasoning that male heads of households would provide the quickest and most reliable inroad into Maasai society, the missionaries had begun work in the early twentieth century establishing schools and community centers designed to attract men rather than women.

But their efforts had the opposite effect. "The enthusiasm of Maasai women for the Catholic Church," wrote Dorothy Hodgson, an anthropologist who has studied the Spiritan mission, "was all the more surprising given the erratic and intermittent nature of religious instruction, administration of the sacraments and pastoral care." In a world shaped by the demands of British colonizers, which placed a premium on men's role as property owners and taxpayers, women found church an important compensation. It offered them social space, a place to socialize, share stories, and develop independence from men. "In addition to providing opportunities for women to come together collectively," Hodgson writes, "the church provided formal and informal leadership opportunities for women. Although men were usually elected or appointed to the formal positions such as 'chairperson' and 'secretary' (which required literacy skills and proficiency in Swahili), women seemed to dismiss, ignore, or at best put up with the presumed authority of these men." In effect, Hodgson concludes, the Maasai Catholic Church offered women social breathing room, allowing them to both affirm the family claim and to subtly undermine it.[8]

SECOND-WAVE FAMILY CLAIM

During the last two decades of the twentieth century, the old question of the family claim reemerged in Christian circles with new urgency and force, spurred in part by the rise of second-wave feminism. Clearly the movement fundamentally shaped the course of the twentieth century. Especially in its broader global context, women's rising aspirations brought about some epic social changes, as charismatic figures like Indira Gandhi, Benazir Bhutto, and Corazon Aquino rose to international leadership, and many lesser local female organizers campaigned for equal rights in marriage, control of sexuality, and access to employment. Though in some quarters changes were slow or nonexistent, they have affected far more than the elite few; in one way or another, women in every modern society have had to grapple with the aspirations the movement unleashed.

But feminism was only one of the new forces affecting the lives of ordinary people. In postindustrial economies like the United

States and Europe, the lines separating work and home—and male and female—had begun to blur and cross each other in complex ways. Technological changes like television, telephones, and computers removed all pretense of home as a sheltered enclave, separate from the secular bustle and flow of the outside world. (As one American fundamentalist noted glumly of television in 1955, "The boast of one network is that it 'brings the world right into your home.' Who wants the world as we know it in our homes?"[9]) The old nineteenth-century divisions of masculine and feminine, public and private, simply made less sense under the fragmenting pressures of modernity.

Economic pressures and rising aspirations also propelled more and more women, including those with school-age children, into the workplace. By the late 1990s, especially in areas of strong economic growth like East and Southeast Asia, over 60 percent of adult women participated in the labor force. Similarly, two-thirds of all mothers in the United States had entered the work force in 1995, a figure that included half of those with children under the age of two.[10] Though conservative churches often decried the erosion of women's domestic responsibilities, they could hardly stem the tide of social change. Studies showed that American evangelical women participated in the work force in almost exactly the same proportion as the population at large; the figure is also basically the same as that of women in more liberal Protestant bodies.[11]

In the midst of such flux, academic theologians and grassroots church leaders struggled to separate the permanent from the transitory. Were women naturally endowed with maternal gifts, and did they imperil both themselves and the wider society by venturing outside the home? Or were the old gendered divisions of labor merely arbitrary social conventions? Social science offered few new certainties; viewed across time and social boundaries, gender categories seemed eminently negotiable, defined more by cultural need than biological necessity. But other scientific research delivered a contradictory word, discovering gender differences deeply fixed in genetics, brain chemistry, and the complex mysteries of prenatal development. What was natural and what was simply imposed by social convention seemed almost impossible to separate.

Within the course of their daily lives, many men and women no doubt experienced the rapid changes of the late twentieth century as both freeing and harrowing, promising much but rarely delivering as anticipated. In Christian circles, of course, the central drama was women's fight for ordination rights. Momentum began building after the first meeting of the World Council of Churches in 1948 and the call for an international forum on "The Life and Work of Women in the Church." Spurred by the ecumenical movement's emphasis on human rights and Christian "essentials," centuries of arbitrary rules against women in the pulpit slowly began to erode. In worldwide Lutheranism, for example, the Slovakian church opened the ministry to women in 1951, and Sweden did so in 1958. During the 1970s, churches in North America, Latin America, and Asia also followed suit, as did African Lutheran churches in the 1980s. By the end of the twentieth century, some 68 percent of the bodies within the Lutheran World Federation ordained women, with those numbers often being matched in other denominations. In 1978, the Lambeth Conference of the worldwide Anglican church allowed women's ordination in principle and within ten years saw the first woman elevated to the office of bishop, when Barbara Harris was elected Suffragan Bishop of Massachusetts. Even among Roman Catholics, where women's ordination was long proscribed by law and custom, the Second Vatican Council opened a range of parish leadership positions to women. As in Protestant churches, women dominated local leadership; in the United States, according to one survey, they accounted for a consistent majority of the laypeople serving in parish councils, eucharistic ministry, and catechism classes.[12]

But timelines and percentages hide as much as they reveal; progress in achieving ordination rights did not necessarily signal changes in the traditional attitudes about gender roles that affected women in

Fig. 10.2. Barbara Harris at her consecration as bishop in the Episcopal Church in 1989. Photo courtesy of the Office of Women's Ministries, Episcopal Church.

church pews and kitchens. The overall thrust of papal teaching on women, capsulized by Pope John Paul II's 1988 encyclical "On the Dignity and Vocation of Women," emphasized women's inherent gifts for domesticity and service. "Woman can only find herself," the encyclical declared, "by giving love to others." Ordination had no justification in either church tradition or its understanding of scripture; because Christ himself had called only men to the apostolic succession, Roman Catholic teaching found no warrant for female priests.

And in fact change was slow everywhere. By century's end, even in some of the more liberal American mainline churches, the percentage of female clergy barely climbed above 15 percent, though women routinely numbered more than half of seminary graduates. Overall the proportion of female clergy had risen no higher than that of women in police and fire departments, around 10 percent. Female clergy also found themselves thwarted by a "stained-glass ceiling" and the expectation that women's primary responsibility to the demands of husband and family would necessarily keep them in smaller, less stable or influential parishes—yet another example of the family claim's continuing power. The slow progress of ordination in local churches in fact signaled that the old gender-based division of labor, with men in leadership and women in silent service, was still very much in operation.

In the postcolonial world, the issues were even starker. In many countries, foreign missionaries had left a legacy of commitment to female education and had modeled the power of educated, independent women. But when Europeans and Americans relinquished their mission stations in the decades following World War II, newly independent indigenous churches found themselves in a delicate position. Conservative attitudes toward women persisted where the minority status of Christian leaders made it difficult for them to challenge social norms. But even more to the point, poverty and urbanization patterns in Third World nations wreaked havoc on traditional family life, as the shifting demands for migrant labor forced many men away from their homes for months, even years on end.

During the 1980s and 1990s, perhaps the most concerted wrestling with religion and the family claim came not from Western

Fig. 10.3. Woman evangelist in India. From *Light and Life,* vol. 49 (1919).

feminists but from Christian women in Africa, Asia, and Latin America. Observing the daily struggle of women with poverty, war, and domestic violence, they found it difficult to press for change. The widespread image of Third World women as silent, patient sufferers lionized their tenacity but also perpetuated a deeply ambiguous stereotype. As Indian theologian Ranjini Rebera declared, "Self-sacrifice is a daily reality of Asian women's experience." Whether rich or poor, educated or uneducated, rural or urban, high caste or low caste, professional or unskilled, all women faced the social demand for marriage and passive acts of selflessness.[13]

The Christian tradition often seemed an uncertain ally of change. The conversation at an Asian consultation of Roman Catholic, Eastern Orthodox, and Protestant theologians in 1978 turned quickly to the gendered dimension of traditional caste structures and the exploitation of women through dowry exchanges—and ended with a critique of the missionary legacy. "Even the missions which established Churches in this country . . . handed down to us a tradition of women's inferior role," one of the women present declared. Though, on the one hand, the church had "always proclaimed loudly the freedom and dignity of all human beings," it rarely acknowledged the contradiction in the traditional view "that the subordinate role of women is the order of creation."[14]

But older, pre-Christian ways posed even more complex challenges. Although many women shared the concern of other Third World theologians for an authentic indigenous Christianity, they warned against resurrecting ancient traditions simply for the sake of doing so. Dorothy Ramobide, a South African writer, spoke for many when she declared that an uncritical acceptance of patriarchal African ways "runs the risk of being party to the legitimization of the domination of women."[15] Her hope was that women would not just protest the errors of the past but play a central role in redefining historic Christian tradition. The overriding message of Christian women outside the Western world was the need for a radical new look at the

Bible, taking the inherited tradition down to its original root.

This made for interesting new wrinkles on the old family claim, as articulate women from traditional cultures struggled to speak both *to* and *for* the many others they represented. To use just one telling example, in the late twentieth century the old Christian discussion about polygamy took a new twist. To be sure, the practice had long been condemned by Western missionaries and also by many feminists. But as one African woman theologian pointed out, none of these arguments took women's point of view seriously. Christian missionaries had always been primarily concerned with persuading the male polygamist to choose just one wife and live only with her. But what of the rest? Turning out a woman with children, who had been with one husband for many years, was hardly merciful. "Since each of the wives is married only to one man," this Christian feminist critic wondered, "could they not be considered for baptism if they so desired?" Could not the wives in a polygamous marriage decide along with their husband which of them would stand for Christian baptism?[16] Was it actually possible that Christian polygamy could exist in modern Africa?

The other rising conundrum of the late twentieth century concerned the role of men. By 1995, at a meeting of the Lutheran World Federation in Geneva, the old pattern of male domination seemed to have thoroughly turned, as the men present found themselves suddenly and unmistakably in the minority. These men responded in time-honored fashion, as many Christian women had a century before, by holding a separate meeting to air their concerns and build solidarity together. Though some of the men were ready to walk out at that point, others urged them to stay and try to influence the proceedings. Most found the experience eye-opening—and deeply frustrating. One Lutheran bishop later confessed to feeling "intimidated" by the

---

African Women's Religious Roles

Religion is an area of life that seems to be able to escape public attention. It is also an area in which individuals may be intimidated to abdicate responsibility for their own lives and to place themselves and everybody else "in God's hands." This should not happen. Christian feminists undertaking "God-talk" must work for the liberation of women from an image of God created for women by men. When examining the role of women in religion in Africa—whether speaking of Christianity, Islam, or African traditional religions—we must face two fundamental questions: what responsibilities do women have in the structures of religion? How does religion serve or obstruct women's development?

—Mercy Amba Oduyoye and Musimbi R. A. Kanyoro, eds., *The Will to Arise: Women, Tradition, and the Church in Africa* (Maryknoll, N.Y.: Orbis Books, 1992), 10–11.

women on the podium, and "helpless and powerless because he was not the one setting the agenda." But he worked far enough through his anger to conclude that "if the way he felt was the way women feel when they are in the minority, then there was an urgent need to do something about it."[17]

The deeper problem, however, was that women simply were not a minority in Christian churches—and had not been so for a long time. If anything, the ferment of the late twentieth century had fixed ordinary women more securely in the center of Christian activism and had rendered men more marginal. Around the world and across many communities, the preponderance of women and the general dearth of men began to raise worries about the social, cultural, and theological effects of religious "feminization."

FUNDAMENTALISM

In the last half of the twentieth century, anxiety about gender found forceful expression in fundamentalism. Especially after the rise of the Taliban in Afghanistan and Islamicist revolutions across the Middle East, the movement became synonymous with conservative views on female sexuality and political rights; yet, in its deepest sense, fundamentalism was not really about Islam, and it was less concerned with proscribing the actions of women than it was with shoring up male authority.

The term "fundamentalism" originated as description of a movement within American Protestantism, joining together conservative, militant voices in response to social and theological changes in the late nineteenth and early twentieth centuries. "Fundamentalists" worried about sliding standards in Christian doctrine and campaigned for a return to basic statements of faith. They decried the loss of biblical authority in an increasingly relativistic moral world, calling for godly separation from the rampant social evils of their age.

But the issues were not just simple matters of correct or incorrect doctrine: fundamentalist protest against secular culture also invoked gender. Many American Protestant fundamentalists were openly critical of women who forsook their appointed moral role, and during the

1920s, they rarely tired of calling down judgments on the "flappers" and "vamps" who smoked and drank in public. They also rejected the popular wisdom that women were more religious than men. Increasingly, fundamentalist diatribes invoked deeply negative portrayals of women as untrustworthy temptresses and, in fact, as symbols of worldly vanity and rebellion against God. The new gender paradigm, emerging out of fundamentalism and exerting a slow but demonstrable influence across other religious communities, turned the old one on its head. No longer the more virtuous sex, and the truest allies of Christianity, women were its bitterest enemies. Godly leadership therefore belonged first and foremost to men.

Recently, scholars and social critics have begun to talk about fundamentalism as a global movement within all of the major world religions. Bruce Lawrence has described it as a "religious ideology of protest" against the forces of modernity: secular nationalism, the rule of technological elites, and the moral relativism of consumer capitalism. But fundamentalists have staged their battle with the best weapons of communication that the latest technology affords, using the resources of the modern world to stake their claim for traditional values. They are, as Lawrence writes, "moderns, but not modernists. . . . at once the consequence of modernity and the antithesis of modernism."[18]

The fundamentalist reassertion of the family claim, therefore, is both deeply conservative and sharply contemporary. When the

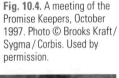

Fig. 10.4. A meeting of the Promise Keepers, October 1997. Photo © Brooks Kraft / Sygma / Corbis. Used by permission.

Promise Keepers movement emerged in the United States in the 1990s, bringing together thousands of men in huge outdoor stadiums to repent of their sins and confirm their commitment to family, some of its most appreciative admirers were feminists. To be sure, the Promise Keepers rarely missed an opportunity for stereotypical language

Fundamentalism and the Family Claim

In the face of . . . frustrations in dealing with external forces beyond their control, fundamentalists have found themselves most able to effect significant change in interpersonal relations, especially within the family. Building upon existing inequalities between women and men, patterns of discrimination against women, and the exclusion of women from positions of power, fundamentalists call for a strengthening of prerogatives for males and elders in the name of a return to "tradition," sanctified as the expression of God's will on earth.

—Helen Hardacre, "The Impact of Fundamentalisms on Women, the Family, and Interpersonal Relations," in Martin Marty and R. Scott Appleby, eds., *Fundamentalisms and Society: Reclaiming the Sciences, the Family, and Education* (Chicago: University of Chicago Press, 1993), 138.

about female dependency and male leadership, and at times their public rhetoric raised angry protests. But the most astute critics of the movement noticed that a Promise Keeper dad, committed to staying at home nights and sharing in child care and housework, was in many ways a feminist's wish come true.

In poorer parts of the world, where father absence is a matter of survival, conservative evangelical religion also played a somewhat paradoxical role. One study of Pentecostal churches in Colombia, for example, found that both men and women were attracted by their highly traditional teaching on male dominance and feminine submission. Pentecostal preachers insisted that men were to be the head of the household, using language drawn from a culture steeped in male machismo. Yet women recognized in that rhetoric an opportunity for family stability. In the long run it made men relatively immune to the more destructive aspects of male culture and answerable to the needs of their wives and children. Pentecostal women found their standard of living, and their own prospects for success, improving as a result of this gender ideology. Instead of buying alcohol or tobacco, Pentecostal fathers brought home their weekly paycheck; instead of spending evenings in bars and clubs, they were busy at church.[19]

Much has been written on fundamentalism, and there is no doubt much more waiting to be said. Few movements demonstrate so starkly both the adaptability and the rigidity of religion in the modern world. One of the best ways to understand the significance of fundamentalism is to approach it as a parable. The literal meaning is not really the point; who is to say whether fundamentalism is "good" or "bad" for either women or men? The effects of its conservative gender ideology are far too ambiguous to allow for a simple conclusion. What's important is the underlying lesson. Clearly, fundamentalism taps deeply into a classic modern problem, tempering the old masculine prerogative of personal autonomy while pressing anew the old family claim on women. And for that reason it is not likely to disappear any time soon.

NEW UNDERSTANDINGS OF OLD IDEAS

Almost everything about ordinary life in the twentieth century seems unprecedented: the unimaginable bloodbath of two world wars and a succession of genocides, the constant flow of startling new technologies, the births and deaths of nations, ethnic groups, animal species, and intellectual paradigms. The world of 1900, comfortably Victorian and dominated by Western hegemony, hardly seems real a hundred years later, when so many easy assumptions have been laid bare by violence and technological change.

Yet it is possible to see the "people's story" of the twentieth century, especially as it relates to religion and gender, as somehow familiar. As the material in this essay suggests, the past one hundred years or so have witnessed not simply the end of tradition but its rediscovery. Contrary to our modern propensity for timelines and horizontal charts, history rarely moves in a linear fashion. More often, what appears to be change is actually a long, slow, three-dimensional spiral; the illusion of forward movement is really a constant circling back onto the same scenery, though each time with a slightly different vantage point. Thus, what might look like the tired spectacle of old battles being fought and refought could well be the work of a new set of people on a quest for contemporary understanding.

There is no simple way to sum up such a long and complicated story, especially one that encompasses so many disparate and invisible personal lives. Perhaps it is best to step back finally and acknowledge the obvious: the mysterious success of religion in the modern world owes much to the vitality of our ongoing conversations around gender and the meaning of personhood. Here emerge some of the deepest, most puzzling questions about what it means to be human, to be at once independent and responsive to the needs of others. It raises a myriad of open queries about the family, both its present-day form and its possible futures, refracted through a maze of cultural lenses. It is a conversation almost guaranteed to be constantly new and constantly beyond the reach of easy answers.

FOR FURTHER READING

Carr, Anne E. *Transforming Grace: Christian Tradition and Women's Experience.* San Francisco: Harper & Row, 1988.

Clark, Elizabeth, and Herbert W. Richardson, eds. *Women and Religion: The Original Sourcebook of Women in Christian Thought.* San Francisco: HarperSanFrancisco, 1996.

Fabella, Virginia, and Mercy Amba Oduyoye, eds. *With Passion and Compassion: Third World Women Doing Theology: Reflections from the Women's Commission of the Ecumenical Association of Third World Theologians.* Maryknoll, N.Y.: Orbis Books, 1988.

Hardacre, Helen. "The Impact of Fundamentalisms on Women, the Family, and Interpersonal Relations." In Martin Marty and R. Scott Appleby, eds., *Fundamentalisms and Society: Reclaiming the Sciences, the Family, and Education,* 129–50. Chicago: University of Chicago Press, 1993.

Melton, J. Gordon, ed. *The Churches Speak On: Women's Ordination.* Detroit: Gale Research, 1991.

Oduyoye, Mercy Amba, and Musimbi R. A. Kanyoro, eds. *The Will to Arise: Women, Tradition, and the Church in Africa.* Maryknoll, N.Y.: Orbis Books, 1992.

Prost, Antoine, and Gerard Vincent, eds. *A History of Private Life.* Vol. 5, *Riddles of Identity in Modern Times.* Cambridge: Belknap, 1991.

Robert, Dana. *American Women in Mission: A Social History of Their Thought and Practice.* Macon, Ga.: Mercer University Press, 1996.

Strawley, John H., ed. *Fundamentalism and Gender.* New York: Oxford University Press, 1993.

PENTECOSTAL TRANSFORMATION IN LATIN AMERICA

LUIS N. RIVERA-PAGÁN

CHAPTER ELEVEN

FATED TO POVERTY

Sidney W. Mintz's *Worker in the Cane: A Puerto Rican Life History*, published in 1960, is a classic text in anthropology. It follows the life and travails of Anastacio (Taso) Zayas Alvarado, a cane worker of poor origins and dismal prospects who from his childhood was destined for the crushing manual labor typical of Caribbean sugarcane plantations. This is, sadly, the story of many Latin Americans who struggle to overcome grievous poverty while striving to confer meaning to a human existence at the margins of any social hierarchy.

Most scholars who examine the text stress the futile efforts of Taso Zayas to forge a brighter economic future for his family. But they frequently have disregarded what truly astounded Mintz: Zayas's unexpected conversion to Pentecostalism. From that dramatic religious experience arose Zayas's profound conviction that, despite the severe social conditions of his life, his existence had now gained an eternal significance, and he had been blessed with heavenly salvation, had become a child of God and temple of the Holy Spirit.[1]

This story of extraordinary healing, both physical and spiritual, gives us a view into the sudden and dramatic irruption of Pentecostal Christianity in Latin America. This charismatic way of conceiving of and living the Christian faith has transgressed the boundaries of what for centuries had been the normative dogmatic and ecclesiastical expression of Christianity in the region. It has reconfigured the self-understanding, family life, and communal existence of millions of working-class men and women.[2] In short, it is a narrative of unexpected transformation that in its particularity becomes paradigmatic of a religious revolution for Latin American Christianity.

Mintz's initial interest in Taso Zayas's life had nothing to do with religiosity. Neither the scholar nor Zayas seemed to care much about sacred issues, matters of doctrine, liturgical rites, or theological creeds. Mintz's scholarly concern was typical of the mid-twentieth century, namely, how the process of modernization and industrialization affected and shaped the existence of rural workers. Taso was one of a multitude of men and women in Latin America who lacked schooling, land, and house, who from cradle to grave were in bondage to an accelerated capitalization of one product, geared toward export and controlled by foreign corporations. In the Caribbean during the first half of the twentieth century, that meant sugarcane. The region had become a huge plantation devoted to sweetening the consumption habits of metropolitan cities all over the world while embittering the lives of so many native workers, modern versions of the African slaves who used to sweat and die in the fields of the islands.[3]

Taso Zayas was nothing more than another worker at a sugarcane plantation, constantly striving and yet failing to make ends meet as he worked from sunrise to sunset to provide food and clothing for his common-law wife, Elizabeth, and his twelve children, of whom three died in their early childhood. Fatherless at the age of ten months (in 1908) and motherless when he was twelve (1920), he suffered from painful aches caused by the hard labor he had to perform daily. His domestic life was plagued by continual bickering with Elizabeth—not exactly an image of happiness and comfort of any kind.

Zayas was not a passive pawn in the winds of social destiny, for at times he was very active in Puerto Rico's general confederation of workers and in the reformist Popular Democratic Party. The 1940s were for him a decade of intensely felt social disillusionment, followed by bitter frustrations. Everything promised to change; everything remained the same. Zayas did not seem to fit well into the social patterns of power struggles. Labor union organizing and political activism resembled Sisyphus's curse.

CONVERSION, SPIRITUAL BAPTISM, HEALING

Yet in 1950, as he was plagued by poverty, pain, and frustration, something astonishing happened in Zayas's life: a radical disruption of his previous self-understanding and existence. As was so frequent though paradoxical in Latin American patriarchal society, the women of the house took the first step. Elizabeth and their oldest daughter, Carmen Iris, went to a Pentecostal healing crusade. They came back with amazing stories of miraculous healings, charismatic happenings, and conversions. Extraordinary events seemed to be taking place, bringing joy where suffering prevailed and hope where despair ruled.

Elizabeth's life was haunted by the sinister memory of her father, who had drunk heavily and mistreated her mother, and by her constant fights with Taso, caused by her suspicions about his possible dalliances with other women. One night in the midst of a Pentecostal revivalist session, she felt herself possessed by a supernatural power that gave her the exceptional capability of speaking in tongues. The preacher's interpretation, to the joyful exclamations of the congregation, was that Elizabeth had been baptized by the Holy Spirit. She had been transformed into a new creature, her soul had been redeemed, and she was assured of eternal salvation.

Mintz was astute enough to perceive the significance of female priority in the religious conversion of this family. Indeed, as happens throughout Latin America, conversion to evangelical Protestantism or to Pentecostalism usually entails a sweeping reconfiguration of family life. It is probably too much to claim that it fundamentally alters the patriarchal hierarchy of authority, for the biblical literalism to which it is closely linked is suffused with notions of masculine primacy. But it frequently transforms the patterns of behavior of the husband/father, who adopts a sterner moral discipline and now abstains from investing money and energy in drinking, womanizing, and betting.[4] The patriarchal hierarchy might be left in place and even theologically reinforced by biblical allusions to female submission in the New Testament epistles (1 Cor. 14:34, Eph. 5:22, Col. 3:18, 1 Tim. 2:11-12, 1 Pet. 3:1), but the shape of masculine behavior is nonetheless substantially reconfigured. The patriarchal household code acquires a benevolent aspect.

Zayas had always considered himself Roman Catholic, but throughout his life he had regarded church activities as something alien to his daily labors, sorrows, and illusions. He heard with some reservations the strange stories narrated by his wife and daughter but decided to attend one of the evangelistic campaigns of a visiting North American preacher. As the evening progressed, Zayas experienced something strange and unexpected: "Brother Osborn[5] began to pray for the sick. . . . I felt something in my body, a thing—an extraordinary thing—while he was praying for the sick. And later, after he finished that prayer, I felt an ecstasy—something strange. . . . And afterward I did not feel that pain that I had been feeling. . . . And up to the present, thank God, I have never felt that pain again."[6]

Fig. 11.1. Healing of blind girl: Photo of Victory Christian Center, Crusade in the Dominican Republic, 2005. Photo © Victory Christian Center, Tusla, Okla.

Miraculous healing is nothing new in Latin American religious traditions. There are several sites considered sacred, where healing divine grace is implored and received. The most famous of all is the basilica of the Virgin of Guadalupe, in Mexico. The basilica brims with thousands of ex-votos of gratitude for the healing miracles performed by the Guadalupe.[7] Since her first alleged appearance to the indigenous man Juan Diego, in December 1531, countless acts of divine healing have been attributed to the Patroness of Mexico and Latin America. Though the Guadalupe has also fulfilled a meaningful role in the formation of the Mexican national identity,[8] it is probably true that common people throughout Mexico, Latin America, and the Hispanic diaspora in the United States look to the Virgin more as a maternal source of extraordinary favors in situations of grave distress than as a patriotic icon.

Miraculous healings are usually attributed to a holy person, most of the time the Mother of Christ, and happen in a sacred place, in this case the Tepeyac. Both the holy person and the place are linked to a sacred myth of origin that first circulated orally and then was recorded in writing. Zayas's healing, however, belongs to a different genre. Stories now abound in Latin America of healings that occur in many scattered places, with no sacred myths of origin, performed after the intercessory prayers of evangelists unrecognized by mainstream churches. Such healings take place under the aegis of churches and congregations of relatively new origins and picturesque names (such as Iglesia del Buen Pastor, Iglesia del Getsemaní, Fuente de Agua Viva, Roca de Salvación), many of them founded by self-appointed preachers. They might take place anywhere—a football stadium, a recently opened storefront church, the town square, places not usually considered sacred—and are performed by ministers not accredited by any theological academy or any of the traditional Christian confessions. One might speak of a radical democratization and popularization of divine healing.

Fig. 11.2. Blessed Virgin of Guadalupe mural, Mexico City. Photo © Rene Sheret/ Stone/Getty Images. Used by permission. Tradition says that the first apparition of the Virgin in Mexico dates from December 1531, when the Virgin appeared to Juan Diego and told him: "*You should know, son, that I am the Virgin Mary, Mother of the true God. I want a house and a chapel, a church to be built for me, in which to show myself a merciful Mother to you and yours, to those devoted to me and to those who seek me in their necessities.*" Adapted by Luiz Nascimento from *Mexican Phoenix: Our Lady of Guadalupe: Image and Tradition across Five Centuries* by D. A. Brading (Cambridge: Cambridge University Press, 2002), 60.

The healings are usually perceived as extraordinary events. But as happens so frequently in the history of the Christian faith, this movement is also a process of the retrieval of a tradition not entirely erased from the memory of the believing community. After all, miraculous healings abound in the Gospels and the chronicles of the first apostles. "Signs and wonders" (John 4:48) were part and parcel of the early Jesus movement and were considered indications of a decisive irruption of divine power and mercy in human history. When John the Baptist had doubts about the identity of Jesus, he sent some of his disciples to question the Galilean. Jesus, true to form, replied indirectly by signaling his acts of healing: "Go and tell John what you hear and see: the blind receive their sight, the lame walk, the lepers are cleansed, the deaf hear, the dead are raised, and the poor have good news brought to them. And blessed is anyone who takes no offence at me" (Matt. 11:2-6). Jesus' first commission to his disciples, according to an early memoir, included the performance of similar "signs and wonders": "Cure the sick, raise the dead, cleanse the lepers, cast out demons" (Matt. 10:8).

Healing

In the moment when Brother Osborn began to pray for the sick, my own case came immediately to my mind. When he began to pray, he spoke in this way: "All those who have sickness in any part—put your hands on the affected place, whoever has different illnesses." And I lifted my hand to the spot where I really felt pain. And while the brother prayed, I felt something in my body, a thing—an extraordinary thing—while he was praying for the sick. And later, after he finished that prayer, I felt an ecstasy—something strange—and then it went away.

—Taso Zayas, quoted in Sidney W. Mintz, *Worker in the Cane: A Puerto Rican Life History* (New York: Norton, 1974 [1960]), 211.

The first controversial public act of the apostles Peter and John was to cure someone lame since birth (Acts 3:1-10). The religious authorities were strongly annoyed, not only because an act of divine grace had taken place outside the margins of the sacred place, in the portico of Jerusalem's temple, but also because the authors were "uneducated and ordinary men" (Acts 4:13) who lacked the social, academic, and ritual credentials traditionally required to mediate divine grace. The "wonders and signs" (Acts 2:43) of those "uneducated and ordinary men" were construed as a serious challenge to the authority of the priesthood and scribal experts.

The "signs and wonders" of Pentecostalism that bewilder so many of its observers are an expression of a characteristic common to most Christian reform movements—an attempt to recover lost dimensions of the early Christian apostolic community. In this case, those lost dimensions are physical healings, reception of the Holy Spirit, glossolalia, passionate devotion to the faith, and priority of the poor ("uneducated and ordinary") people in the worshiping community.

Zayas's healing was neither unique nor peculiar. In twentieth-century Latin America healing divine grace seemed to abound, manifesting itself in multiple forms outside the boundaries of the established church. Acts of healing and exorcism occurred thanks to the intercession of evangelists whose ministry was ignored by most mainstream churches, and they benefited common people like Taso Zayas. Once again, as so many times before in history, divine grace seemed to surpass and overwhelm the hierarchical patrolling of ecclesiastical frontiers.

Despite the constant attribution to Latin American Pentecostalism of ethereal spiritualism and otherworldliness, researchers are astounded by the importance of corporeal healing for many charismatic Pentecostal churches. The body recovers the centrality that it enjoyed in the early Jesus movement. There are sensible reasons for this. These are men and women whose physical and social survival is predicated upon their ability to perform hard manual labor and who therefore need to have strong and healthy bodies to provide for the well-being of their families. They are poor and do not have the financial resources to pay for expensive medi-

Fig. 11.3. Honduras Church Leaders Conference and Crusade with Rev. Dr. Jae-Rock Lee. Photo © Urim Book USA. Used by permission.

cal services. They are also denizens of nations lacking adequate social health institutions. Thus, a debilitating illness becomes a matter of life and death. In such a grave situation, sometimes the only hope of the powerless appears to be divine intervention. For countless rural and urban poor workers, serious sickness becomes the occasion to implore the Virgin or to attend a healing crusade with anxious hope in their hearts that they might become beneficiaries of merciful divine power.

In the twentieth century new and more accessible healing competitors to the Virgin suddenly began to spread across Latin America. Divine grace took a more popular and democratic shape. Dozens of uneducated and ordinary men and women became mediators of divine healing power.[9] This process simultaneously implied a critical downgrading of the Virgin Mary's role in creedal faith and religious rites, a dimension of the antagonism of Latin American evangelicals and Pentecostals toward Roman Catholicism.

Physical healing might have been the starting point, but conversion, as Zayas explained to Mintz, entailed other decisive dimensions. After attending the worship services of the Pentecostal chapel in his barrio for several weeks, Zayas experienced an extraordinary event usually known in that ecclesiastical tradition as baptism by the Holy Spirit. He was a man of few words, but his narration of the blessing of the Holy Spirit had subtle tinges of deep spiritual gratification: "And while one is praying one feels as if something comes and fills one. . . . I received a blessing . . . at the same time one receives the tongues. And when one is baptized with the Spirit . . . one feels most content. . . . When a person thus receives the blessing of the Holy Ghost, it is a great joy that a Christian feels. . . . One is exceedingly happy."[10] A man whose life had been extremely difficult—in continuous bondage to strenuous work and poverty, plagued by debilitating pain, in perennial marital stress, and with a history of disappointments in labor union and political affairs—suddenly felt joyful thanks to the divine blessing of baptism by the Holy Spirit. His taciturn and somewhat trite witness lacks eloquence but nonetheless expresses the radical newness of his self-understanding by stressing that he felt "full": "One receives the Spirit . . . that comes and fills one. . . . Yes something comes and fills one."[11] Plenitude has displaced hollowness at the core of his mind and heart.

The experience of an uneducated and ordinary person speaking in divine tongues under the blessing of the Holy Spirit is not only memorable; it also leads to a momentous reappraisal of his or her entire existence. The hearing of the gospel, preached in clear, simple words, awakened in Zayas a deep sense first of guilt and then of absolution. "In truth at times one feels, eh—guilty of many things. . . . All of those things must be changed."[12] Zayas was not one to belabor the things he used to do that he now considered sinful, and it would be unfair to attempt to fill in the blanks, but the idea is emblematic of many similar experiences: a rejection of a former lifestyle now perceived as violating God's will, the sense of having been forgiven, and the decision to lead a holier life. Sanctification is taken seriously as a necessary consequence of spiritual baptism.

In this narration, the emphasis is not upon the traditional baptism by water, but upon the spectacular event of the reception of the Holy Spirit. Elizabeth was more loquacious, more expressive with words, and her description of the baptism by the Spirit was more dramatic than Taso's. "There came this peculiar thing. It invaded my whole body. . . . I began to tremble. . . . My body was moving more . . . until at last something . . . compelled me to dance. . . . I could not control myself. . . . And then I spoke in other languages, like Hebrew or something like that. . . . Mean-

---

Guilt and Absolution

Now, in that moment that I felt—eh—eh—guilty, it was because I used to do many things they prohibit. That is the guilty part of what I was feeling. Before, as I said, Elizabeth and I used to have our differences and we used to quarrel and such things. And when they explain these things, then one feels guilty. I felt guilty, and she [Elizabeth] must have too.

—Sidney W. Mintz,
Worker in the Cane: A Puerto Rican Life History (New York: Norton, 1974 [1960]), 217.

while . . . there were those strong movements in my body . . . and for the sheer pleasure of it, one goes speaking in tongues. . . . I felt as if my face were being lighted up by a flashlight. And I felt more alive than ever, and happier than ever."[13]

A poor woman—who had seen her mother mistreated by her drunkard father, felt disregarded by her husband, had suffered three of her children dying in their infancy, and was overworked in caring for her other children—suddenly felt "more alive than ever, and happier than ever" after being baptized by the Holy Spirit. She felt that divine power—"there is something powerful . . . beyond the firmament one sees"[14]—had entered into her and conferred on her amazing gifts.[15] Elizabeth and Taso describe their incorporation into a Pentecostal church, but curiously neither mentions the traditional

Figs. 11.4 and 11.5. A large-scale Protestant religious ceremony at the Maracaña soccer stadium in Rio de Janeiro, Brazil, in the summer of 2004. Although this ceremony was open to all denominations, most Protestants in Rio de Janeiro are Pentecostals. Photos © Marshall Roderick.

sacrament of water baptism. It probably took place, but as a sacramental event it was overshadowed by the spiritual baptism. This constitutes an important, though usually overlooked, recasting of the theological understanding of baptism. Baptism by the Spirit, not by water, becomes the decisive transforming and empowering experience.

One important outcome of conversion and spiritual baptism is peace of mind. Joy and hope displace anger and frustration. It is first expressed in family life. The bitter fights between husband and wife disappear. "When you seek God," according to Taso, "then you are made a new creature and then you have peace in your home, then you have contentment."[16] But his wider communal context also changed. This is signaled mainly by his continual references to the members of his church as "brothers" and "sisters," an indication that Taso and Elizabeth are now members of a new type of family and that their church functions not only as a place for common worship but also as a network of vital support and solidarity. For Taso, the solutions once searched for in the labor union or in the political party are now to be found in the community of believers. Indeed, Pentecostal congregations in Latin America frequently perform useful services of solidarity in situations of social distress so common in the lives of their members.

BECOMING PEOPLE OF THE BOOK?

Conversion did not drastically change the socioeconomic situation of Zayas and his family. They were poor before it and remained poor afterward. "His work takes him to the cane, along the railroad tracks and on the spurs, eight hours a day in the sun. . . . He and Elí and seven of their children live in their little house, eating their rice and beans and drinking black coffee, entertaining themselves with the Bible and the tambourine and the gossip of the barrio."[17] In fact, one might suspect that the midcentury decline of sugarcane production on the island and its replacement by small manufacturing plants requiring higher levels of technological skills possibly placed his family under even worse economic stress.

Despite the connections that some scholars predict, in a too-facile optimistic Weberian mood, between conversion to a morally stern religiosity and socioeconomic upward mobility, more frequently than not the poor remain poor. After all, modern economic globalization never truly intended the elimination of poverty. Its preferred biblical mantra is probably Matthew 25:29 ("for to all those who have, more will be given, and they will have in abundance.")

And indeed, the second half of the twentieth century was not generous to the Latin American poor. The glad tidings of socialist revolution, national security military juntas, liberation theology, and neoliberal globalization had all been proclaimed, leaving behind a trail of broken promises and frustrated hopes. However, millions of Latin Americans, in the midst of dreadful poverty and turbulent revolutions, still believed firmly that their lives had changed significantly. They held fast to the conviction that, thanks to the Holy Spirit, they possessed a new identity and were now "children of God," members of the community of saints, chosen for eternal salvation. They gathered assiduously in austere temples and chapels, built by their own hands and devoid of the grandeur of Roman Catholic sacred architecture, to praise God, study the Bible, perform acts of exorcism, heal the sick, and share in the tribulations and good news of their fellow brothers and sisters.

The story of Zayas and his wife is superbly narrated by Sidney Mintz, but the anthropologist could not hide his surprise at their conversion to the newly introduced Pentecostalism. Mintz was no apologist for the newcomer evangelists, and his last sentences poetically betray his secularist perspective. "Taso's story has no moral. . . . Or perhaps the reader will see the waste I think I see: the waste of a mind that stands above the others as the violet sprays of the *flor de caña* tower above the cane."[18] A wasted mind? Maybe from the perspective of an academician who values intellectual achievement, but that is not how Taso and Elizabeth perceived themselves. When asked, they emphasize the healing of their bodies and the salvation of their souls. They have been healed, have received the blessing of the Holy Spirit, and have the Bible, as the word of God, constantly within reach. They are now members of the community of believers and possess the assurance of eternal redemption. They have come to see themselves as privileged citizens of the kingdom of heaven. They even learned to play the tambourine.

At the core of all of these phenomena lay another crucial change in the minds of people like Taso and Elizabeth that seems to have escaped Mintz: They have become *readers*. In the more than two hundred pages of Mintz's study of Taso's life before his conversion, it is obvious that Taso did not care for books or any type of reading. He apparently was not analphabetic, but certainly illiterate. Totally absorbed in daily labors, he had neither time for nor interest in books or journals. After their conversion, he and his wife may still not be people of books, but they have certainly joined the company of the people of the Book. Now Taso and Elizabeth read the Bible constantly, in the congregation and in their house.

Conversion entails a novel source of certainty regarding the place of humanity in the divinely ordered cosmos. The Bible is now perceived as the word of God. In the middle of the twentieth century, evangelicals in Latin America could be distinctly recognized by a book they carried constantly and quoted ceaselessly, the Bible. It was always at the center of the congregation and in the living room of the house. It was seen as an infallible font of firm convictions and ideas. It functioned symbolically as a talisman, an apotropaic (intended to ward off evil) amulet, when risky activities were to be undertaken. Only after the reforms approved by Second Vatican Council, in the mid-1960s, would the Roman Catholic Church promote a similar mass publication of the Bible in easily accessible editions.

Zayas explains how in his church they gathered around the Bible and in a collegial way conversed about biblical doctrines. "Any other doubt I might have I resolved in the Scriptures," he affirms with confidence.[19] Notice the prominence of the "I" in this statement; it is not the case that the believers receive a body of doctrines from a hierarch equipped with credentials of ecclesiastical authority. What they now share is a sacred book to be read and interpreted by many uneducated and ordinary men and women—people like Zayas. They have become the people of the Bible, but the Bible has also become the book of the people.

Merely one book is indeed a rather limited intellectual horizon. Yet if someone, no matter his or her educational background, diligently reads the poetry of the Psalms, the biographical narrations of the Gospels, the irate apostrophes of the prophets, or the subtle theological deliberations of Paul, it is difficult not to surmise that such a practice would indeed expand their repertoire of words, images, and ideas. Taso and Elizabeth did not become biblical scholars by any means. Their textual interpretations might be naïve, but it is hard to imagine their not acquiring a wider stock of linguistic and intellectual skills simply by reading what is, after all, not an undemanding text. Their reading of the Word increases their repertoire of words and, what for them might be even more decisive, simultaneously transforms drastically their understanding of the world.

THE KINGDOM OF GOD AND THE KINGDOM OF THIS WORLD

Several scholars currently take a critical view of Christian Lalive d'Epinay's thesis about the otherworldliness and lack of political awareness of the Pentecostal churches in Latin America. This rethinking takes place in the wake of the emergence of Neo-Pentecostal megachurches and evangelical political parties all over Latin America. Demographic growth has increased their political power and influence. Numbers do make a difference when votes are counted.[20] The time has come when many Pentecostal churches take more interest in the kingdom of this world and in earthly citizenship, and the debate is now shifting its focus to the shape of their social engagement (including the intriguing question about the possible emergence of a Pentecostal theology of liberation).

The political awareness and activism of the Pentecostal churches in Latin America, however, is a rather new process that has mainly taken place since about 1990. In the mid-twentieth century the community of the saints stressed separation and distinction from the world, functioning as a refuge from its sorrows and temptations. When prompted and challenged to confront controversial political and social matters, most evangelical and Pentecostal churches would quote Jesus' words to Pilate as the legitimizing text for their political abstention: "My kingdom is not of this world" (John 18:36). The severe Johannine strictures against the "world" were some of their favorite biblical leitmotifs. The "world" was conceived as ruled by demonic powers, under the tyranny of Satan. The most that could be asked of the state was its protection of the right of the new churches to preach and expand. Religious freedom might indeed have important consequences for the democratization of any society, and mainstream Protestant churches were usually aware of the link. Yet the concern of most midcentury Pentecostal congregations was their right to proclaim their charismatic version of the gospel free from restrictions by the state or any legally established church.

For their part, Taso and Elizabeth seemed undisturbed by the midcentury political and social turbulences taking place in Puerto Rico, including the formation of a strong independence party, a nationalist insurrection, the industrialization of the island, and the establishment of the Commonwealth of Puerto Rico, an ambiguous juridical relationship with the United States.[21] In the midst of poverty and sociopolitical transformations, Taso and Elizabeth were relatively serene, for their minds and hearts revolved around the community of saints, the joy of the Spirit, and the promise of eternal salvation. In political issues, they tended toward quietism rather than activism.

Taso did not continue his work in union-related and political matters. He sees those activities as part of his former self, from which he has been freed. The church now became the center of his aspirations and exertions. We cannot tell from Mintz's account whether at a later date Taso became disenchanted with the church as well, but it can be ascertained that some years after his unexpected and dramatic conversion, he still felt at home immersed in church activities. "He seems serene" is Mintz's terse description.[22]

TRANSFIGURING LATIN AMERICAN CHRISTENDOM

The spread of evangelical charismatic Christianity across Latin America has not left the social situation intact. The growth of these congregations has indeed changed the continental public landscape considerably.

Since their colonial inception, Latin American nations were characterized by an official linkage between the state and the Roman Catholic Church. The royal patronage exercised by the Iberian crowns entailed the acknowledgment by the church of the sovereignty and authority of the metropolitan state, but also the state's recognition of the Roman Catholic Church's exclusivity in religious affairs.[23] It was sometimes the source of acute conflicts, whenever the ethical conscience of priests, missionaries, and theologians clashed with the severe exploitation of the native communities.[24] Yet it was a convenient arrangement for both partners, for it conferred a sacred aura to the metropolitan sovereignty and conversely provided the church with state protection.

The governments of the new states, which emerged after the nineteenth-century wars of independence, promptly recognized the advantages of royal patronage and tried to preserve it. This heritage forged a particular brand of Christendom closely linking the state and the Roman Catholic Church in Latin American countries, a condition juridically inscribed in many national constitutions and Vatican concordats.[25]

This official connection between church and state was venerable but also vulnerable. It became embroiled in countless disputes of jurisdiction that sometimes resembled the renowned dispute between Henry II and Becket, though most of these never produced martyrs deserving similar fame or memory. Sometimes archbishops and bishops became decisive protagonists in the national drama, diminishing the powers of the state and restricting the possibilities of religious competition; at other times, the sword of the state curtailed severely the rights and powers of the church. In a critical phase of the Mexican Revolution, the church lost legal recognition, its property was nationalized, and religious houses were closed. During the Colombian civil war, on the other hand, Catholics massacred members of the evangelical minority under the excuse that the Protestants usually aligned themselves with the Liberal faction. In general, only the Roman Catholic Church had the legal and political credentials to influence national destinies.

Conversion experiences like those of Taso and Elizabeth have substantially changed and dramatically complicated the religious landscape of Latin America. Titles like that of David Stoll's book—*Is Latin America Turning Protestant?*[26]—might be hyperbolic and misleading, but it is indeed true that evangelical and Pentecostal churches of all kinds and varieties are sprouting up all over Central America. In Guatemala, Nicaragua, Costa Rica, Brazil, and Puerto Rico, on any given Sunday morning possibly more hymns are sung, sermons are preached, exorcisms are performed, and prayers are offered to God in Protestant churches than in Catholic ones. The exceptional growth of the variegated Pentecostal expressions of the Christian faith has indeed reshaped the religious configuration of the entire region.[27]

In changing the religious landscape, widening the horizons of religious liberty, and forging a ferocious competition for the souls and hearts of believers, these charismatic congregations have fragmented the traditional Latin American model of Christendom. Their presence and activities constitute one of the most important transformations of the Latin American human

Fig. 11.6. Mother Church of the Christian Congregation in Brazil, located in the Italian Braz District, in Sao Paulo, Brazil. The Christian Congregation in Brazil is also called Congregação Cristã no Brasil.

landscape of the past century. No history of twentieth-century Latin America is complete if it leaves outside its margins the evangelical and Pentecostal reshaping of the continental religious configuration. It has become a meaningful part of the story of many men and women who, in very severe socioeconomic straits, strive simultaneously to create an earthly home for their bodies and to affirm their belonging to a heavenly home.

Some scholars have made the case that despite their initial isolation from the public and political arenas and their tendency toward a conservative stance regarding ethical issues, the evangelical and Pentecostal churches widen the democratic character of Latin American societies. They point out, first, that to become a member of any of these congregations, which lack the aura of traditional social legitimation, requires a free and conscious decision—a crucial building block of any democracy. Second, these churches' tend to be more participatory and less restricted by a professional clergy, thus inspiring a less passive attitude on important community issues.[28]

It is probably safer to say that the jury is still out regarding the political consequences of the increase in the diversity of evangelical and Pentecostal expressions of Christianity in Latin America. Some of these new churches tend to be very congregational and participatory; others, however, are under the iron-fisted control of their founders and self-designated apostles and tend to mirror the autocratic character of traditional haciendas and plantations. Some might question traditional norms of social conduct; others, on the contrary, espouse very conservative social and sexual ethics. What is undeniable is that traditional monopolistic Christendom, as known for centuries in Latin America, has been superseded by a bewildering variety of forms of living and thinking the Christian faith. The actions of the Holy Spirit, contrary to Augustine's restriction of the Spirit within the confines of the Catholic

> ### Speaking in Tongues
> And while I was glorifying, I know that at one point I wanted to say, "Glory to God, Hallelujah," and I could not. I swallowed my tongue, and then I spoke in other languages, like Hebrew or something like that. The pastor said I was going to something in tongues; and then I heard Brother Juan say, "She has received it! She has spoken in tongues, in spiritual tongues." And meanwhile, while I was in that state, there were those strong movements in my body. Something comes—comes to where one is, and for the sheer pleasure of it, one goes on speaking in tongues. One does not know what one is saying, and one is left speaking that way without knowing how.
> —Sidney W. Mintz, *Worker in the Cane: A Puerto Rican Life History* (New York: Norton, 1974 [1960]), 242.

Church, seem to promote diversity, division, and, from time to time, even bitter competition for the hearts and souls of the people. Under the proclaimed aegis of the Spirit, Latin American Christendom is indeed undergoing a dramatic and profound religious transfiguration.

PROVISIONAL PREDICTIONS

It is too early to predict with a high degree of confidence the long-range consequences of the impressive growth of Pentecostal Christianity in Latin America, but some provisional suspicions can be suggested.

There has been a dramatic battle for the spirit of the poor between the Pentecostal churches, with their pneumatological emphasis, and the Catholic ecclesial base communities inspired by liberation theology. Liberation theology made the preferential option for the poor a cardinal theological and ecclesiastical principle. It also foregrounded the primacy of the hermeneutical perspective of the poor. Ernesto Cardenal's famous *The Gospel in Solentiname* (first published in 1978) became its poetical hermeneutical paradigm. Many poor, however, have opted for the religiosity of the Spirit rather than for a theology of political and social resistance. This tendency does not necessarily lead us to the dirge of liberation theology prematurely sung by some conservative critics. But it certainly complicates the image of the historical protagonism of the poor, in the midst of continuing poverty and the new waves of enthusiasm for drastic social transformation shaking Latin America during the first decade of the twenty-first century. Intriguingly enough, since the 1990s there have been increasing signs of an emerging Pentecostal Latin American theological production.[29] The script of Latin American liberation theology might yet be redrafted, this time with surprising charismatic contours.

If we speak of the Latin American poor, then their racial and ethnic identities must also be taken into account. Many of them are indigenous (most prominently in Guatemala, Bolivia, Peru, Ecuador, and Mexico), African Americans (in Haiti, Brazil, Dominican Republic, Cuba, and Puerto Rico), or mestizos, generated by the multiple forms of miscegenation that have taken place during the past five hundred years. These ethnic and racial communities have suffered social discrimination and degradation, and many are now attracted to the promise of spiritual dignity conveyed by the religions of the Spirit.

"Syncretism" has always been a risky and potentially misleading term in religious matters, but it is difficult to avoid the impression of certain intimate interactions, in several autochthonous (indigenous) communities, between the spirits of the ancestors and the Spirit of the new Pentecost thriving all over Latin America. The boundaries between the Christian Spirit and the spirits of indigenous and African religiosities are frequently porous and symbiotic. It is not necessarily a conscious synthesis, but the primacy of orality in their liturgy, the narrative style of their homilies, and their flexibility in integrating popular rhythms and melodies into their worship constitute points of contact of many Pentecostal churches with the spirituality enshrined in the aesthetic traditions of autochthonous peoples. This has led some scholars to perceive indigenous Pentecostalism in Latin America, the Caribbean, and Africa as part and parcel of a process of ethnic revitalization.[30]

Religion matters in Latin America. And it matters even more in its increasing and astounding variety. The traditional binary confrontation between the secular state and the Roman Catholic Church is now being displaced by an array of multiple relations among religiosities of assorted theological and ritual configurations. The proliferation of many of these congregations with their tendency to break off from each other suggests a complex and confusing Latin American religious map in the future. Such a spiritual configuration promises to become a bewildering and ever-winding maze analogous to the fantastic labyrinths found in some of Jorge Luis Borges's stories. Diversity and complexity seem to be decisive hermeneutical keys in the religion of the Spirit of this postmodern zeitgeist.

Scholars and missiologists have recently stressed a crucial change in the global demographics of Christianity.[31] While the proportion of Christians in the Western and Northern churches diminishes, the churches in the South are growing geometrically. Some even predict the emergence of a "next Christendom," dominated by the churches of Latin America, sub-Saharan Africa, and Southeast Asia. If that is a valid point, then much of the credit belongs to the explosion of indigenous Pentecostal churches throughout the Third World. Future historians might consider twentieth-century Pentecostalism as the most significant global religious upheaval since the birth of Islam and the Protestant Reformation.

What this might entail for the political and social conflict engendered by neoliberal globalization is hard to envisage. The leadership of many of these churches is frequently authoritarian, conservative, isolationist, and fundamentalist. As has been shrewdly observed, the hierarchies of some Pentecostal churches, influenced by the North American "theology of prosperity," seem more interested in apostolic success than in apostolic succession. Nevertheless, a growing body of critical Pentecostal literature, open to political radicalism, challenges the prevailing socioeconomic powers and is ready to engage in ecumenical dialogue with other Christian partners. The future might be less bleak than the one foreseen by many contemporary Cassandras.

Indeed, the vigorous spread of Pentecostal churches and movements in the twentieth century has complicated enormously another of the main dimensions of that century of Christianity—the ecumenical movement. Ecumenical dialogue has taken place mainly among mainline Protestant churches, Roman Catholicism, and Eastern and Oriental Orthodox churches. With few exceptions, the Pentecostal movement, the fastest growing sector of Christianity during the past hundred years, has kept its distance from the ecumenical dialogue and has frequently viewed it with some degree of distrust. The Pentecostal churches are very young and still rather anxious to forge a clear sense of their own identity. They have emerged and developed in a social and ecclesiastical environment of contempt and disdain, engendering their tendency toward isolation and clear boundaries of separation.

The time may come when many of them will look more positively toward dialogue and ecumenical collaboration with other Christian churches. The success of Pentecostalism has promoted a mimetic reaction in other branches of Christianity, as attested by the increasing popularity of the charismatic renewal movement in many Roman Catholic Latin American dioceses. The enthusiastic Pentecostal style of worship is also strongly influencing mainstream Protestant congregations. This has led some scholars to perceive, in analogy to Paul

Tillich's "Protestant principle," a Pentecostal principle, a tendency toward "pentecostality" that is not restricted to Pentecostal denominations but is shaping the liturgical practices of many other Christian churches.[32] This liturgical convergence might constitute a bridge of ecumenical dialogue and rapprochement between churches that usually have stressed their doctrinal and theological differences.

Several times in the history of Christianity, an age of the Spirit has been foreseen, predicted, and desired. The hierarchical church, with its emphasis on orthodox doctrine, traditional liturgy, and accredited priesthood, has frequently looked with distrust at these enthusiastic aspirations, for it well knows how difficult it is to control and restrain their possible consequences. The Spirit tends to overwhelm and transgress the boundaries so carefully drawn by ecclesiastical hierarchies. "For the *pneuma* [spirit/wind] blows where it chooses . . . but you do not know where it comes from or where it goes" (John 3:8).

This chapter began with Sidney Mintz's engaging story of the astounding conversion to charismatic and Pentecostal Christianity of Taso Zayas and his wife, Elizabeth, two "uneducated and ordinary people" from the Latin American Caribbean. Some skeptical minds might recall John Locke's ironic observation regarding this type of charismatic enthusiasm: "I ask how shall any one distinguish between the delusions of Satan, and the inspirations of the Holy Ghost?"[33] Still, for many other trustful believers, their story of healing, spiritual baptism, and conversion was one of many similar signs that the age of the Spirit had finally arrived. Like the wind from the Caribbean Sea, whose storms bring disarray and redesign so many constructions in the sands of human affairs, the new Pentecost of the Spirit seems to be reconfiguring in unexpected ways the contours of the people's history of Christianity.[34]

FOR FURTHER READING

Anderson, Allan H., and Walter Hollenweger, eds. *Pentecostals after a Century: Global Perspectives on a Movement in Transition.* Sheffield: Sheffield Academic, 1999.

Chesnut, R. Andrew. *Competitive Spirits: Latin America's New Religious Economy.* Oxford: Oxford University Press, 2003.

Cleary, Edward L., and Hannah W. Stewart-Gambino, eds. *Power, Politics, and Pentecostals in Latin America.* Boulder: Westview, 1997.

Escobar, Samuel. *Changing Tides: Latin America and World Mission Today.* Maryknoll, N.Y.: Orbis Books, 2002.

Gutiérrez, Benjamin, and Dennis Smith, eds. *In the Power of the Spirit: The Pentecostal Challenge to Historic Churches in Latin America.* Arkansas City: Asociación de Iglesias Presbiterianas y Reformadas en América Latina; Centro Evangélico Latinoamericano de Estudios Pastorales; Presbyterian Church (U.S.A.), Worldwide Ministries Division, 1996.

Míguez Bonino, José. *Faces of Latin American Protestantism.* Grand Rapids: Eerdmans, 1997.

Shaull, Richard, and Waldo Cesar. *Pentecostalism and the Future of the Christian Churches: Promises, Limitations, Challenges.* Grand Rapids: Eerdmans, 2000.

Sigmund, Paul E., ed. *Religious Freedom and Evangelization in Latin America: The Challenge of Religious Pluralism.* Maryknoll, N.Y.: Orbis Books, 1999.

Silveira Campos, Leonildo. *Teatro, templo e mercado: Organização e marketing de um empreendimento neopentecostal.* Petrópolis, Brazil: Editora Vozes, 1997.

Stoll, David. *Is Latin America Turning Protestant? The Politics of Evangelical Growth.* Berkeley: University of California Press, 1990.

NOTES

Introduction. Invitation to a People's History of Christianity

1. The original version of this paper was presented as a lecture at New Orleans Baptist Theological Seminary on 20 April 2004. A refined, German version was published as "Eine neue Agenda für die Kirchengeschichte," in J. Bohn and T. Bohrmann, eds., *Religion als Lebensmacht: Eine Festgabe für Goffried Küenzlen*, (Leipzig: Evangelische Verlagsanstalt, 2010), pp. 22–34. A slightly revised English version was published as "Invitation to the New Church History" in the online *Journal for Baptist Theology and Ministry*, 8 (2011), 97–105. The final revision is published here.

Chapter One. Jesus Movements and the Renewal of Israel

1. Discussed more extensively in Richard A. Horsley, *Jesus and the Spiral of Violence: Popular Jewish Resistance in Roman Palestine* (Minneapolis: Fortress, 1993 [1987]), esp. chaps. 2 and 4.

2. Compared with studies of protests by modern urban crowds in ibid., 90–99.

3. Examined critically in Richard A. Horsley, "Popular Messianic Movements around the Time of Jesus," *CBQ* 46 (1984): 471–93; "'Like One of the Prophets of Old': Two Types of Popular Prophets at the Time of Jesus," *CBQ* 47 (1985): 435–63; "Popular Prophetic Movements at the Time of Jesus, Their Principal Features and Social Origins," *JSNT* 26 (1986): 3–27; and, more accessibly, in Richard A. Horsley with John S. Hanson, *Bandits, Prophets, and Messiahs: Popular Movements in the Time of Jesus* (Harrisburg, Pa.: Trinity Press International, 1999 [1985]).

4. See further my *Jesus and Empire: The Kingdom of God and the New World Disorder* (Minneapolis: Fortress, 2003), chap. 3.

5. The following discussion of Jesus movements draws heavily on my recent treatments of Q and Mark in *Whoever Hears You Hears Me: Prophets, Performance, and Tradition in Q,* with Jonathan Draper (Harrisburg, Pa.: Trinity Press International, 1999), and *Hearing the Whole Story: The Politics of Plot in Mark's Gospel* (Louisville: Westminster John Knox, 2001).

6. Fuller critical examination in Horsley, *Whoever Hears You Hears Me,* and Horsley, *Hearing the Whole Story.*

7. More fully analyzed and discussed in Richard A. Horsley, *Galilee: History, Politics, People* (Valley Forge, Pa.: Trinity Press International, 1995); and *Archaeology, History, and Society in Galilee* (Harrisburg, Pa.: Trinity Press International, 1996).

8. See especially James C. Scott, "Protest and Profanation: Agrarian Revolt and the Little Tradition," *Theory and Society* 4 (1977): 3–38, 211–45.

9. Horsley, *Galilee,* 147–57.

10. On the Herodian estates in western Judea, see David Fiensy, *The Social History of Palestine in the Herodian Period* (Lewiston, N.Y.: Mellen, 1991), 32–43; on the question of land tenure and royal estates in Judea and Galilee in historical political-economic context, see Horsley, *Galilee,* chap. 9.

11. Summary of evidence and analysis in Horsley, *Galilee,* chap. 10. Most of the buildings that archaeologists label as "synagogues" date to late antiquity. This suggests that village communities were not yet constructing such buildings at the time of Jesus and his movements.

12. Fuller analysis of the mission discourses in Horsley, *Whoever Hears You Hears Me,* chap. 10.

13. Building a movement by sending envoys to work in village communities sounds similar to the activities of at least two known organizations, Der Bundshuh and Der Arme Konrad, which sent delegates to towns up and down the Rhine Valley in the decade prior to the Peasant War of 1524–25 in southwest Germany. See Peter Blickle, *The Revolution of 1525: The German Peasants' War from a New Perspective* (Baltimore: Johns Hopkins University Press, 1977).

14. On the fishing enterprise under Herod Antipas, see K. C. Hanson, "The Galileans' Fishing Economy and the Jesus Tradition," *Biblical Theology Bulletin* 27 (1997): 99–111.

15. Horsley, *Galilee,* 147–57.

16. The following discussion draws upon the fuller analysis in Horsley, *Whoever Hears You Hears Me,* chap. 9, and Horsley, *Hearing the Whole Story,* chap. 8.

17. James C. Scott, *The Moral Economy of the Peasant: Rebellion and Subsistence in Southeast Asia* (New Haven: Yale University Press, 1976).

Chapter Two. Food, Ritual, and Power

1. Leonardo Boff and Clodovis Boff, *Introducing Liberation Theology* (Maryknoll, N.Y.: Orbis, 1987), 1.

2. See Mary Douglas, "Food as a System of Communication," in *In the Active Voice* (London: Routledge, 1982), 82–124.

3. The ancient terminology was more varied, and these groups included the Jewish meal clubs known as *haburoth.* See further Jacob Neusner, "Two Pictures of the Pharisees: Philosophical Circle or Eating Club," *Anglican Theological Review* 64 (1982): 525–38.

4. See Dennis E. Smith, *From Symposium to Eucharist: The Banquet in the Early Christian World* (Minneapolis: Fortress, 2003).

5. Ibid., 47–65.

6. See Dale Martin, "Tongues of Angels and Other Status Indicators," *Journal of the American Academy of Religion* 59 (1991): 547–89.

7. Michael Townsend, "Exit the *Agape*?" *Expository Times* 90 (1979): 356–61.

8. See Peter Garnsey, *Food and Society in Classical Antiquity* (Cambridge: Cambridge University Press, 1999), 12–21.

9. See Jonathan Klawans, "Interpreting the Last Supper: Sacrifice, Spiritualization, and Anti-Sacrifice," *New Testament Studies* 48/1 (2002): 1–17.

10. This sort of elaboration of the meal is well attested in North Africa around the year 200; see, for instance, Tertullian, *Against Marcion* 1.14.1, and also the *Martyrdom of Perpetua and Felicitas* 4.9–10. On these cases, see Andrew McGowan, *Ascetic Eucharists: Food and Drink in Early Christian Ritual Meals* (Oxford: Clarendon, 1999), 95–115.

11. The early third-century date, authorship, and even title of the supposed *Apostolic Tradition* by Hippolytus of Rome, assumed through much of the twentieth century, must now be scrutinized and almost certainly rejected; see Paul F. Bradshaw, Maxwell E. Johnson, and L. Edward Philips, *The Apostolic Tradition: A Commentary,* Hermeneia (Minneapolis: Fortress, 2002), 1–17.

12. On these issues, see the essays in Gerd Theissen, *The Social Setting of Pauline Christianity: Essays on Corinth* (Philadelphia: Fortress, 1982).

13. McGowan, *Ascetic Eucharists,* 143–74.

14. The original story need not be understood as a direct reference to the eucharistic meal, but it should be understood as making use of images also applied to it for a more general christological purpose.

15. Translation adapted from *New Testament Apocrypha,* 2 vols., ed. Wilhelm Schneemelcher (Louisville, Ky.: Westminster/John Knox, 1992), 200–201.

16. See Andrew McGowan, "The Inordinate Cup: Issues of Order in Early Eucharistic Drinking," *Studia Patristica* 35 (2001): 283–91.

17. Adapted from the translation of Kirsopp Lake, *The Apostolic Fathers,* Loeb Classical Library (Cambridge: Harvard University Press, 1965).

18. See Enrico Mazza, *The Origins of the Eucharistic Prayer* (Collegeville, Minn.: Liturgical, 1995).

19. Andrew McGowan, "'Is There a Liturgical Text in This Gospel?' The Institution Narratives and Their Early Interpretive Communities," *Journal of Biblical Literature* 118 (1999): 77–89.

20. On these issues, see Kathleen E. Corley, *Private Women, Public Meals: Social Conflict in the Synoptic Tradition* (Peabody, Mass.: Hendrickson, 1993).

21. See John D'Arms, "The Roman *Convivium* and the Idea of Equality," in *Sympotica: A Symposium on the 'Symposium',* ed. Oswyn Murray (Oxford: Clarendon, 1990), 308–20.

22. The study by Ute Eisen is useful: *Women Officeholders in Early Christianity: Epigraphical and Literary Studies* (Collegeville, Minn.: Liturgical, 2000).

23. The treatment by Charles A. Bobertz ("The Role of the Patron in the *Cena Dominica* of Hippolytus' *Apostolic Tradition,*" *Journal of Theological Studies* n.s. 44 [1993]: 170–84) is helpful. The present chapter assumes a different chronology and character for that work, but the issues raised are still relevant.

24. See Joan R. Branham, "Women as *Objets de Sacrifice*? An Early Christian 'Chancel of the Virgins,'" in *De la cuisine à l'autel. Les sacrifices en question dans les sociétés de la méditerranée ancienne,* ed. S. Georgoudi, R. Koch Piettre, and F. Schmidt, Bibliothèque de l'École des Hautes Études, Sciences religieuses (Paris: Brepols, forthcoming).

25. Augustine provides evidence for North African practice around 400 and how it differed from Italian; *On the Morals of the Catholic Church* 34.75 and *Conf.* 8.27.

26. The shrine of Felix at Nola, accepted and even advocated as a legitimate site of sacrificial practice by Paulinus; see Dennis Trout, "Christianizing the Nolan Countryside: Animal Sacrifice at the Tomb of St Felix," *Journal of Early Christian Studies* 3 (1995): 281–98.

Chapter Three. The Practice of Christianity in Byzantium

1. Cyril of Scythopolis, *Life of Sabas,* 80; *Miracles of Artemios* 5; Theodore of Studios, *Life of Theoktiste of Constantinople*, 884b–845a.

2. Symeon of Thessalonike, PG 155.688–89.

3. For a reassessment of icon veneration and iconoclasm, see Leslie Brubaker, "Icons before Iconoclasm?" in *Morfologie sociali e culturali in Europa fra tarda antichità e alto Medioevo* (Spoleto: Presso La sede del Centro, 1998), 2:1215–54, and Leslie Brubaker and John F. Haldon, *Byzantium in the Iconoclast Era (ca. 680–850): A History* (Cambridge: Cambridge University Press, 2003).

4. For an excellent overview, see John Binns, *An Introduction to the Christian Orthodox Churches* (Cambridge: Cambridge University Press, 2002).

5. John Tzetzes, *Ep.* 104; ed. P. L. M. Leone, *Ioannis Tzetzae epistulae* (Leipzig: Teubner, 1972); trans. in Paul Magdalino, "The Byzantine Holy Man in the Twelfth Century," in *The Byzantine Saint,* ed. Sergei Hackel (San Bernardino, Calif.: Borgo, 1983), 54.

6. David Brakke, *Athanasius and the Politics of Asceticism*, Oxford Early Christian Studies (Oxford: Clarendon, 1995), 182–98.

Chapter Four. Medieval Revivalism

1. Frederick Morgan Davenport, *Primitive Traits in Religious Revivals: A Study of Mental and Social Evolution* (New York: Macmillan, 1905), 42, 184, 217.

2. William James, *The Varieties of Religious Experience* (London: Longman, Green, 1902), 227–28.

3. Norman Zacour, "The Children's Crusade," in *A History of the Crusades*, ed. Kenneth M. Setton (Philadelphia: University of Pennsylvania Press, 1962), 2:325–42, quotation at 328.

4. Emile Durkheim, *The Elementary Forms of the Religious Life*, trans. J. W. Swain (London: Allen & Unwin, 1964), 241.

5. André Vauchez, *Sainthood in the Later Middle Ages*, trans. Jean Birrell (Cambridge: Cambridge University Press, 1997), 245 ("the manifestations of collective enthusiasm of the *devotio*").

6. Translated from Robert of Rheims, *Historia Iherosolimitana*, in *The Crusades: Idea and Reality, 1095–1274*, ed. L. and J. Riley-Smith (London: Edward Arnold, 1981), 44.

7. Translation from the *Chronicon universale anonymi Laudunensis* in *Medieval Popular Religion: A Reader*, ed. J. Shinners (Peterborough, Ont.: Broadview, 1997), 395.

8. Salimbene de Adam, *The Chronicle*, ed. and trans. Joseph L. Baird, Giuseppe

Baglivi, and John Robert Kane (Binghamton, N.Y.: Medieval and Renaissance Texts and Studies, 1986), 47.

9. See Salimbene de Adam, *Cronica*, ed. Giuseppe Scalia, new ed. (Bari: G. Laterza, 1966), 1:426–27, 527, 567; 2:675–77.

10. Cited from Jean Lemoine, *Extravagantes communes* (Lyons, 1559), 152, in Gary Dickson, "Revivalism as a Medieval Religious Genre," *Journal of Ecclesiastical History* 51 (2000): 473–96, quotation at 495.

11. Poem by Sacchetti cited in Daniel E. Bornstein, *The Bianchi of 1399: Popular Devotion in Late Medieval Italy* (Ithaca, N.Y.: Cornell University Press, 1993), 117.

12. John Donne, "Holy Sonnets," in *The Penguin Book of English Verse*, ed. John Hayward (Harmondsworth, U.K.: Penguin, 1964), 84–85.

13. *Rodulfus Glaber Opera: Historiarum Libri Quinque*, ed. and trans. John France (Oxford: Clarendon, 1989), xixff., 194–97.

14. Revised from B. G. Babington's translation of the Mortemer chronicle in J. F. C. Hecker, *The Epidemics of the Middle Ages*, 3rd ed. (London: Trübner, 1859).

15. Selection from the *Annales S. Iustinae Patavini*, revised from the partial translation of William Heywood, *Palio and Ponte* (London: Methuen, 1904), 18.

16. Translated from the *Cronaca del Graziani* of Perugia by Heywood in *Palio and Ponte*, 154–55.

17. Orderic Vitalis, *Ecclesiastical History*, ed. and trans. Marjorie Chibnall (Oxford: Clarendon, 1973), 4:332–33.

Chapter Five. Reforming from Below

1. *The Collected Works of Thomas Müntzer*, ed. and trans. Peter Matheson (Edinburgh: T & T Clark, 1988), 335.

2. *Erasmus*, ed. Richard L. DeMolen (London: Edward Arnold, 1973), 134.

3. *The Essential Carlstad*, trans. and ed. E. J. Furcha (Waterloo, Ont.: Herald, 1995), 104, 116.; see also *Anticlericalism in Late Medieval and Early Modern Europe*, ed. Peter A. Dykema and Heiko A. Oberman, Studies in Medieval and Reformation Thought, vol. 51 (Leiden: Brill, 1993).

4. See also the interesting article by the Marxist historian Adolf Laube, "Social Arguments in Early Reformation Pamphlets and Their Significance for the German Peasants' War," *Social History* 12 (1987): 361–78.

5. See Thomas A. Brady, *Ruling Class, Regime and Reformation at Strasbourg, 1520–1555* (Leiden: Brill, 1978), 294; Miriam Usher Chrisman, *Conflicting Visions of Reform: German Lay Propaganda Pamphlets, 1519–1530* (Atlantic Highland, N.J.: Humanities, 1996).

6. Carlo Ginzburg, *The Cheese and the Worms: The Cosmos of a Sixteenth-Century Miller,* trans. John and Anne Tedeschi (London: Routledge & Kegan Paul, 1980).

7. *Argula von Grumbach: A Woman's Voice in the Reformation*, ed. Peter Matheson (Edinburgh: T & T Clark, 1995), 89f.

8. J. H. Hexter, *Reappraisals in History* (Chicago: Chicago University Press, 1979), 266; see also Brad Gregory, *Salvation at Stake: Christian Martyrdom in Early Modern Europe* (Cambridge: Harvard University Press, 1989).

9. *Die Chroniken der deutschen Städte*, vol. 25 (Leipzig: Hirzel, 1896), 208, my translation.

10. Robert W. Scribner, "Is There a Social History of the Reformation?" *Social History* 4 (1976): 499.

Chapter Six. The Dream of a Just Society

1. Adolf Laube, "Radicalism as a Research Problem in Early Reformation," in *Radical Tendencies in the Reformation: Divergent Perspectives*, ed. Hans J. Hillerbrand (Kirksville, Mo.: Sixteenth Century Journal, 1988), 9–23.

2. Heiko A. Oberman, "The Gospel of Social Unrest," in *The German Peasant War of 1525: New Viewpoints*, ed. Bob Scribner and Gerhard Benecke (London: Allen & Unwin, 1979), 39–51.

3. Heinz Schilling, "Confessional Europe," in *Handbook of European History, 1400–1600*, ed. Thomas A. Brady Jr., Heiko A. Oberman, and James D. Tracy (Leiden: Brill 1995), 2:641–81.

4. W. Ian P. Hazlett, "Settlements: The British Isles," in Brady, Oberman, and Tracy, *Handbook of European History, 1400–1600*, 2:480: "They embodied the Kirk's aspirations rather than achieved reality. Yet their educational, social welfare, and disciplinary policies appealed to ordinary people."

5. Günther Franz, *Der deutsche Bauernkrieg* (Darmstadt: Wissenschaftliche Buchgesellschaft, 1977), 62–79; Tom Scott, *Freiburg and the Breisgau: Town–Country Relations in the Age of Reformation and Peasants' War* (Oxford: Clarendon, 1986), 173–89, where the Fritz conspiracies are presented as indubitable matters of fact.

6. Oberman, "Gospel of Social Unrest," 40.

7. Miriam Usher Chrisman, *Conflicting Visions of Reform: German Lay Propaganda Pamphlets, 1519–1530* (Atlantic Highlands, N.J.: Humanities, 1996), 65–89.

8. Ulrich Bubenheimer, *Thomas Müntzer: Herkunft und Bildung* (Leiden: Brill 1989).

9. See *The German Peasants' War: A History in Documents*, trans. and ed. Tom Scott and Bob Scribner (Atlantic Highlands, N.J.: Humanities, 1991), 19–28.

10. Adolf Laube, "Lotzer, Sebastian," and "Schappeler, Christoph," in *The Oxford Encyclopedia of the Reformation*, ed. Hans J. Hillerbrand (New York: Oxford University Press, 1996), 2:454–55, 4:1. Laube prefers Lotzer as single author of the *Twelve Articles*: "Whether Schappeler had directly participated in the formulation of the Twelve Articles—the most widely circulated program of the German Peasants' War—is controversial. In all probability the wording is solely that of Sebastian Lotzer."

11. Text in Peter Blickle, *The Revolution of 1525: The German Peasants' War from a New Perspective*, trans. Thomas A. Brady Jr. and H. C. Erik Midelfort (Baltimore: Johns Hopkins University Press, 1981), 195–201.

12. Text in Scott and Scribner, *German Peasants' War*, 130–32.

13. Peter Blickle, "Republiktheorie aus revolutionärer Erfahrung (1525)," in *Verborgene republikanische Traditionen* (Tübingen: Bibliotheca Academica, 1998), 195–210.

14. Abbreviated text in Scott and Scribner, *German Peasants' War*, 269–76.

15. Oberman, "Gospel of Social Unrest," 48.

16. Hans-Jürgen Goertz, *Thomas Müntzer: Apocalyptic Mystic and Revolutionary*

(Edinburgh: T & T Clark, 1993), 173–207: R. Emmet McLaughlin, "Apocalypticism and Thomas Müntzer," *Archive for Reformation History* 95 (2004): 98–131.

17. Werner O. Packull, "The Image of the Common Man in the Early Pamphlets of the Reformation (1520–1525)," *Historical Reflections* 12 (1985): 253–77.

18. Blickle, *Revolution of 1525*, 185.

19. James M. Stayer, "The Passing of the Radical Moment in the Radical Reformation," *Mennonite Quarterly Review* 71 (1997): 147–52.

20. Franz Lau, "Der Bauernkrieg und das angebliche Ende der lutherischen Reformation als spontaner Volksbewegung," *Luther-Jahrbuch* 26 (1959): 109–34.

21. Bruce Gordon, *The Swiss Reformation* (Manchester: Manchester University Press, 2002), 146–90, 283–316; see also Amy Nelson Burnett, "Basel and the Wittenberg Concord," *Archive for Reformation History* 96 (2005): 33–56.

22. Thanks are due to Tom Scott for his invaluable advice in the composition of this chapter.

Chapter Seven. Expansion and Change

1. For an excellent overview of scholarly discussion of the term "modernization" and its relation to religion, see Michael Saler, "Modernity and Enchantment: A Historiographic Overview," *The American Historical Review* 111, no. 3 (June 2006): 692–716.

2. Thomas Paine, *Common Sense* (1776; New York: Penguin, 1976), 76, 98.

3. Gregory Evans Dowd, *War under Heaven: Pontiac, the Indian Nations, and the British Empire* (Baltimore: Johns Hopkins University Press, 2002); Michael Hittman, *Wovoka and the Ghost Dance* (Lincoln: University of Nebraska Press, 1997).

4. Amanda Porterfield, *Mary Lyon and the Mount Holyoke Missionaries* (New York: Oxford University Press, 1997), 68–86.

5. Amanda Porterfield, *Healing in the History of Christianity* (New York: Oxford University Press, 2005), 152–57.

Chapter Eight. New Ways of Confronting Death

1. Edward Shills, "Ritual and Crisis," in *Center and Periphery: Essays in Macrosociology, Selected Papers of Edward Shills,* (Chicago: University of Chicago Press, 1975), 2:154.

2. Saint Gregory, *Dialogues*, book 4, chap. 57, p. 266

3. Roland H. Bainton, quoting Johann Tetzel, in *Here I Stand: A Life of Martin Luther,* (New York: Abingdon, 1950), 78.

4 . Martin Luther, "On the Misuse of the Mass" (1521), in *Luther's Works*, vol. 36, *Word and Sacrament II*, ed. Abdel Ross Wentz (Philadelphia: Fortress, 1959), 191.

5. Joannis Calvini opera quae supersunt omnia, ed. By W. Baum, E. Cunitz, and E. Reuss (Braunschweig, 1863-1900), 59 vols. Hereafter cited as CO, by treatise, volume, and page number: Commentary on the Acts of the Apostles, CO 48.562.

6. John Calvin, *De christiani hominis officio in sacerdotiis papalis ecclesiae vel administrandis vel abiiciendis*, CO 5. 304.

7. John Calvin, *Institutes of the Christian Religion* (1559), 4.18.1 Translated by

Ford Lewis Battles; edited by John T. McNeill, 2 vols. (Philadelphia, 1960). Cited by book, chapter, and subchapter.

8. Martin Luther, "First Invocavit Sermon," in *Luther's Works*, vol. 51, *Sermons I*, ed. Helmut T. Lehmann (Philadelphia: Fortress, 1959), 70.

9. *The Works of James Pilkington*, ed. James Scholefield (Cambridge: n.p., 1842), 318, 543. Quoted by David Cressy, *Birth, Marriage and Death: Ritual, Religion, and the Life-Cycle in Tudor and Stuart England* (Oxford: Oxford University Press, 1997), 399.

10. Robert Hill, *The Pathway to Prayer and Pietie* (1610), 197, 229.

11. Juan Eusebio Nieremberg, *De la diferencia entre lo temporal y lo eterno. Crisol de desengaños con la memoria de la eternidad, postrimerias humans y principales misterios divinos*, in *Obras escogidas del R.P. Juan Eusebio Nieremberg*, ed. Eduardo Zepeda-Henríquez, 2 vols, (Madrid: Ediciones Atlas, 1957), 2:223.

12. Diego Murillo, *Discursos predicables sobre todos los evangelios* (Zaragoza, 1611). Cited in Ana Martínez Arancón, *Geografía de la Eternidad* (Madrid: Tecnos, 1987), 79.

13. Jean Delumeau, *Sin and Fear: The Emergence of a Western Guilt Culture, 13th–18th Centuries*, trans. Eric Nicholson (New York: Palgrave Macmillan, 1990); Piero Camporesi, *The Fear of Hell: Images of Damnation and Salvation in Early Modern Europe*, trans. Lucinda Byatt (University Park: Pennsylvania State University Press, 1991).

14. François Rabelais, quoted in D. J. Enright, ed., *The Oxford Book of Death* (Oxford: Oxford University Press, 1987), 330.

15. Thomas Paine, *The Age of Reason*, being an investigation of true and fabulous theology (1794), part 2, chapter 3. Edited by Daniel Edwin Wheeler, *The Life and Writings of Thomas Paine: Containing a Biography by Thomas Clio Rickman* (New York, 1908), 274–75.

16. Denis Diderot, quoted by Paul Johnson, *A History of Christianity* (New York: Touchstone, 2005), 350ff.

17. Jonathan Edwards, "Sinners in the Hands of an Angry God" (1741), in *A Jonathan Edwards Reader*, ed. John E. Smith, Harry S. Stout, and Kenneth P. Minkema (New Haven: Yale University Press, 1995), 97–87.

18. Philipe Ariès, *The Hour of Our Death*, trans. Helen Weaver (New York: Oxford University Press, 1981), 506–56.

19. William Shakespeare, *Hamlet*, 1.5.9–13.

Chapter Nine. Multiplicity and Ambiguity

1. Conversation with Cesar del Rio, November 1, 2006.

2. "The Key to the Churches in the Diocese of Visby" (Church of Sweden, 2001).

3. Jim Forest, *The Resurrection of the Church in Albania: Voices of Orthodox Christians* (Geneva: WCC Publications, 2002), 37.

4. Masao Takenaka, *God Is Rice: Asian Culture and Christian Faith* (Geneva: WCC Publications, 1986), 6–7. The quote from Watanabe comes from Masao Takenaka, "Sadao Watanabe—The Man and His Work," in *Biblical Prints by Sadao Watanabe*, Sadao Watanabe and Masao Takenaka (Tokyo: Shinkyo Shuppansha [Protestant Publishing Co.], 1986).

5. Joseph Healey and Donald Sybertz, *Towards an African Narrative Theology* (Maryknoll, N.Y.: Orbis, 1996), 123–24. The authors are Maryknoll missionaries.

6. *New St. Joseph's People's Prayer Book* (New York: Catholic Book, 1980, 1993), 442.

7. One of the most recent and complete is volume 9 of the Cambridge History of Christianity Series, *World Christianities c. 1914–c. 2000*, ed. Hugh McLeod (Cambridge: Cambridge University Press, 2006).

8. In *Icons of American Protestantism: The Art of Warner Sallman, 1892–1968* (New Haven: Yale University Press, 1994), the editor, David Morgan, cites an estimate by Sallman's publisher, Kriebel and Bates, Inc., that *Head of Christ* has been reproduced more than 500 million times and has been distributed around the world (210n1).

9. Kwok Pui-lan has creative things to say about this process in "Discovering the Bible in the Non-Biblical World," in *Lift Every Voice: Constructing Christian Theologies from the Underside*, ed. Susan Brooks Thistlethwaite and Mary Potter Engel, revised and expanded edition (Maryknoll, N.Y.: Orbis Books, 1998), 276–88.

10. Estimates of the numbers of Christians in the world and in various parts of the world tend to be just that—estimates. One of the most frequently cited sources is David B. Barrett, George T. Kurian, and Todd M. Johnson, eds., *World Christian Encyclopedia*, 2 vols. (Oxford: Oxford University Press, 2001), 1:4, 12. Scholars like Philip Jenkins in *The Next Christendom: The Coming of Global Christianity* (Oxford: Oxford University Press, 2002) advise caution in using statistics about how many Christians there are in the world and where they are, and points to discrepancies in various sources. In "Counting Christians in China: A Cautionary Report," *International Bulletin of Missionary Research* 27, no. 1 (January 2003): 6–10, Tony Lambert relates that "the last two decades have seen no resolution to the problem posed by the yawning gulf between statistics issued by the Chinese government or state-approved church representatives, and those figures published by some Christian agencies elsewhere" (6). One place to keep track of numbers of Christians and the percentage of the population they comprise in a given continent or country is on the website of the World Christian Database: http://www .worldchristiandatabase.org/wcd/esweb.asp.

Chapter Ten. Gender and Twentieth-Century Christianity

1. Pauli Murray, *Song in a Weary Throat: An American Pilgrimage* (New York: HarperCollins, 1987), 435.

2. See David Barrett, George Kurian, and Todd M. Johnson, eds., *World Christian Encyclopedia*, vol. 1, *The World by Countries, Religionists, Churches, Ministries*, 2nd ed. (New York: Oxford University Press, 2001), 4, 682–85; Roger Finke and Rodney Stark, *The Churching of America, 1776–2005: Winners and Losers in Our Religious Economy*, 2nd ed. (New Brunswick, N.J.: Rutgers University Press, 2005), 23.

3. Figures cited in Wendy Murray Zoba, "A Woman's Place," *Christianity Today* 44, August 7, 2000, 4.

4. Jane Addams, "The College Woman and the Family Claim," *Commons* 29 (September 1898): 6.

5. Anthony Fletcher, "Beyond the Church: Women's Spiritual Experience at Home and in the Community, 1600–1900," in *Gender and Christian Religion*, ed. R. N.

Swanson (Woodbridge, U.K.: Published for the Ecclesiastical Society by Boydell, 1998), 190.

6. Horace Bushnell, *Woman Suffrage: The Reform Against Nature* (New York: Charles Scribner, 1869), 51, 83.

7. "Appeal to the Ladies of the Methodist Episcopal Church," *Heathen Woman's Friend* 1 (1869): 1.

8. Dorothy Hodgson, *The Church of Women: Gendered Encounters between Maasai and Missionaries* (Bloomington: University of Indiana Press, 2005), 180–81, 184.

9. R. W. Battles, "What about Television?" *Sunday School Times*, November 26, 1955, 942.

10. Estelle B. Freedman, *No Turning Back: A History of Feminism and the Future of Women* (New York: Ballantine Books, 2002), 151.

11. Sally Gallagher, *Evangelical Identity and Gendered Family Life* (New Brunswick, N.J.: Rutgers University Press, 2003), 134.

12. See Gary L. Ward, "Introductory Essay: A Survey of the Women's Ordination Issue," in *The Churches Speak On: Women's Ordination*, ed. J. Gordon Melton (Detroit: Gale Research, 1991), xvi–xvii.

13. Ranjini Rebera, "Introduction: Difference and Identity," in *Affirming Difference, Celebrating Wholeness: A Partnership of Equals*, ed. Ranjini Rebera (Hong Kong: Clear-Cut, 1995), 12.

14. Quoted in Constance F. Parvey, "Third World Women and Men: Effects of Cultural Change on Interpretation of Scripture," in John C. B. Webster and Ellen Low Webster, eds., *The Church and Women in the Third World* (Philadelphia: Westminster, 1985), 110.

15. Dorothy Ramobide, "Women and Men Building Together the Church in Africa," in Virginia Fabella, and Mercy Amba Oduyoye, eds., *With Passion and Compassion: Third World Women Doing Theology: Reflections from the Women's Commission of the Ecumenical Association of Third World Theologians* (Maryknoll, N.Y.: Orbis, 1988), 15.

16. Lloyda Fanusie, "Sexuality and Women in African Culture," in Mercy Amba Oduyoye and Musimbi R. A. Kanyoro, eds., *The Will to Arise: Women, Tradition, and the Church in Africa* (Maryknoll, N.Y.: Orbis, 1992), 114.

17. Musimbi R. A. Kanyoro, "Introduction: Background and Genesis," in *In Search of a Round Table: Gender, Theology, and Church Leadership*, ed. Rachel Kanyoro (Geneva: World Council of Churches, 1997), ix–x.

18. Bruce Lawrence, *Defenders of God: The Fundamentalist Revolt against the Modern Age* (San Francisco: Harper & Row, 1989), 2.

19. Elizabeth Brusco, *The Reformation of Machismo: Evangelical Conversion and Gender in Colombia* (Austin: University of Texas Press, 1995).

Chapter Eleven. Pentecostal Transformation in Latin America

1. David Martin is one of the few scholars who has noticed the importance of the conversion of Taso Zayas to Pentecostalism in Mintz's text. See David Martin, *Tongues of Fire: The Explosion of Protestantism in Latin America* (Cambridge, Mass.: Blackwell, 1990), 191–97.

2. On Pentecostalism, see the useful essays in Allan H. Anderson and Walter Hollenweger, eds., *Pentecostals after a Century: Global Perspectives on a Movement in Transition* (Sheffield: Sheffield Academic, 1999). Harvey Cox, *Fire from Heaven: The Rise of Pentecostal Spirituality and the Reshaping of Religion in the Twenty-First Century* (Reading, Mass.: Addison-Wesley, 1995), is an informative text in which the former "secular city" theologian becomes an advocate of the "spiritual city." For a sociological analysis of global Pentecostalism, see David Martin, *Pentecostalism: The World Their Parish* (Oxford: Blackwell, 2002). Martin is another theoretician of secularization now bewildered by the new Pentecostal religious revival. Stanley M. Burgess, Gary B. McGee, and Patrick H. Alexander, eds., *Dictionary of Pentecostal and Charismatic Movements* (Grand Rapids: Zondervan, 1988), is a useful reference text.

3. See the splendid study of the cultural consequences of the sugarcane plantation for the Caribbean by Antonio Benítez-Rojo, *The Repeating Island: The Caribbean and the Postmodern Perspective* (Durham, N.C.: Duke University Press, 1992 [1989]). Sidney Mintz has written an elegant and intelligent text on the development of the sugarcane plantations in the British Caribbean. Sidney Mintz, *Sweetness and Power: The Place of Sugar in Modern History* (New York: Penguin Books, 1986).

4. See Elizabeth Brusco, "The Reformation of Machismo: Ascetism and Masculinity among Colombian Evangelicals," in Virginia Garrard-Burnett and David Stoll, eds., *Rethinking Protestantism in Latin America* (Philadelphia: Temple University Press, 1993).

5. Tommy Lee Osborn (sometimes spelled Osborne) was a self-appointed American evangelist who conducted healing crusades through the Caribbean (Jamaica, Puerto Rico, and Cuba). His book *Healing the Sick* (Tulsa, Okla.: Harrison House, 1986 [1951]) has sold over one million copies. It contains a short summary and photos of the healing campaign (February 1950) in which Taso Zayas alleges to be healed (Osborn, *Healing the Sick*, 416–21).

6. Sidney W. Mintz, *Worker in the Cane: A Puerto Rican Life History* (New York: Norton, 1974 [1960]), 211–12.

7. D. A. Brading, *Mexican Phoenix: Our Lady of Guadalupe: Image and Tradition across Five Centuries* (Cambridge: Cambridge University Press, 2001).

8. See Jacques Lafaye, *Quetzalcóatl and Guadalupe: The Formation of Mexican National Consciousness, 1531–1813* (Chicago: University of Chicago Press, 1976). According to Octavio Paz, the Virgin of Guadalupe has been the main source of the Mexican sense of nationhood, more influential in its shaping than the official nationalist myths of the several republican and revolutionary governments of the last two centuries. Octavio Paz, *Sor Juana, or, The Traps of Faith* (Cambridge: Harvard University Press, 1988), 478.

9. Miraculous healings have not been restricted to the first wave of Pentecostal evangelization in Latin America. The phenomenon has also been one of the keys for the exceptional growth of the Brazilian Universal Church of the Kingdom of God, considered by some scholars as a Neo-Pentecostal church that promises social and economic prosperity and not only spiritual benefits. See Leonildo Silveira Campos, *Teatro, Templo e Mercado: Organização e marketing de um empreendimento neopentecostal* (Petrópolis: Editora Vozes, 1997). See the theological conversation about "healing and deliverance" between the Pentecostal Cheryl Bridge Johns, the Roman Catholic Virgil Elizondo, and the Reformed feminist Elisabeth Moltmann-Wendel in Jürgen Moltmann and Karl-

Josef Kuschel, eds., *Pentecostal Movements as an Ecumenical Challenge* (Maryknoll, N.Y.: Orbis, 1996), 45–62.

10. Mintz, *Worker in the Cane*, 220–21.

11. Ibid., 223.

12. Ibid., 216.

13. Ibid., 241–44.

14. Ibid., 231.

15. It would be interesting to compare the ecstatic experiences of Taso and Elizabeth with that of John, a rather skeptical young man and the protagonist of James Baldwin's novel *Go Tell It on the Mountain* (first published in 1953). John's possession by the Holy Spirit takes place in the early '50s, in a storefront Harlem Pentecostal church with the significant name, the Temple of the Fire Baptized.

16. Mintz, *Worker in the Cane*, 217.

17. Ibid., 276.

18. Ibid., 277.

19. Ibid., 225.

20. See Christian Lalive d'Epinay, *The Haven of the Masses* (London: Lutterworth, 1969); and Paul E. Sigmund, ed. *Religious Freedom and Evangelization in Latin America: The Challenge of Religious Pluralism* (Maryknoll, N.Y.: Orbis, 1999).

21. See Raymond Carr, *Puerto Rico: A Colonial Experiment* (New York: Vintage Books, 1984); José Trías Monge, *Puerto Rico: The Trials of the Oldest Colony in the World* (New Haven: Yale University Press, 1997); and Efrén Rivera Ramos, *The Legal Construction of Identity: The Judicial and Social Legacy of American Colonialism in Puerto Rico* (Washington, D.C.: American Psychological Association, 2001).

22. Mintz, *Worker in the Cane*, 276.

23. For the Iberian royal patronage in Latin America, and the debates it engendered, see William Eugene Shiels, S.J., *King and Church: The Rise and Fall of the Patronato Real* (Chicago: Loyola University Press, 1961), and Luis N. Rivera-Pagán, "Formation of a Hispanic American Theology: The Capitulations of Burgos," in Daniel Rodríguez-Díaz and David Cortés-Fuentes, eds., *Hidden Stories: Unveiling the History of the Latino Church* (Decatur, Ga.: Asociación para la Educación Teológica Hispana, 1994), 67–97. For the history before and after the independence of the Latin American nations, see Hans-Jürgen Prien, *La historia del cristianismo en América Latina* (Salamanca: Ediciones Sígueme, 1985).

24. See Luis N. Rivera-Pagán, "Violence of the Conquistadores and Prophetic Indignation," in Kenneth R. Chase and Alan Jacobs, eds., *Must Christianity Be Violent? Reflections on History, Practice, and Theology* (Grand Rapids: Brazos, 2003), 37–49, 239–43; Luis N. Rivera-Pagán, "A Prophetic Challenge to the Church: The Last Word of Bartolomé de las Casas," *Princeton Seminary Bulletin* 24, no. 2, new series (July 2003): 216–40; and Luis N. Rivera-Pagán, "Freedom and Servitude: Indigenous Slavery in the Spanish Conquest of the Caribbean," in Jalil Sued-Badillo, ed., *General History of the Caribbean,* vol. 1, *Autochthonous Societies* (London: UNESCO and Macmillan, 2003), 316–62.

25. See, for example, the intelligent discussion of the history of the juridical bonds between the state and the Roman Catholic Church in Argentina by José Míguez Bonino, in his article "Church, State, and Religious Freedom in Argentina," in Sigmund, *Religious*

Freedom, 187–203. Samuel Silva Gotay has made an important recent contribution to the study of the relations between the Roman Catholic Church and the state in Puerto Rico, first in the nineteenth century, when the island was a colonial possession of Spain, and then during the first decades of the twentieth century, when it became a territory of the United States. Samuel Silva Gotay, *Catolicismo y política en Puerto Rico bajo España y Estados Unidos: Siglos XIX y XX* (San Juan: Editorial de la Universidad de Puerto Rico, 2005). The classic text about the whole region is that of J. Lloyd Mecham, *Church and State in Latin America: A History of Politicoecclesiastical Relations* (Chapel Hill: University of North Carolina Press, 1966).

26. David Stoll, *Is Latin America Turning Protestant? The Politics of Evangelical Growth* (Berkeley: University of California Press, 1990).

27. For the spread of Pentecostalism in Latin America, see the variety of perspectives in Benjamin Gutiérrez and Dennis Smith, eds., *In the Power of the Spirit: The Pentecostal Challenge to Historic Churches in Latin America* (Arkansas City: Asociación de Iglesias Presbiterianas y Reformadas en América Latina; Centro Evangélico Latinoamericano de Estudios Pastorales; Presbyterian Church [U.S.A.], Worldwide Ministries Division, 1996); and Edward L. Cleary and Hannah W. Stewart-Gambino, eds., *Power, Politics, and Pentecostals in Latin America* (Boulder: Westview, 1997).

28. See, for example, Michael Dodson, "Pentecostals, Politics, and Public Space in Latin America," in Cleary and Stewart-Gambino, *Power*, 25–40.

29. See Carmelo Álvarez, *Pentecostalismo y liberación* (San José, Costa Rica: DEI, 1992); Richard Shaull and Waldo Cesar, *Pentecostalism and the Future of the Christian Churches: Promises, Limitations, Challenges* (Grand Rapids: Eerdmans, 2000); Douglas Petersen, *Not by Might Nor by Power: A Pentecostal Theology of Social Concern in Latin America* (Oxford: Regnum Books, 1996); and Eldin Villafañe, *The Liberating Spirit: Toward an Hispanic American Social Ethic* (Grand Rapids: Eerdmans, 1993).

30. See the doctoral dissertation of the Chilean Pentecostal theologian Juan Sepúlveda, *Gospel and Culture in Latin American Protestantism: Toward a New Theological Appreciation of Syncretism* (Ph.D. diss., University of Birmingham, 1996).

31. Andrew Walls, *The Missionary Movement in Christian History: Studies in the Transmission of Faith* (Maryknoll, N.Y.: Orbis, 1996); Lamin Sanneh, *Whose Religion Is Christianity? The Gospel beyond the West* (Grand Rapids: Eerdmans, 2003); Philip Jenkins, *The Next Christendom: The Coming of Global Christianity* (Oxford: Oxford University Press, 2002).

32. Bernardo Campos, *De la Reforma Protestante a la Pentecostalidad de la Iglesia: Debate sobre el Pentecostalismo en América Latina* (Quito: Ediciones CLAI, 1997).

33. John Locke, *An Essay Concerning Human Understanding* (New York: Dover, 1959 [1690]), vol. 2, bk. 4, chap. 19, par. 13, 438.

34. A note of gratitude to Susan Richardson, who reviewed the draft of this chapter, saved the author from many linguistic infelicities, and enabled him to write a more readable and elegant text. The author also wants to acknowledge the collaboration of Luiz Nascimento, a Brazilian doctoral student at Princeton Theological Seminary, for the selection of illustrations.

INDEX